Praise for

"What makes Susan D. Mustafa and Sue Israel such powerful chroniclers of man's darkest deeds? Their compassion for all involved, especially the victims and those who loved them, and their ability to tell a true story in dramatic yet empathetic fashion. *Dismembered* shows their sensitivity in revealing the stories of those who commit senseless, violent acts."

—Michael McCall, author and journalist, Associated Press

"When it comes to true crime stories, there are 'should' reads and 'must' reads. *Dismembered* falls in the latter category. Authors Mustafa and Israel give us a unique insight into the mind of horrific serial killer Sean Vincent Gillis, from inception as a novice killer to a nightmarish national murderer and cannibal. With first-hand accounts, the book details a journey from the disturbed to the psychotic. Get the book, but keep the lights on."

—Stone Grissom, legal analyst, journalist

BLOOD BATH

"So expertly written and reported . . . It scared the bejesus out of me!"

—Alanna Nash, author of *Let's Play House: Elvis Presley and the Women Who Loved Him*

"Takes us into the mentally bizarre world of a real serial killer as he stalks and defiles beautiful and talented women whom he hates for being 'too good' for him."

—Edward Morris, reviewer for *BookPage* and *ForeWord* magazines

"Mustafa invited horror into her home, looked it in the eye and squashed it with a creative energy used to produce a book that touches the soul.".

—Dave Moormann, *Southeast News*

"Mustafa walked the steps of the killer and the victims . . . She tells the story as if she hovered overhead while it was happening . . . This chilling sequence of events will have women locking their doors and looking around corners for days."

—Dr. Amber Reetz Narro, Southeastern Lousiana University

"A complete and compelling story of murder."

—Lily Jackson, *Gambit Weekly*, BestofNewOrleans.com

"A must read. [It] doesn't just tell you the story, it takes you on the journey . . . There were certain parts I read without breathing."
—Jodi Carson, Clear Channel Radio, 96.1, The River

DISMEMBERED

Susan D. Mustafa
and Sue Israel

PINNACLE BOOKS
Kensington Publishing Corp.
http://www.kensingtonbooks.com

Some names have been changed to protect the privacy of individuals connected to this story.

PINNACLE BOOKS are published by

Kensington Publishing Corp.
119 West 40th Street
New York, NY 10018

Copyright © 2011 by Susan D. Mustafa and Sue Israel

All rights reserved. No part of this book may be reproduced in any form or by any means without the prior written consent of the Publisher, excepting brief quotes used in reviews.

If you purchased this book without a cover, you should be aware that this book is stolen property. It was reported as "unsold and destroyed" to the Publisher and neither the Author nor the Publisher has received any payment for this "stripped book."

All Kensington Titles, Imprints, and Distributed Lines are available at special quantity discounts for bulk purchases for sales promotions, premiums, fund-raising, and educational or institutional use. Special book excerpts or customized printings can also be created to fit specific needs. For details, write or phone the office of the Kensington special sales manager: Kensington Publishing Corp., 119 West 40th Street, New York, NY 10018, attn: Special Sales Department, Phone: 1-800-221-2647.

Pinnacle and the P logo Reg. U.S. Pat. & TM Off.

ISBN-13: 978-0-7860-2361-5
ISBN-10: 0-7860-2361-9

First printing: July 2011

10 9 8 7 6 5 4 3 2 1

Printed in the United States of America

For all the women who walk lonely streets at night,
may the stars guide you safely home.

At Confession

The reporter shook his head, not quite believing what he was hearing. "But, Sean, why did you kill all of those women?" he asked.

Sean shrugged his shoulders, leaning closer to the glass partition, which separated them, and said, "They were already dead to me."

July 16, 2004

1. *I found her driving around, searching.*
2. *I found her at or near the corner of Prescott and Geronimo Streets.*
3. *We did not talk much, just about price and for what, you know.*
4. *She was smoking.*
5. *There were no advances. Sex was not my intent.*
6. *She did not anger me.*
7. *Late at night, around three or four in the morning*
8. *Nylon zip tie*
9. *I still do not know the why of anything, much less the arm, leg, nipples.*
10. *I had no dope on me. If I did, I would have been home in bed. The only dope I use is pot.*
11. *Maybe at the end, she knew for sixty seconds or so.*
12. *We had no sex. None, zip, nada.*

I was in a real bad place. I was pure evil. No love, no compassion, no faith, no mercy, no hope. I've been there many times in the past ten years. She was so far gone that night I really do not think she knew what was happening to her. I don't know why, but how—strangulation with a nylon tie lock. I still puzzle over the post mortem dismemberment and cutting. There must be something deep in my subconscious that needs that kind of macabre action. I really don't know what my damage is. In time the wounds will be easier to live with. There is a reason for everything, even such senseless acts of violence. Until ten years ago, I never so much imagined harm to anyone. Please tell me more about Donna. I think I would have liked her.

Excerpts from a series of letters written by Sean Vincent Gillis to a fellow inmate who was a friend of his last victim.

Body on Ben Hur

As they drove along Ben Hur Road in Baton Rouge, Louisiana, James Andernann and his girlfriend, Lauren Keller, stared out the car windows and looked for their dog, which had run off that morning. The twenty-year-olds drove slowly past the fields where Louisiana State University's Agriculture Research Station grows a variety of beans and vegetables in an effort to determine the best conditions for growth. Goats and sheep bleated their morning songs on the opposite side of the road, but the couple did not see the dog running among the animals. He had been gone for more than an hour, and although there was not much traffic in this remote area between the more populated Nicholson and Burbank Drives, residents did sometimes use it as a through street, and the couple worried that the dog might have been harmed by a vehicle traveling just a little too fast.

As they approached the bridge that provides access over a small canal, they noticed something that didn't look quite right. They stopped and stared at what appeared to be a naked person on the west bank of the canal, about twenty-five yards from the bridge. From their vantage point, they thought the person didn't seem to be real, so James backed the car off the road and decided to get closer. James and Lauren got out of the car they had parked near an old broken gate and began walking toward the canal to get a better look.

All thoughts of their dog disappeared when they saw the woman. She wasn't moving. From ten feet away, they could see that she was indeed real. And that she was dead.

James hurriedly dialed 911 on his cell phone, and the couple anxiously waited for police to arrive.

It was cool and sunny on the morning of February 27, 2004, when crime scene technician Van Calhoun got the call that a body had been found in the canal on Ben Hur Road. It was still early, only 9:17 A.M., when he arrived.

He had been with the East Baton Rouge Parish Sheriff's Office (EBRSO) for about six years, first working at the parish prison before moving into the Crime Scene Division in May 2002. His job was to document crime scenes with his camera and to process and collect evidence. Throughout his years with the sheriff's office, he had witnessed many murders, but this one seemed more gruesome than most.

The woman has been positioned on her stomach with her buttocks raised slightly in the air. A jacket had been placed over her face and her right arm. Calhoun noticed that her back was covered with abrasions, like she had been dragged down the embankment and placed facing west in the ravine. The canal was littered with debris, and she had been dragged through it.

Her left arm had been severed at the elbow, and a piece of flesh was missing from her right thigh. Trauma to her anus and vagina were evident by the dried blood that surrounded those areas. Calhoun suspected that the killer had wanted her to be seen like this. It was evident from the positioning of her body.

Calhoun roped off the area and began taking photographs and making notes as other detectives arrived on the scene.

He and Lieutenant Terry Felton did a walk-through around the perimeter of the body and onto the south side of Ben Hur Road, west of the canal. They noticed immediately that a set of tire tracks were visible in the field that parallels the canal. The tracks showed that a vehicle had pulled into the field, just past the gate, and then backed up to the incline, where the victim had been dumped. It was there that Calhoun noticed what looked like a piece of cartilage that had been dropped on the ground behind where the tire tracks stopped. He bagged the discarded piece of human tissue and continued his search for clues.

He counted thirteen empty Budweiser Light cans and gathered them as evidence. He then made casts of the tire tracks. After he had completed his search, he returned to the body.

Calhoun carefully removed the jacket that covered the victim's face and saw that blood had spattered on the inside of it. He placed the jacket in a bag and tagged it with the identification code *1VC*. He took swabs from the woman's right arm, her wrist, her shoulder, and her buttocks, then rolled her over onto a homicide sheet.

It was then he saw how she had died. Ligature marks encircled her neck, partially hidden by a large slash in her throat. He could see several deep cuts above where the victim's arm had been amputated. Then he saw the cuts to her nipples. The nipple and areola had been completely severed from both of her breasts. It was obvious that her killer had taken his time, had enjoyed his dissection. The absence of blood indicated that the mutilations to her body had occurred postmortem.

After taking more swabs and then fingerprinting her right hand, Calhoun carefully searched the area but could not find any of the woman's missing body parts. He shook his head, disgusted that someone could do something like this.

The woman was placed in a body bag and tagged with the number *0001182.*

It was a little after one o'clock that afternoon when Calhoun left the scene to return to his office and store the evidence. He didn't know it then, but the casts he had made of the tire tracks would lead police to the woman's killer—to a serial killer who had been preying on women in Baton Rouge and the surrounding areas for almost ten years.

But the police in Baton Rouge were unaware that this serial killer existed or that he had already savagely killed and dismembered seven other women.

As he watched the media coverage of his murders, the killer laughed with the knowledge that he had outwitted police again, that no connection had been made between the eight women he had so viciously mutilated. To him, it was a sick game, and he was always the winner.

Until he killed his last victim, Donna Bennett Johnston.

First Blood

The biker's voice was getting louder as he argued with the scantily clad stripper. He wore a jacket that bore the Sons of Silence logo, a gang known for the quick tempers of its members. Terri Lemoine watched from across the bar, ever aware that things could get nasty at any moment.

The Key Club, located on Plank Road in an area of Baton Rouge known for its prostitutes and easy drug access, was not the best place to work, but Terri loved it. She liked the excitement generated by the dancers and the mostly friendly guys who came there to ogle the girls and live out their sexual fantasies. But sometimes the men were not so friendly, and those were the ones she watched. This one, with the long, dark hair and thick moustache and beard, had an air about him, an air of danger. He looked tough, rougher than most of the bar's regular customers.

Terri was a pretty girl, with straight blond hair and a slender body. She enjoyed the attention men gave her, the flirting, the feeling of being desired. She had been married once and had left the marriage for something a bit more exciting—the nightlife in the capital city of Louisiana. She had been hurt by the men in her life, and Terri was not about to let any man hurt her again. She had developed a tough exterior to hide the frightened, lonely woman who resided behind a great wall erected for self-preservation. Inside that wall lived a woman who had no confidence, no thought other than to go to the bar every night and revel in the attention she got. It was worth the life she had given up—the children who lived with their father or grandparents, the husband who had bored her, the responsibility she did not want or need.

The young woman truly had loved only once—a good-looking, sweet man named Louis Michael Gaar. He had loved her, too. She had felt secure, safe—for the first time in her life—but after Terri gave birth to his daughter, Christine, Louis suddenly had to go away. Terri missed him terribly, but she was still in her twenties and had a lot of life left to live. She didn't want to miss out on anything.

Then Norbert "Norby" David Dees walked into the bar, and everything changed. Terri watched for a moment as he argued with the stripper, edging closer and closer. When the biker slapped the girl, Terri was ready. She jumped between them.

"Go to the dressing room," she told the girl, who ran off quickly, eager to get away from the man who had hit her.

Terri turned to look at the biker, unafraid, and stared him dead in the eyes. "Does this make you feel like a big man?" she said before turning to walk away.

Norby picked up a pool cue and swung, breaking it across Terri's back.

Terri turned around slowly, carefully. "Have you lost

your fucking mind?" she yelled, bending to pick up the half of the stick she could reach.

In a rage, she began hitting him, over and over. Norby tried to ward off the blows, but the jagged edge of the stick kept stabbing at him.

Bleeding from his head and chest, he fell to the floor, but Terri couldn't stop. She hit him again and again. The biker rolled onto his stomach, desperately hoping his back could better take the blows.

Patrons simply watched as Terri kept hitting him. In dives like the Key Club, there's nothing better than a good bar fight, and rarely did anyone get to see a girl beating up a biker, especially one from a gang as notorious as the Sons of Silence.

The dancer whom Terri had been protecting ran from the dressing room, holding a knife. She began stabbing Norby in his back, while Terri continued to hit him with the cue in his head, in his back.

Until he was dead.

The barroom fell silent as realization dawned. The biker wasn't moving, wasn't breathing. The blood from his wounds that saturated the floor had stopped flowing.

Terri backed away, breathing heavily, the weapon still in her hand. The dancer dropped the knife, her hands shaking, her shoulders heaving.

Someone called the police.

Terri and the dancers who worked at the club spent the night of March 13, 1987, at East Baton Rouge Parish Prison. The police arrested all of them, but not before saying, "Thanks, girls" as they looked at the gang member lying dead on the floor.

Three days later, after sorting through the stories of witnesses and interviewing the girls, Terri and the others were released but ordered by police to "find another profession." Norby's death was deemed self-defense.

To this day, more than twenty years later, Terri carries photos in her wallet of Norbert Dees bleeding on the floor of that barroom. The photo of the man she killed—her reminder that she would never again let a man mistreat her.

Ann Bryan

St. James Place, located on a long stretch of road known as Lee Drive near Louisiana State University (LSU), was the first upscale retirement facility built in Louisiana. Situated on fifty-two acres decorated with lush landscaping and oak trees more than two hundred years old, this land was originally part of the Duplantier Plantation. Old Southern charm once seeped through the porches and walls of the rambling plantation house whose adjoining structures housed slaves named Abraham, Isaac, Jean Baptiste, Hercules, and Samson. Elegance and grace, long past, had left their mark on the grounds, where the elderly now sit and sip tea or enjoy a leisurely stroll punctuated with the steady whistling of crested wood ducks along pathways lined with sweeping branches that shade their way.

What had begun as a vision of parishioners at St. James Episcopal Church in Baton Rouge had turned into a sprawling luxury home for seniors who wanted to enjoy their golden years surrounded by friends and family. Built in 1983, the retirement facility provided an atmosphere of fun and happiness where residents could dance to Cajun music on a portable wooden dance floor, enjoy crawfish boils on lazy summer days, or enjoy private parties catered on site. This innovative approach to retirement was wildly successful, and it wasn't long before the facility was filled to capacity and bustling with activity. Seniors there made friends by participating in a variety of activities, like Ping-Pong, arts and crafts, woodworking, and golf. Healthy living was stressed by the staff, and seniors were afforded the best in health care and exercise facilities that catered to longevity. For those who lived there, life couldn't have been better.

Across the street, a Circle K convenience store provided easy access to milk and bread and snacks. Seniors often made the short walk to the store to pick up small items they might need during the week. Many were not aware that the store had a history of being robbed, as those robberies often happened at night when they were safely sleeping in their comfortable beds. Terri Lemoine knew about the robberies, though. She had experienced them firsthand, at gunpoint, seven times to be exact, but she continued to work the night shift, liking the slower pace better than the nonstop stream of customers who stopped to get gas and cigarettes during the day.

Back then, there were no gates to limit access in or out of the retirement facility. Anyone could walk along the sidewalks that led to individual wings that housed numerous apartments. From the windows inside the Circle K, Terri could watch people come and go at St. James Place when she was bored, although the traffic in and out became minimal as night progressed.

Today, large wrought-iron gates and wooden fencing around the facility prevent access. No longer can anyone view the beautiful grounds from the street. A guard in the guard station at the entrance stops every vehicle that approaches and asks drivers for identification and a reason for being on the property. For those visiting residents, a call must be made to ensure that the visitor is welcome. Security is very tight at St. James Place, but there's good reason for that. In 1994, administrators of the facility learned the hard way that extra security measures must be in place for the protection of their elderly residents.

When Ann Bryan chose St. James Place as her new home, she had thought she was safe. In 1990, she had fallen and broken her left shoulder and could not use her arm or hand. For most people, that would be an inconvenience, but for the lovely woman whose face did not bear the usual signs of aging, the fall had been devastating. She had been born without a right hand, and this accident had left her incapable of caring for herself.

Ann had never been one to let the lack of a hand stop her from doing anything. Throughout her life, she had always painted—beautiful still lifes of the magnolias that could be found everywhere in Louisiana, and occasionally a bowl of colorful fruit. She also played piano and had learned to drive when automatic transmissions made it possible to drive using only one hand. Even though these activities were more difficult for her than for others, she had a creative streak that could not be stemmed by her handicap. She resolutely worked around it.

Born in 1911, Ann moved to Baton Rouge to attend LSU when she was only sixteen. She had graduated high school early, salutatorian of her class. At first, she was very homesick for her family, and sometimes she cried at night when she missed them. One night, the dean of women saw her sitting alone and crying; she asked her why.

"I want to go home," Ann said between sniffles.

At that moment, the dean spotted another student, William Paul Bryan, walking across the campus. She stopped him and asked him to comfort the young girl, hoping that he would be able to cheer up Ann. William was very comforting, but Ann went home that night and cried again. This time, because she only had one hand. She knew that the sweet young man would never be interested in her. Ann was wrong.

The next morning, William was waiting for her. The slender girl with the beautiful skin and dark hair had captured his heart through her tears. He asked if she would go out with him to the picture show. Ann was delighted, but her parents had always warned her never to get in a car with someone she didn't know.

"How will we get there?" she asked.

William put his head down, embarrassed. "We'll have to take the streetcar because I don't have a car," he said.

"That's perfect," Ann replied, laughing. "I'd love to go out with you."

She enjoyed every minute of the evening she spent watching *Ben-Hur* with her new beau.

The couple married in 1929, and Ann gave birth to their first son, William Jr., the next year. Two more children followed, George and Rachel. William worked as an engineer with the Louisiana Department of Transportation, and Ann stayed home with her babies. When the youngest child, Rachel, was nine, William had a stroke, and Ann spent the next thirteen years caring for and comforting the man who had always given her so much comfort. When William passed away, Ann cried once again, this time for the man whose life had been shortened dramatically by a stroke.

Even without her William, Ann lived a happy life for many years, one made happier by her wonderful sense of humor and ability to keep herself busy with artistic endeavors. Art and music gave her purpose, brought beauty into her life, and she shared that beauty with her children and grandchildren, who loved her dearly. Her children loved to tease her because she had taught them to take her handicap with a grain of salt, just as she did. When she had a little difficulty accomplishing a task, they would laugh and say, "What's wrong with you? You act like you only have one hand." Ann would laugh, too, undaunted by their teasing. She knew how much they respected her.

And when Ann broke her shoulder, her children knew only too well how devastating that was. Ann could no longer pick up a paintbrush or stroke the keys of her piano. She could no longer do anything without help. St. James Place, with its manicured lawns and attractive apartments, seemed to be the perfect solution. The nursing staff was well equipped to care for her and to help the still-beautiful woman in her late seventies adjust to her new life. Ann sold her home and moved into her small apartment, in the same manner she had done everything in her life—with resolve that she would make the best of the situation.

For several years, that is just what she did. Although she was plagued by headaches, she had no other real health problems and might have lived for many more years. But in the early morning hours of March 21, 1994, Ann's life would come to an abrupt and horrific end. The sweet eighty-two-year-old woman, who had faced life so bravely, would leave this world in terror, her body mutilated.

From her perch across the street, Terri did not see the

bushy-moustached man sneaking onto the property in the predawn hours. He was cloaked by the shadows of darkness. Ann's murder would remain unsolved for ten long years; and even when resolution came, her family could never be certain.

A Rocky Beginning

"I'll shoot him," Norman Gillis screamed, holding the gun with a shaking hand to the head of his one-year-old son, Sean. "I'll kill you, too."

Norman's wife, Yvonne, stood in the door of the bedroom for a moment, petrified.

She couldn't believe this stranger with a gun was the fun-loving man she had married two years before. She didn't like to be around guns and had been afraid when Norman had walked into the house carrying this one. She had consoled herself with the fact that men liked guns. But then he had become angry because she didn't jump to do his bidding.

Norman had grabbed the gun and run into Sean's room. Yvonne had run after him.

"I'm serious, Yvonne. I'll kill him."

"Oh no, you won't!" Yvonne yelled, spurred to furious action by his words.

She charged toward him, determined to get the gun.

Norman put his finger on the trigger. Just before he pulled, Yvonne managed to get to him. She desperately tried to wrestle the gun away from her husband. She fought him fiercely. Yvonne would not let this crazed man kill her son. When she realized the gun was in her hands, she ran into the bathroom, hurriedly locking the door behind her.

Yvonne leaned back against the door for a moment, catching her breath. The window above the sink provided an avenue of escape. She jumped on the counter, gun still in her hand. A tall, slender woman, she had no trouble maneuvering herself out the window and to the ground below. She ran to her neighbor's house and called Norman's father.

Yvonne watched as Norman Gillis Sr. brought her husband out of the house; then she hurried inside to get her baby. She held him tightly, tears streaming down her face as she promised her son that she would never let anything bad happen to him again.

That night as she lay in bed, Yvonne wondered what had happened, how Norman could have done something like this. She didn't understand. They had been so happy together. As she lay there, crying, Yvonne went over the details of their first meeting in her mind.

She had met Norman while pursuing a graduate degree at Louisiana State University in the late 1950s. One night, Norman's roommate, a friend of Yvonne's, had invited her to a cast party. Norman studied acting and sometimes performed in college plays. Yvonne had thought Norman was cute, but she only talked with him for a moment at the party that night. It wasn't until the following semester that she saw him again in one of her classes. They began talking every day, and the handsome young man finally asked her out.

"I'm going to marry you, you know," he told her on their first date.

"You've got to be kidding." Yvonne laughed, and her heart beat just a little faster.

"I'm very serious," he assured her.

Yvonne didn't believe him. Boys didn't say things like that on a first date. She knew that true love took time to develop, but his words excited her.

Yvonne was a good Catholic girl. Her brother was a priest and her sister a nun. While she had chosen to pursue a college education instead of the life of a nun, her religious beliefs were strong. She liked that Norman's intentions had been so clearly stated, that his intentions seemed pure. The two had discovered that they liked a lot of the same things, and Yvonne had been taken with his good looks. He had made her laugh and seemed to be a kind young man.

On Thanksgiving Day in 1960, just a year after that first date, the couple spoke the vows that would bind them in holy matrimony at the elegant St. Ann's Catholic Church in Mamou, Louisiana. Yvonne could not have been happier. Norman was the man of her dreams—smart, funny, good-looking. With stars in her eyes, Yvonne held on to her new husband's hand tightly as they drove away from the church to begin their life together. She couldn't believe her luck. God had certainly shown his favor to her.

But there was much that Yvonne didn't know about Norman. Born in 1935, Norman had grown up in New Orleans, although he had lived in the small town of Picayune, Mississippi, for a short period. His had not been a particularly happy childhood. His parents had divorced when he was four years old. His father was an alcoholic, and his mother was not pleasant to be around. Norman would later tell Yvonne that his mother didn't beat him or hurt him, he just didn't like her. It wasn't long before he moved in with his grandmother, a Sunday school teacher who spent much of her time teaching him the Bible.

As a teenager, Norman liked to collect coins and guns. He had amassed quite a collection of coins one year and decided to take one to the carnival that had come to town. When he spent it, he didn't think much of it, but when his grandmother asked him about it, she cried as he told her he'd spent a valuable piece from his collection.

"It hurt her that I had done that," Norman said. "That taught me that I did not ever want to hurt anyone again. I did not like to see her cry."

Norman scraped his way through school, barely getting by. After his high-school graduation, he decided to join the military. He spent four years in the navy, but those were not happy years, either, and he occasionally got into trouble. Once, in Honolulu, Hawaii, he was found wandering through the streets, drunk and naked. He was taken immediately to a mental hospital, where he spent a few days being psychoanalyzed.

In another incident, Norman was in a bar in Honolulu drinking with a friend when a chaplain came in to take him back to the base. On the bus ride back, Norman attacked the chaplain and tried to jump out of the bus. Again, he was sent to a mental hospital, this time for eight days. When he was released, he was discharged from the military and told he could not reenlist.

Not quite knowing what to do next, he enrolled in Louisiana State University, taking advantage of the GI Bill. His grades there were not good, but Norman was outgoing and soon made a lot of friends. When he met Yvonne, he saw a chance to make a stable life for himself. The idea of getting married and having his own family was attractive to him. He had not experienced much love in his life, outside of his grandmother, and Yvonne represented stability and love to him. He did not dare rock that boat by telling her that he sometimes had problems—with drinking, with coping. He did not tell her that he wondered about his own sexuality, that sometimes he struggled with his identity, that he wondered whether he was feminine or masculine.

Norman had serious mental problems, but he hid those from the pretty girl who held his hand so tightly, the girl who had vowed to love him forever. He just knew that he had been given a chance to make a happy life for himself, and he did not ever want to hurt her or to make her cry, like he had made his grandmother cry. He wanted a normal life. And for a while, he was successful in his effort to achieve that dream.

Norman and Yvonne rented a small apartment on West Chimes, a bustling street near LSU's campus. They lived there for a few months; then they moved to another apartment on St. Charles Street. Norman worked at Sherwin-Williams in the accounting department, while Yvonne worked as a receptionist for a local radio station. Yvonne settled happily into her role as a wife, but Norman struggled to be the man she wanted him to be. It wasn't easy, and soon he found himself slipping back into his old patterns.

At first, he hid his drinking from Yvonne, but eventually he began staying out, later and later. Yvonne began to worry, just a niggling thought in the back of her mind, that she had made a mistake. Norman wasn't the same when he drank. He didn't laugh and have fun with her. He was meaner, more demanding. She didn't like that side of him very much, but she didn't know what to do to change things.

Then she discovered she was pregnant. On June 24, 1962, Sean Vincent Gillis was born. As Yvonne held him to her breast, she looked down with fascination at this beautiful baby boy she had created. He was to be her salvation. She prayed that her husband would now become more responsible, would stop the drinking, would be a good father to this gift from God.

Her prayers were in vain. Norman got worse after Sean was born. The couple bought a house on West Roosevelt Street, and the pressure of raising a family, of being responsible, became too much for Norman to handle. He began hanging out in the bars even more and started drinking at home. He was always irritable, and Yvonne struggled to keep him happy while taking care of their son.

Norman wasn't helping matters. He had lost his job at Sherwin-Williams and had begun working as a door-to-door encyclopedia salesman. He did not make enough money to take care of their needs; so Yvonne, even though she wanted to stay home with her baby, went to work writing commercials for WBRZ-TV, channel 2, in Baton Rouge. A babysitter cared for Sean and cleaned the house while Yvonne worked.

Although hers was not the happy life she had envisioned, Yvonne made the best of it and tried to stay positive. She loved Norman and hoped he would come to his senses. She prayed for him every night before she went to sleep. She remembered the good times, the times when Norman had been so attentive and made her laugh. She wondered if she was doing something wrong and tried harder to make him happy. Nothing she tried worked.

And then he came home with the gun, and her marriage was over. He had never been violent before, but she would take no chances with Sean's life.

Norman committed himself to the East Louisiana State Hospital in Jackson, Louisiana, where he spent a month before being released. When he got out, he called Yvonne's brother, Father Francis Bourgeois, and told him he wasn't going back to her. Then he called Yvonne.

"I'm leaving," he said. "I don't ever want to hurt you or Sean, so it's best if I just go."

Yvonne hung up the phone and bowed her head, praying for the strength to raise her son on her own. As a Catholic, she knew that her marriage was supposed to last forever. After she had wiped the tears from her eyes, Yvonne went to get Sean from his bed. She hugged him close to her.

"Everything will be all right," she promised. "I'm going to take good care of you."

She would spend the rest of her life living up to those words. It would be many years before she heard from Norman again. However, he took the time to forge her name to a check or two soon after he left her.

Norman spent the next years in and out of mental institutions. He was a lost soul searching for some comfort in a world he did not understand. He went to the Veterans Administration for help and was once again hospitalized. The tranquilizers he took in the hospital gave him hallucinations, and his condition worsened. While there, he sliced his wrist, but he survived. Norman was tired, tired of trying, tired of not knowing who he was. He was referred to a domiciliary for veterans in Los Angeles, but he did not get any better there. It was determined that he was disabled, and he was placed on Social Security and disability. In December 1969, he checked himself out.

"I had money saved and went to Mexico for a week," Norman remembered. "I came back and went to San Diego Hospital. I didn't feel like I could function outside. Everything was so scary to me. I didn't feel comfortable trying to get a job."

After Norman left that hospital, he made his way to

San Francisco. It was the "Summer of Love," and he found himself in Haight-Ashbury, living in a Bohemian subculture that felt like home to him. The area, with its abandoned multistory buildings, had become a haven for hippies, who lived together in peace and harmony. Norman got a room in a large brownstone that housed a commune on the corner of Haight and Ashbury Streets and began taking LSD with his new friends. Sometimes he went with them to feed people in Golden Gate Park, amid huge cherry trees and rose and tulip gardens.

For a while, Norman seemed to enjoy his life, but the darkness always came back. It rose up and engulfed him. When that happened, he knew it was time to let someone else take care of him. He did not really want to die or to hurt anyone else. He checked himself into another hospital.

This time, he was given electroshock therapy, but he continued to have problems. Nothing worked. Nothing made him feel normal. Nothing helped him cope with life.

Norman was committed to mental institutions nineteen times in the years after he left Yvonne. He would spend a total of four and a half years institutionalized, working sporadically in the interim.

Yvonne did not hear from him and received no financial support during those years. But the death of Norman's father in 1978 would bring the family back together.

A Killer in the Making

Sean was a sweet, loving little boy. Yvonne often referred to him as her blue-eyed angel, and she doted on him. She read to him each night, sometimes familiar stories heard by other children and sometimes more elevated material. While other children were learning about the three little pigs, Sean was listening to the works of the great masters: Charles Dickens, Mark Twain, John Milton. Each time she finished one book, Yvonne would pull another from the room that was lined from floor to ceiling with books, in the back of the house. She had the complete works of William Shakespeare, Dante Alighieri, Ernest Hemingway, Edgar Allan Poe.

"Lew Wallace wrote *Ben-Hur,*" she explained to her young son before she turned to the first chapter. She felt it was important that he know the author of the books she read to him. Sean listened quietly, lulled to sleep most nights by the sound of his mother's voice bringing to life the books she loved.

"Sean was a child who was in awe of things," Yvonne recalled. "He was very respectful. I used to think he was my little genius, but one of his teachers told me he was just an average child."

Sean was like every other boy, except that he didn't have a father. Sometimes the children at school would tease him, and he would come home upset. "Where is my daddy?" he would ask his mother. Yvonne didn't quite know how to answer that question.

The two spent a lot of time with Norman's family while Sean was growing up. Yvonne wanted her son to know his family, and Sean saw his grandfather almost every day. "You might have divorced our son, but you didn't divorce us," Norman Sr. was fond of telling his former daughter-in-law. Together, they often went to feed the ducks that waddled around the LSU lakes or to the grocery store or to get ice cream.

And although his mother worked hard at the television station, Sean did not lack for attention. As he grew older, he hung out at the station with her, learning the ins and outs of production and sales. Sometimes he would sit near Yvonne's desk, reading one of the books she had brought for him. Yvonne didn't make a lot of money, but they made do on her salary. She always made sure her son had food before she ate. And though meeting her obligations was often difficult, Yvonne was eventually able to make a down payment on a house located on Burgin Avenue.

The neighborhood was nice, just a block off Lee Drive in a growing area of Baton Rouge, only a few miles from LSU. A magnolia tree in the front yard provided shade for the three-bedroom, two-bath home. Yvonne liked that she would have enough room for her bookcases in the extra bedroom. Although the living room was small, there was plenty of room for her and her son. A large backyard, which provided ample space for running and playing, could be seen from the sliding glass door in the dining room. Yvonne knew that this home would bring the two of them great happiness. She especially liked the bricked sculpture surrounded by flowers that centered the backyard. Sean liked to call it "my mother's shrine."

"Sean was about ten when they moved here," said Carolyn Clay, a neighbor who had moved across the street in 1971, two years before Yvonne moved in. "He gave the other kids in the neighborhood the willies. There was just something strange about him. He played Dungeons and Dragons with my son once in a while, but my daughter avoided him."

Yvonne didn't think there was anything strange about her precious son. He seemed perfectly normal to her. He liked *Star Trek* and snakes, reading books and assembling model cars. He went through an Evel Knievel stage, like other boys. He behaved well, and Yvonne only had to spank him once. She used a thin belt, which left marks on the back of his legs, and that had hurt her heart.

"It hurt me more than it hurt him," she said. "After that, I took away his television privileges, when he needed to be punished."

Sean attended several schools: St. Agnes School, University Terrace Elementary School, and St. Anthony Elementary School, even though it was sometimes difficult for Yvonne to raise the tuition for the parochial schools. She wanted Sean to have a good Catholic education, so she cut corners to be able to afford it. His grades were okay, but Sean did not have the motivation to be an overachiever. Yvonne saw him as one, though. She knew how smart he was, even if his teachers did not.

It was at St. Anthony that Sean met John Green, one of the two boys who would become his best friends.

"Sean was a very neat kid," Green remembered. "He was different, offbeat, smart. He had a lot more going on mentally than others. He used to carry a briefcase with a *Star Trek* sticker to elementary school, and he taught me to play chess. We were like-minded and had a lot of classes together. He was very respectful to adults and very helpful. If one of us needed help, Sean was always there. If he didn't know what he was doing, he was a quick study and would learn. He also had a fantastic sense of humor."

When in the seventh grade, Sean began attending Redemptorist High School, the circle grew to include John Rosas. He, too, liked that Sean was so smart. Together, the three boys went to the movies or to the Mall at Cortana or just to each other's houses. They would often sit around and talk about girls. "Sean was like a brother to me," Rosas said. "We had the same ideals, liked the same television shows, had the same characteristics. I could count on him."

Yvonne liked Sean's friends and even called them her "sons" on occasion. Sean was a latchkey kid, so she was glad that he had such good friends to play with after school. She didn't have to worry so much when she worked late.

"Sean was my first experience with a single-parent household," Green said. "His mom was a very pleasant lady, hardworking. She treated Sean more like an adult than a child. It made him a survivor."

As the boys grew older, they did get into a spot of trouble from time to time, but no more than other teenagers. They went through a phase where they were intrigued with the idea of Devil worship, and when Green told Sean about a place where it was rumored that Devil worshippers hung out, Sean insisted they check it out.

"We would go there, adventure seeking sometimes," Green recalled. "We soon found out other teenagers did the same thing."

They all gathered at the end of South Harrell's Ferry

Road, a rural area in the southeastern part of Baton Rouge. A gate with brick pillars on either side led the way. One of the boys would open the gate, while the other would back the car down the road past a dilapidated house to the edge of the field. When they got to the end of the road, if they listened very hard, they could hear people chanting. They wondered if they were making sacrifices, but they never got the nerve to get close enough to find out what was really going on. On Friday nights, they liked to park by the gate, shining their lights on other approaching teenagers to scare them off. One night, as they drove down the road, someone shot a gun at them. They took off in a hurry that night.

"Most of what we heard there was in our imaginations," Green recalled, laughing. "It was exciting stuff for us."

Smoking marijuana was also exciting for the three boys, and together, they experimented with the drug, although Sean liked it more than the other two. Yvonne knew nothing about that. The Sean she had raised would never do anything illegal. She had the utmost confidence in him, and he intended to keep it that way. He kept many of his activities well hidden from his mother.

For fourteen years, Yvonne worked at WBRZ, enjoying her job and her life. In 1976, she decided it was time to move on and took a job with Goudchaux's department store in its advertising department. She had not done a bad job of raising her son by herself. Although money was tight at times, she did her best to make sure that Sean had everything he needed. And when he earned extra money, he would buy her books to add to her collection. By now, he was well versed in the classics, and he knew that reading books pleased his mother. He liked to please her, and she him. They depended on each other for everything, and Yvonne was very proud of the young man Sean was becoming.

From her view across the street, Carolyn Clay worried about the person Sean was becoming. "I knew something was wrong with him," she said. "One night, about three in the morning, I awoke to a loud noise coming from their yard. Sean was in the front yard beating wildly on some garbage cans. He told another neighbor that he was frustrated because he didn't have a girlfriend. He was prone to fits of anger like that. He was an angry young boy."

But Yvonne didn't see that part of her son's personality, or she simply ignored it.

Family Reunion

Norman Sr. passed away at Christmastime when Sean was seventeen. Yvonne called her ex-husband to tell him that his father had died. It was the first time they had spoken in years. Norman got on a plane and headed back to Louisiana, nervous because he knew he would see his son for the first time since Sean had been a year old.

At the funeral, Yvonne introduced Sean to his father.

"Sean was hostile to me," Norman said.

Yvonne had a different version of that story. "We spent about a week there, and they talked a lot," she said. "They began writing to each other after that."

The father and son would meet again in Shreveport, Louisiana, in 1979. In the years since Sean had grown up, much had changed in Norman's life. He was now working as the manager of patient transport at Stanford Hospital in Palo Alto, California. His mental condition had improved enough to allow him to hold a job, although he still went through rough patches. He had married and divorced during that time as well, but he still struggled with his sexual identity.

Norman decided it was time to develop a relationship with his son. He had spent many years feeling guilty because he had not participated in Sean's upbringing and wanted to make amends. The trip to Shreveport did a lot to mend fences between the two, and they enjoyed horseback riding together, visiting an amusement park, and catching up on what they had missed in each other's lives. Norman left out the bad stuff, but, then, so did Sean. They both left feeling the meeting had been successful, with hope that they could have a real relationship.

And when Sean graduated from Redemptorist High School in 1980, Norman was sitting beside Yvonne, as proud as any other father in attendance. Yvonne was beaming. She had done her job and had done it well. Sean had graduated from high school and was ready to begin his life armed with the tools she had given him. She had high hopes for her son. So did Norman.

Happy that he had been able to watch his son graduate, Norman decided to celebrate. He went out that night and got drunk, something he had not done in a while. When Yvonne's brother, the priest, found out, he sent Norman to the bishop for confession. The bishop gave him penance and told him to read the Epistle of James. Norman did, and spent a fitful night.

The next morning, he felt better. *I've done penance, gone to confession, and read James. I'll have a beer now,* he thought as he pulled back the tab. As he drank his beer, he looked out the bathroom window and saw an apparition: a disheveled man in a cage riding with a traveling circus. Norman offered him a sip of whiskey if he would bite off the head of a chicken. When Norman came out of his hallucination, he called Alcoholics Anonymous. Two men came and brought him to Baton Rouge General, where he was placed in intensive care.

"Sean, can you pick up a few things I left in the room I rented in New Orleans?" Norman said into the phone, worried that he would lose his possessions while he was in the hospital. "The car I rented also needs to be returned."

"Sure, Dad," Sean replied before getting directions.

Sean called John Green and another friend, John LeBlanc, and asked them to go along with him. Green followed Sean in Yvonne's car.

"The room was in the French Quarter," Green said. "I had never been there before. We drove up a small street and stopped at the address. There was a group of people walking by, and one person had a T-shirt on that read, 'Gay is the way.' That struck me."

The trio walked through a gate and into a courtyard, where two men were sitting in old wicker chairs. The boys made their way to a small bedroom, where Norman had left a suitcase and a few personal items. As they packed his things, Sean's friends noticed some photographs on the nightstand. They picked them up and began looking through them.

Naked men in various sexual positions stared back at them.

"It was revolting," John Green said. "I was a homophobe back then and couldn't believe what I was seeing. Sean just kind of stood there in shock. I could tell he was swallowing emotion, but he kind of grinned and shook it off. I knew he was upset."

The boys hurriedly gathered the rest of Norman's things, then headed back to Baton Rouge. Sean was very quiet on the ride home. He was mortified that his friends had seen those pictures. He was horrified by the thought that his dad was homosexual. The pictures had made that very clear.

"When he got home, Sean was very peeved at his dad," Yvonne said. "I was a little ticked off at Sean because he had taken my car without permission."

Norman committed himself for thirty days to a chemical dependency unit. That was the last time he ever drank. When he got out of the hospital, Norman immediately returned to California. His secret was finally out, and he did not want to face his son or Yvonne just then. He joined Alcoholics Anonymous and, after a few weeks, called Yvonne and invited her and Sean to come to California to attend one of his meetings so that he could apologize.

"They didn't want to come, so I assumed they wanted to write me off," Norman said. Disgusted with himself, he continued attending his meetings and began reading the Bible. He asked God to take his illness away from him, to bring some sort of stability to his life and to his thoughts. When Norman found the Body of Christ Church, he knew God had heard his prayers. Through the church, Norman was able to rebuild his life and reconcile his sexual identity. He eventually remarried and became an ordained minister. The years he had spent searching for himself melted into the past, and the Bible replaced the alcohol and drugs that had previously ruled his life. For the first time in his life, Norman found peace.

Sean, however, could find none. He struggled to deal with what he had seen and what he had learned about his father in that sleazy little room in the French Quarter.

Separation

Sean was arrested for the first time for criminal trespass a few months before he graduated high school. It was the first of several times he would be arrested in the ensuing years, although he was never arrested for any violent crimes. After he graduated, he went to work with his old friend, John Rosas, for Southland Corporation, which owned the 7-Eleven chain of convenience stores.

"Sean was a hard worker. We started on the dog shift, from eleven at night until seven in the morning, and Sean would come sit with me and help me out, and vice versa," Rosas explained. "We also worked together at the Wilson's (department store) on College Drive for a while."

Throughout the next few years, Sean would change jobs often, never content to stay in one place too long. He didn't really like to work, preferring instead to sit at home in front of his newest discovery—a personal computer. It fascinated him. Long before most people had home computers, Sean was busy learning every detail of how to operate one. He attended a community college to get his certification in computers and passed all of his courses.

He couldn't wait to get a job where he could utilize his knowledge. That would not happen for a while.

Sean still lived at home, but Yvonne didn't mind. He kept her company. She was in no hurry for him to leave, although she did like it better when he was working. She worried about him sometimes, about his lack of motivation and the fact that he was grown now, but still living off her. *He'll grow up,* she thought. *These things take time.* Sean saw no need to change anything.

For the next ten years, they lived together, until Yvonne decided to move to Atlanta. She had been offered a job as a broadcast manager with the Richards Agency, and she was excited about the prospect. She asked Sean to go with her.

"No," he said. "I'll just stay here."

"Well, I'll pay the mortgage, so all you have to worry about are the utilities," Yvonne told him.

Sean smiled and assured Yvonne that he would be okay living there by himself. Although she was a little worried about leaving him alone, Yvonne left for her new life in Atlanta.

It was 1992, and Sean was alone for the first time in his life, alone to spend his time on his computer, surfing the emerging Internet, discovering the excitement of the pornography that could be found there.

On August 26 of that year, Hurricane Andrew swept through Baton Rouge, bringing with it moderate winds and minor flooding in some parts of town. Sitting in front of his computer, Sean could not be bothered to clean up the mess caused by the few inches of water that had seeped into the house. He put newspaper down on the floors to sop up the water, but he did not pick up his mother's books that had begun floating across the back room. *I'll do it later,* he thought, but he never did. When his friends came over, he just grinned and said, "Excuse the mess," then lit up a joint. No one seemed to mind the dried-up newspaper everywhere or the moldy smells that lingered in the house.

Yvonne would have been horrified, but she didn't know. Whenever she called, Sean assured her that everything was fine. His neighbors didn't think so. Sometimes late at night, they could hear Sean outside, howling at the moon and cursing his mother for leaving him.

"He got worse after his mother left," Carolyn Clay said. "My son and daughter-in-law lived next door to him, and one day my daughter-in-law saw him behind her house peeping into her window. She called the police."

"My cat got into her yard, and I was looking for it," Sean told the officer who arrived to investigate the complaint. "I wasn't looking in her window. I was looking for the cat."

Sean had outstanding warrants for traffic violations, so the officer arrested him. "He asked me to go in his house and make sure the cat had food in her bowl," Carolyn said. "An officer went with me. When we got inside, the house smelled like pot. It was so messy that we only had a pathway where we could walk to the kitchen. There was stuff everywhere. I thought it looked like stolen stuff, but the officer could not do anything because he didn't have a search warrant."

Sean got out of jail in a few hours and returned home. Carolyn wished they had kept him longer. She had hoped he would grow up and move away. She knew that her daughter-in-law had been correct, that Sean had been peeping in the window, and she worried for her safety. She didn't like what was going on in the Gillis house.

"Sometimes he had parties there, and I always thought he was dealing dope out of the house," Carolyn said. "On

Veterans Day one year, he had a party, and I watched as Sean and some friends led an obviously drunk black girl into the yard. I don't know if she's dead, but if she is, all of those boys were involved. I never trusted him, not even when he was a young boy. There was just something about him."

A Chance at Love

Terri Lemoine barely noticed the man with the bushy moustache when he walked into the store behind her friend Sharon. It was early in her shift at Circle K, and she was happy to see her friend. She loved it when people dropped in to see her; it broke up the monotony that the long nights could bring.

"Terri, this is Sean," Sharon said, stepping back a little so Terri could see the man behind her. "Sean, this is Terri. Y'all have to get to know each other. Y'all have so much in common."

Terri leaned toward her friend and, through clenched teeth, said, "Get him out of here."

"No." Sharon laughed before walking out of the store, leaving Sean behind.

Terri looked uncomfortably at the man her friend had brought to meet her. She thought he was rather good-looking in a geeky sort of way. He wasn't tall, only about five feet seven inches or so, but she didn't mind. He had brown hair and pretty blue eyes, which looked at her through wire-rimmed glasses. He was slender and had a short beard. He didn't look too bad, so she decided it might be better to make the most of the situation her friend had thrust upon her.

"Hi," she said.

Sean smiled. "Hi." Already he liked the girl behind the counter. She was pretty, with long bleached-blond hair and brown eyes, hidden behind her glasses like his.

Sean and Terri spent that night in early March 1994 talking in between the occasional customer. They discovered they had quite a lot in common. Both were Trekkies. Both liked the same movies, the same television shows, the same food. They talked about everything that night— politics, religion, their past lives. When Sean finally left early the next morning, just before Terri's shift ended, each knew that they wanted to see the other again. But Terri was a little scared.

In the years since she had left the Key Club the night she had killed the biker, she had married, this time to a Palestinian. Her life had changed dramatically when she met her second husband. She had been introduced to a whole new culture and soon began dressing the part. Mazen was interesting to Terri. She liked that he was different, that he taught her another way of life. They lived together in America until he finished his schooling, and then they moved to Kuwait for a while.

They soon returned to Baton Rouge, where they lived for two years. By this time, Terri was deeply immersed in Arab culture and had become president of the local American Palestinian Arab Corporation (APAC). Terri had no problem dressing in the *abayas* and *thobes,* which Arab society demanded women wear. She liked the attention, and Terri had always enjoyed dressing up. People noticed her in the long, flowing robes and shawls that hid the fact that she was gaining weight. They noticed that her skin was paler than most women who wore those robes. They wondered about her. She liked that.

Terri and Mazen soon returned to the Middle East, this time to Jordan to stay with his family for a while, but they came back to the United States in 1992. In the years since they had met, living with Mazen had become more and more difficult. According to Terri, he had hit her on occasion.

One night, he came into the kitchen with his fist raised.

"Don't do it," Terri said, her voice calm, her stance ready.

He hit her. Terri grabbed the meat cleaver, which was on the counter, and sliced her husband's arm wide open. Mazen backed away, holding his arm. He was bleeding all over the floor and was shocked that his wife could do such a thing.

"I told him not to do it," Terri said later.

She filed for divorce, but the marriage had left some serious scars. And Terri did not feel as attractive as she had been before. "I was stunned by how much weight I had gained," she said. "All those years of wearing robes, you never really take a good look at yourself."

By the time Terri met Sean, her divorce was almost final. It had been two years since she had left her husband, and she was ready for some excitement. With Sean, she found more than that. She found a friend, a companion, someone who understood her, someone who didn't mind that she had epilepsy and occasionally suffered with grand mal seizures. He was like her, interested in collecting things. He knew every title of every episode of *Star Trek* that had ever aired.

When Sean asked her out, Terri said yes. She couldn't wait to see this unusual man again. And she couldn't believe she felt that way. Because of her prior experiences with men, she had been certain she would be alone for the rest of her life, and she had been content with that thought. Her life was fine. She lived in her apartment with her cats, had many things to occupy her time, and she liked her job. Sean would change all of that.

She felt like she could talk to him, but she wasn't sure she trusted him. One night, not long after they began dating, the two got into a minor argument. Terri slapped him, hard across his face. Sean looked at her for a moment, stunned, his fists clenching and unclenching at his sides. Then he began stomping his feet, tears seeping from the corners of his eyes.

"Girls don't hit boys, and boys don't hit girls!" he yelled before running from the room.

Terri was relieved. She knew then that she could trust him, that he would not hit her, would not try to hurt her, as the others had done. She told him she was sorry and that she would never hit him again. There would be no more violence in their relationship.

Sean soon fell madly in love with Terri. He visited her often at her two-story town house apartment on Jennifer Jean Drive near Burbank, a road used by many students heading toward LSU to avoid the heavy traffic on Nicholson Drive and Highland Road. Knee-high weeds filled most of the yards on the street, and sheets doubled as curtains in many windows of the homes that looked much the same, one after the other.

Terri's apartment was always clean. She prided herself in her ability to decorate and make the most of whatever home she had. She liked things to be tidy. The first time she walked into Sean's home, she was appalled.

"It was horrible," she said, her nose wrinkling at the memory. "The house had been flooded by Hurricane Andrew, and it was in bad shape. The gold shag carpet still had the newspapers on it that Sean had used to soak up the water."

Terri set about cleaning up the mess. Many of Yvonne's books had been ruined, but when Terri tried to throw them away, Sean yelled, "For God's sake, don't get rid of those books! Those are my mother's. She'd get mad if I threw them away."

As she cleaned up the books as best she could before returning them to the shelves, she wondered if Sean was afraid of his mother. It had sounded like he was.

Terri worked furiously on the house. Soon the moldy smell was gone, and she could see shiny floors and clean carpet beneath her feet. She took pictures of her handiwork and sent them to Yvonne.

When they first met, Sean drank heavily—Jack Daniel's or Crown Royal and water. "He drank and drank and drank," Terri remembered. "And he didn't work. All he did was sit all day at the computer he had built. His mother sent him money for the bills. She spoiled him, gave him everything he wanted. They didn't talk much, but she always sent him money. I couldn't see him being able-bodied and sitting in front of a computer all day. It bothered me."

Other things about Sean bothered Terri, but the men in her past had been brutal, and Sean was affectionate and kind. He called Terri "Honey Bunny." She loved him in return, grateful that she had found someone with whom she had so much in common. Sean appreciated that she could sew, that she was creative, that she knew as much about *Star Trek* as he did. He was her admiral fleet commander, and she adored him. She knew that with a little motivation, Sean would be the man she wanted. She soon got him a job at the Circle K, where she worked. Terri worked at night, and Sean worked during the day, so they didn't see each other that often, but the relationship deepened over those first few months.

Their sex life, however, left much to be desired. Sean had made no serious advances, but Terri decided one night that it was time to have sex. She cooked him one of her specialties, lasagna, and the couple laughed and talked as they ate. Terri soon led him to the bedroom.

"He was very nervous, like he wasn't sure if he knew what to do," Terri said. "I thought he was a virgin but found out later he wasn't. I think he had sex with one girl before me."

Terri showed him what to do, but Sean was still nervous. He didn't seem to be enjoying it.

Sean and Terri only had sex two or three more times throughout the course of their ten-year relationship. It bothered Terri tremendously, and she questioned him about it on many occasions.

"I'm just not interested in sex," he would tell her.

"Is something wrong with me?" she prodded.

"No. It's not you," Sean responded.

"Am I too fat?"

"No. I just don't like it," Sean explained. After a while, Terri quit caring. She had been through her share of men, and although Sean's lack of interest in sex seemed strange to her, it was nice that she could spend so much time with a man and not have sex. And besides, Sean was affectionate with her. He would come up behind her and hug her as she washed dishes. He held her hand. He told her he loved her.

It wasn't until she moved in with him in 1995 that she discovered the real reason he did not want to have sex with her. Sean was addicted to pornography. She would often find balled-up T-shirts behind the couch or the bed stained with the evidence that he had been masturbating when she wasn't around.

Sometimes, when Terri found a shirt that she knew he had used to clean himself after he masturbated, she would sneak up behind him as he sat at his computer and lay the shirt over his head. Sean would scrunch down in his seat and grin, knowing he had been caught. Terri would rub the shirt over his head before throwing it in the washing machine. Sean tried to hide his proclivities from her, but Terri now knew why he wouldn't have sex with her. Worried about it, she consulted her mother.

"Well, if that's what gets him off, then that's what gets him off," her mother had said. "It has nothing to do with you."

But Terri still wondered about it. Sometimes she thought something might have happened to Sean when he was younger that made him that way. She noticed that he hated homosexuals and did not ever want to be viewed as one.

"Did something happen to make you not like women?" she asked him.

"No, no, no," Sean replied vehemently. "I like women."

Terri finally gave up, and sex became a nonissue in their relationship. The love and the friendship she had with Sean were much more important to her. She could tell him anything—even that she had killed a man. She showed him the picture she kept in her wallet, the one of the dead biker on the floor of the bar covered in blood. She told Sean about Louis, the father of her youngest child, whom she had loved so much. She told him about her second husband, how he had beaten her. She showed Sean pictures of her battered face. She told him she had sliced her husband's arm open with a meat cleaver. Sean didn't care. To him, Terri was special.

Senseless Slaughter

On the night of March 20, 1994, Ann Bryan was not feeling well. During a trip to the mall with her daughter, Rachel Ehricht, a few days before, Rachel had been forced to slam on her brakes. Ann, who was sitting in the backseat, had been thrown forward and had broken a couple of ribs. Those ribs had been hurting her all day, and she had been unable to play bridge with her friends at St. James Place that night.

Ann was an avid bridge player. Three or four times each week, several of her friends would gather at her apartment to play. These women were part of her bridge club, the non-daters who were more interested in spending time with each other than chasing the crotchety old men, as some of the other women liked to do. Ann also enjoyed playing Scrabble and was considered unbeatable—a walking Scrabble dictionary.

Ann enjoyed her life at the assisted-living facility. She had been there for about five years and had adjusted nicely. It wasn't like her old home, of course, but she always made the best of things. The other residents liked her. They liked her spirit, her sense of humor. She always made them feel welcome.

Some of the housekeeping staff would fuss at her sometimes for leaving the door to her apartment unlocked, but Ann felt safe. Hers was the first apartment as you entered the hallway from the exterior door in the E wing, but that door was always locked at night. She had never feared for her safety there and liked to leave her door open so that the nurses and housekeeping staff would not have to wait in the hallway for her to open the door when they knocked. It was getting harder and harder for the elderly woman to get around, and sometimes getting to the door took a while.

Ann liked to be considerate of others, and the friends she had made there appreciated her thoughtfulness. A lot of the other residents left their doors unlocked at night, too. One of the things that had attracted them to living there had been the promise of security. Paying the expensive residence fee and then the monthly fees to live there afforded them the best in security measures.

Many of the residents sold their homes to be able to pay for this new life in luxurious surroundings, complete with whatever assistance they needed. Their residence fees varied, depending on the size and amenities of their apartments, but many cost more than fifty thousand dollars. Their monthly service fees ran more than nine hundred dollars. Ann felt privileged to be living there. She felt like this place was for rich people, and she had never been rich. But the sale of her home and her Social Security had helped to get her accepted into St. James Place.

Her apartment was not the most expensive, but it was nice. A foyer featuring a storage closet led to a large room that served as a living-dining combination. Her china cabinet rested against a wall near the dining-room table. The small but functional kitchen was perfect because Ann didn't cook much, anyway. It was easier just to order her meals each day, one of the perks of living at that particular facility. A Bible always adorned her coffee table, along with a few other religious books. Her home was small but contained all the important mementoes from her life. Photographs of her three children were displayed on tables throughout her apartment.

As she prepared for bed that evening on March 20, Ann decided to leave her front door unlocked. She thought the nurse might want to check on her during the night and bring her medication in the morning. Everyone knew she had hurt herself and might require assistance.

Ann put on her pink nightgown and climbed into bed.

Around 3:00 A.M. on March 21, she heard a noise. She thought it might be the nurse coming to check on her, so she was not alarmed.

Until the male figure loomed over her.

She could not see him clearly in the shadows of the dark room, but she felt his presence. She knew something was wrong. This man did not belong in her bedroom.

She screamed when he touched her. She screamed louder when he climbed on top of her and tore at her panties. She would not stop screaming, but no one heard her cries. He had closed the door, and the walls between the apartments were thick.

Ann screamed again and again, her hands and feet flailing desperately in an attempt to ward off her attacker.

She caught a glimpse of the steel blade of the knife just before he began slashing at her, stabbing the eighty-two-year-old woman as she lay, defenseless, in her bed. Frustrated that she would not be quiet and let him do what he had come to do, his fury mounted with each stab.

Ann screamed again, the last time any sound would

ever leave her lips. In a vicious swipe of his knife, the man sliced her throat open with such force that he almost decapitated her.

Thankfully, Ann passed quickly, but the man was not finished. He stabbed at her over and over, enjoying the experience, relishing it.

He knew she was dead, but he didn't care. She had stopped screaming. That was all that mattered.

He cut her stomach until her intestines and bowels extruded. He slashed her right breast until it was attached by only a few shreds of skin. He sliced her genitals, her face, between her breasts.

Forty-seven times, he stabbed the sweet old lady before he was finally sated.

He left as quietly as he had entered, enjoying the glory of his first kill. The only clues police found were a bloody knife print in the beige carpet and a shoe print. But there was another clue in the room that would be overlooked by police for more than ten years. It was a clue that would become a signature of a serial killer.

Carmen Cook, Ann's neighbor, read through *The Advocate* as she did every morning, then folded it neatly. She liked to keep it neat for Ann. She always brought it to her when she finished reading, and the morning of March 21 was no different. She knew Ann's door would be unlocked, so she didn't bother to knock. She didn't want to wake her. She put the paper on the table by the foyer. She didn't see Ann, so she assumed she was sleeping. Carmen went back to her room, unaware that anything was amiss.

* * *

St. James Place employee Louise Molbert saw that JoAnn Stevenson was busy and offered to help her out. "I'm going up to the front," she said. "I have to take somebody else's medicine, so I'll take Miss Ann's."

"Thanks," JoAnn replied. Louise often helped her while she set up medications and counted the narcotics. It was already 8:15 A.M., and she had not yet clocked in. She liked to get that chore completed first.

A few minutes later, Louise ran back into the health care center, hysterical, and hurried to the nursing director's office.

"What's wrong?" JoAnn said when Louise came out of the office.

"Mrs. Bryan is dead," she said as she went past. "I knocked on the door, then called her name. I called it again and again, but got no response. Then I went into the bedroom and found her."

The director, Marie Thibodeaux, was right behind her.

JoAnn got up and hurried toward Ann's room. She hated to hear this news and wanted to verify it for herself. Along the way, she ran into Charles Brady, the marketing director for St. James Place. Together, they made their way to Ann's apartment.

"Nothing looked out of the ordinary," JoAnn recalled about entering the apartment. "It looked like it always did, until you got to the bedroom. But when you saw the sheets . . . they were pink sheets with a pink coverlet on the bed. They were soaked in blood. Miss Ann was lying on the floor, with one leg on the floor and one leg on the bed. There wasn't much blood underneath her because she had bled out on the bed. Her throat had been cut, and I found out later that she was almost decapitated. There was an incision over the bowel, and the bowel loop was coming out. Then I quit looking."

It would be more than an hour before police were notified of the death. When it was finally called in to police, there was no mention of a murder, which would have made it a priority. It was called in as a regular death. The administrators of St. James Place did not want the media to show up with the police, but precious time had been lost—time that could have been spent searching for clues. In any murder, the clock is ticking, and the first forty-eight hours are the most important.

Terri Lemoine did not hear about the murder that had happened across the street from the Circle K until she got to work that night.

The Investigation Begins

Police were dispatched to Lee Drive at 10:22 A.M. When Officer Ben Odom arrived, uniform patrol officers were already inside the apartment. Needing to preserve the integrity of the scene, Odom asked everyone to step outside, then cordoned off the area around the apartment. He called headquarters and asked that Homicide Division detectives Keith Bates and Donald Armstrong be sent over immediately. Odom then surveyed the apartment.

He moved from the foyer to the living room, noticing that nothing seemed out of place. The kitchen revealed nothing out of the ordinary, either. Everything was neat and orderly.

He walked over to the sliding glass door, which led to a patio, and noticed no signs of forced entry there. Odom leaned down for a closer look, spotting a fingerprint that he made a mental note to have tested.

It wasn't until he reached the bedroom that evidence of the brutality of the crime emerged. He noticed the dresser, decorated with family photographs and toiletries. Closed drapes covered the window, which appeared to be locked.

Baskets under the window containing implements for sewing—scissors, thread, fabric—were undisturbed. A purple-and-white comforter lay over a wicker chair, which held bags of clothes. A wooden crucifix lay on the floor between the bed and the chair.

The bed was covered with a pink-orange-and-white spread. White-and-pink pillowcases covered the two pillows on the bed. Odom noticed an adult diaper wedged between the mattress and the headboard. Near one of the pillows, he saw a white hand towel, just above a large pool of blood. The other pillow was spattered with blood, as were the sheets and blanket. The telephone book, located on a table on the far side of the bed, was also spattered with blood. Red slippers were tucked neatly on the floor by the bed.

And on the floor near the table was the lifeless body of Ann Bryan. Her slight frame was facing the closet, and her right leg and foot were on the bed. Her left foot was bent under her right leg, and she was lying on a heating pad. Ann's left hand was balled into a fist near her neck. Blood spatters on the closet door indicated to the detective than Ann had been dropped from the bed onto the floor.

The killer had torn open the pink nightgown Ann had donned the night before, and had deliberately left her most private areas exposed for police to see.

Odom noticed multiple stab and slash wounds all over Ann's body. It was a vicious slaughter, her neck slashed from left to right, almost to the point of decapitation.

Her right breast was now a gaping hole, where the killer's weapon had cut through it in an effort to excise it. Odom noticed that no blood surrounded the area. This had been done after Ann had died. Other postmortem wounds became obvious—cuts to her upper abdomen and a slash to her lower abdomen that exposed her bowels and intestines.

Stab wounds between her breasts, stab wounds to her vulva, stab wounds to her cheek and chin. Ben Odom swallowed the bile that rose in his throat. He had to turn away for a moment.

It was then that he saw two bloody footprints on the floor adjacent to where Ann's body lay.

He moved to the bathroom, where he observed that the attack had been so forceful that blood had flown through the air and landed on the sliding doors that covered the closet. He turned away. He had seen enough.

When Keith Bates entered the apartment, he was unprepared for what he encountered. He had worked homicide with the Baton Rouge Police Department (BRPD) for five years and had experienced his fair share of gruesome murders. A tall, good-looking black man, Bates's soft-spoken voice and gentlemanly manners belied his toughness. Many a murderer had been convicted because Bates rarely relied on technology to solve a crime. He believed that crimes should be solved using instinct—his gut and what it was telling him. The cause, the manner, and the mechanism of the death were all he needed to put him on the path to a killer.

Bates had come to the Baton Rouge police from the military, where he served in the Army Police Corps. It wasn't long before his superior officers discovered he had a knack for reconstructing traffic accidents. Bates discovered he had a strong interest in law enforcement, and after three years, he returned to Baton Rouge to begin his career as a police officer. He started in the Traffic Control Division in 1980. Chief of Police Greg Phares soon realized that Bates commanded attention, and asked him to teach accident investigation at the police academy.

In 1986, Bates moved into criminal investigation, working on juvenile and sex crimes cases. By 1988, he had progressed to homicide. Methodical by nature, Bates thrived in his new environment. He enjoyed putting the pieces of crimes together and solving murders. It was his way of keeping safe the town where he had been born and raised. He felt he had an advantage. He knew the city inside and out. He understood the criminal mind. But when he walked into Ann Bryan's apartment, he would be faced with a crime more gruesome than most.

"It was Ben Odom's case. We were just support," Bates explained. "It was a very calm, isolated scene, confined to the bedroom. I had never seen a case like this before—the number of stab wounds, the brutality of the murder, the posing of the body. It was a retirement community, a nice area. The who, what, when, where, how, and why of this case became very challenging. If I knew then what I know now, I would have investigated it differently."

But hindsight is twenty-twenty, and Bates began doing what he always did—talking to neighbors, asking them if they had seen or heard anything. No one had. He investigated the security there. He talked to staff members. He asked the hard questions.

"The apparent cause and positioning of the body was alarming to me," he said. "This was not a typical murder, and I had not experienced anything like it before. Academically, I was aware that these things happened. You can sit in a class all day long, but when you actually see it, it's a different ball game. You're in shock when you see something like this."

Bates returned to the apartment to see if any evidence had been discovered. He and Ben Odom heard the crime scene technicians entering and returned to the living room. They watched as evidence was bagged and an alternate light source was used to determine if semen was present on the victim. No semen was found, and nothing in the apartment seemed to be missing or out of place. It appeared that rape or robbery had not been the motive of the attack. This killer only wanted to kill.

Rachel Ehricht walked into Robert E. Lee High School carrying dozens of eggs to be used in her home economics class. It was a day like any other—she had woken early, dressed, and hurried to the school in time for her first class. On her break, she went to Albertsons to purchase the necessary food for the next day's lectures. Another teacher was waiting for her when she got back to her classroom. Rachel knew by the look on her face that something was wrong.

"It's your mom," the teacher said.

"What? Did her blood pressure go up?" Rachel joked, setting the bags down. She was used to getting news about her mom's health through school personnel who took the calls from St. James Place.

"No. It's worse. She passed away."

Rachel couldn't believe it. She quickly ran to her car, anxious to get to St. James Place to find out what had happened. She knew her mom had been suffering because of her ribs, but she had seemed fine, other than that, when Rachel had seen her only days before.

When she arrived at the retirement facility, less than a mile down Lee Drive from the school, Rachel threw her car into park and ran inside, quickly making her way to the office. "I'm here because I got a call about my mom, that she died," she frantically said to the receptionist. A staff member hurried over and led Rachel into a private room.

"How did she die?" Rachel asked.

"She was murdered."

"She was what?"

"I'm sorry, Rachel. She was murdered last night. We found her this morning," the woman said.

Rachel could not comprehend what she was hearing. Who would kill her mother? Who would kill such a sweet, harmless old lady? She leaned back in her chair, a million questions mingling with her grief. She was still sitting there when the principal of Robert E. Lee High School arrived to comfort her. John, Rachel's husband, had called the principal to tell him what had happened and ask him to keep Rachel from leaving the school alone. John had been too late. Rachel had already been told the news, but she didn't understand. It was insane. It was awful.

"Do you know who did this?" she asked the woman.

Nobody knew.

It would be ten years before anyone had a clue, years that Rachel and her family would spend searching for the person who had so mercilessly killed an eighty-two-year-old woman in her bed. By 1997, when the murderer still had not been caught, Ann's family offered the public a fifteen-thousand-dollar reward for information leading to an arrest. They hired a private detective. They came up with theories about what had happened based on information gleaned from police.

One particular clue led the family to believe that Ann's death was somehow mixed up in Louisiana politics. Two calls had been made from her room the night of her murder, one to a prominent attorney in New Orleans who was embroiled in a multimillion-dollar lawsuit. There was no reason for Ann to call an attorney in the early-morning hours just before she was killed. Not long after Ann died, this same attorney was appointed as the head of the Gaming Control Board in Louisiana, which oversees the state's gambling industry. Ann's children came to believe that her death had been meant to send a message to the governor at the time, Edwin Edwards.

Edwards's mother lived only a few apartments away from Ann in St. James Place. Ann's family felt the murder was an intended message to Governor Edwards, which was, "This could have been your mother." They wondered about this for years and became even more convinced when the attorney was removed from the Louisiana Gaming Control Board the week after Edwards's mother passed away. But all of this was only speculation. They couldn't know for sure, and the terrible way in which their mother had died lingered over them like a dark cloud lingers on the horizon just before a storm.

Police spent the next few months following clue after clue. Fingerprints taken from near a window in the back of the apartment where a screen had been torn could not be identified. Photographs of the crime scene revealed the bloody imprint of a lock blade knife that could not be seen with the naked eye. The bloody footprints yielded no clues. Neighbors were interviewed, but nobody had seen anything. No one had heard the screams as Ann had fought for her life.

An arrest was eventually made. William Stevenson, the son of JoAnn Stevenson, one of the nurses on duty that day, had bragged to friends that he had committed the murder, that he knew the weapon that had been used. This information was relayed to police, but the case didn't stick. There was simply not enough evidence, and his story did not match the evidence.

Ben Odom would spend the next ten years haunted by the death of Ann Bryan. Even when the case went officially cold, he would not forget about this particular murder and would never stop chasing new clues as they were presented to him during the ensuing years. He could not know that Ann's killer would one day strike again.

Keith Bates went over and over the cause, manner, and mechanism of the case, hoping that he would find something that had been overlooked, hoping that a clue would emerge. The case stayed with him, mostly because this wasn't a body that had been dumped on the side of the road. This was an elderly woman who had been brutalized in her home, where she had felt safe. He knew the perpetrator had stayed with her for a while. Keith prayed he could bring her murderer to justice. He couldn't. Back then, no one could. There simply wasn't enough evidence.

St. James Place, its image of luxury and safety tarnished by the murder, quickly installed wrought-iron gates around the perimeter of the facility and placed a guard station at the entrance. Administrators tried valiantly to minimize media coverage of the murder. They did not need the bad publicity, and they reassured tenants that everything possible was being done to ensure that nothing like this would ever happen again. The retirement home eventually settled a lawsuit with each of Ann's children, who sued on the grounds of inadequate security, after it had come to light that only one guard watched the entire facility at night, and that it was his job to empty the trash in all of the bins on the premises during his shift. The administrators of St. James Place would not make that mistake twice.

A Normal Family

"Sean, can you please get off that computer? I fixed you spaghetti. Come on," Terri said, frustration evident in her voice. Sean stayed on the computer night and day when he wasn't working. That was the only thing they ever fought about.

When Sean got upset, he would sometimes tear things up, but that didn't scare Terri. She already knew he would never hurt her. He was much too timid. He liked her too much, although he didn't like to be around other people. He hated even to go to the store, unless it was to look at electronics. He just liked to stay in the living room and play Donkey Kong or other games on the Nintendo. Sometimes Terri and Sean curled up on the couch and watched *Star Trek* together. But mostly, Sean played on his computer, preferring to spend his time discovering the world through the magic of the Internet.

"Terri, come see this," Sean called.

"What?" Terri responded.

"Look what I found." Sean seemed excited, so Terri

bent over the computer to take a look. What she saw troubled her.

"It's a Web site of dead women," Sean said.

Terri looked again at the photographs of nude women posed in various positions. They were all dead.

"That's sick," she admonished him.

Sean just laughed and went back to viewing the women. He was enjoying his new discovery. He memorized the name of the Web site so he could find it again when Terri went to work. He tried to be respectful of her and usually only looked at porn when she was at work. While she worked at night, he stayed up, wading through site after site searching for naked women, dead or alive. He didn't want her to know the depths of his depravity and obsession.

Terri knew, but she had learned to ignore it. Sean was usually so sweet that she let him have that one secret. And when he wasn't on the computer, he was fun to be around. They went out to dinner once in a while, mostly for special occasions like anniversaries and usually for steak, which was Sean's favorite meal.

And when the Renaissance Festival came to nearby Hammond, Louisiana, Terri would sew costumes, and they would spend the weekend making merry with the burly Englishmen and the wenches who frequented the festival. Sean liked to dress in a burlap tunic and matching pants, while Terri wore elaborate costumes made from curtains and tablecloths. She loved the festival, felt like she had a real connection with the people there, because she believed her great-great-great-grandfather was William Wallace, whose story was portrayed in the blockbuster movie *Braveheart*. She liked to collect swords, her tribute to her ancestor's bravery. The dining-room walls in their home showcased her collection.

The couple enjoyed collecting a variety of things. Sean had collected stamps throughout his childhood and displayed them in numerous books. He also liked to amass *Star Wars* and *Star Trek* cards, as did Terri. They took special care of their collections and proudly showed them off to the occasional visitor.

Sean also took special care of Terri because she suffered with grand mal seizures, a result of hitting her head on a coffee table when she was three years old. He drove her to work every night at eleven o'clock and picked her up the following morning at seven, because she couldn't drive. Sean didn't mind. His shift didn't begin until three in the afternoon, and he got off from work in time to bring Terri to the store. He couldn't wait to get home most nights. He hated to work, and only did so when Terri made him.

While there were things Terri didn't like about her boyfriend, he had many good qualities that outweighed the bad. If he sometimes went in the backyard and smoked a joint with his buddies, that was okay, although she didn't like it. If she found Crown Royal bottles hidden under the sink after he had promised her he would stop drinking, that was okay, because when he kissed her on the cheek for no reason, her heart melted. And he had helped mend the rifts she had experienced with her three children: Christine, Katie, and Jimmy. Before Sean came along, she had not seen her children for thirteen years. He had helped the family come together and had gone out of his way to make holidays special.

Sean loved Christmas and always helped decorate the tree. He would put on his Santa hat and give out presents on Christmas Day. A big grin always creased his face when he opened his own gifts, hoping for the latest electronic gadget or game. He would sit on the couch petting his striped gray cat, Heather, and watch as Terri and the kids admired each other's gifts. He enjoyed his family on this day more than at any other time. Terri would smile at him, aware that he was just a big kid at heart who loved playing with all the toys they exchanged.

She was unaware that he had a dark secret, a side that she never saw. For her, theirs was a happy family, the family she had always wanted. Sean gave her stability, peace, and love. It was all she needed.

It would be all he needed, too, for almost five years. But then he got bored.

June 7, 2004

My dearest Terri,

Thank you so much for the picture. Your smile keeps me going on in the time of darkness in my life. I so wish that I could be with you now. It is so true that you don't know what you've got until it is gone. I will kiss your picture goodnite and good morning. Of all the things in my life; movies, games, my computer, the car and Star Trek, your sweet voice and kind face is all I can say that I really miss. Thanks Honey Bunny. For the best years of my life so far.

With so much love,
Sean

Katherine Hall

Downtown Baton Rouge hosts a plethora of governmental buildings, among them the State Capitol, built by Governor Huey P. Long in 1930 through 1932, and rising 450 feet above the Mississippi River (and where Long was later assassinated in 1935); the historic Pentagon Barracks, a two-story brick military fort built in 1825, which also served as the site of Louisiana State University from 1884 until 1926; and the elegant Governor's Mansion, inspired by the architecture of Oak Alley Plantation and built in 1963 by Governor Jimmie Davis, better known for starring in several B movies and for his recording of the country-western song "You Are My Sunshine." Most of Louisiana's politics today are conducted in these buildings and in the coffee shops and restaurants that line streets that have been revitalized recently in an effort to bring life to a dying downtown. Decaying buildings have been bought and remodeled into gleaming structures meant to invite tourists and conventions to the area.

The *Hollywood Casino* and the *Belle of Baton Rouge,* gaming riverboats that cater to rich and poor alike, float on the Mississippi just blocks from the State Capitol Building. The Shaw Center for the Arts, the Arts Council of Greater Baton Rouge, and the Louisiana Art & Science Museum, complete with a planetarium designed to bring locals downtown, provide the beginnings of the cultural district that is the goal of the Downtown Development District (DDD). And on some Fridays during the fall, and again in the spring, "Live after Five," an outdoor concert series, features Louisiana blues and funk, with acts like John Lisi, Sundanze, or the Chris LeBlanc Band, who entertain area professionals leaving work at the end of a long week as they dance in the streets with beers in hand.

Life here seems good—well-lit streets, luxury apartments with courtyards housed above new businesses, restaurants and bars to provide entertainment.

But on the other side of Interstate 110, another world exists. On streets like Winnebago, Hollywood, North, Plank, and Geronimo, prostitutes hooked on cocaine hustle those driving by in hopes of earning enough money for another rock of crack. During the night, no self-respecting Baton Rougean would be caught traveling those streets. It simply isn't safe.

Here, life is about survival, staying alive long enough to make one more score. Old shacks, with peeling paint and torn curtains in windows, are a sharp contrast to the more modern buildings located just blocks away.

Many of the hookers who work these streets once lived a normal life. They had families and jobs. Some had husbands who held them close each night. Some had children whose hair they combed and whose small bodies they bathed, fed, and clothed. Each could remember what family and love felt like. But drugs had changed all of that. All had once thought this could never happen to them.

Now they lived in a world filled with danger and

heartache. They learned early on to trust no one and to never let anyone get too close. The buying and selling of sex was a competitive business, and hookers had to work long hours to get as many johns as they could to make enough money for drugs and food, in that order. Sex comes cheap on these streets—sometimes as little as ten dollars for oral sex, which isn't enough to feed habits that have grown through the years.

The men who frequent and live in this area either pay for their pleasure or make their livings on the backs of these women, whose faces reflect their painful existence. Many of these women hold their heads high but rarely smile, afraid to show teeth rotted by the chemicals they take to get through each night. Their too-thin bodies and fragile bones barely fill the short skirts and low-cut blouses they wear to attract customers. None of that really matters, though. Despite an unstable economy, business is always good on darkened corners and in trash-filled alleys in the heart of North Baton Rouge.

The Baton Rouge Police Department does try to curb activity on these streets, but there is simply not enough money and manpower to eliminate a way of life. Cameras positioned on lampposts monitor the comings and goings of those who enter this area, and undercover cops make regular busts of drug dealers and prostitutes. However, bail money is readily available, and then it's back to business as usual.

When prostitutes go missing, as often happens, investigations are useless, as lips are sealed. Nobody sees or hears anything. In this area, it's a regular occurrence—murdered prostitutes vulgarly displayed and discarded along with the rest of the trash. Perhaps a pimp will notice one of his girls hasn't shown up for work, but no one else cares.

The upper echelon of society—those who live in mansions along the picturesque Highland Road—are blinded to the plight of the poor and hopeless by power, position, and wealth. North Baton Rouge is a world away from the catered parties attended by rich politicians, business owners, doctors, and lawyers who sit in fancy parlors and sip expensive wines. They do not want to know about drug deals or murders that take place on inner-city streets. It's too ugly to think about, too intrusive.

Sean Gillis liked to think about those streets. He drove them regularly at night while Terri was working. He liked to pick out women and think about what he would do to them. Those thoughts excited him. It wasn't the sex. It was the death. Naked dead women posed like he had seen on the Web site.

He looked for small women, ones he could easily overpower. He wasn't a big man or strong. He was of average build and had never done any manual labor. He didn't like to fight. He wanted this to be easy. It had been a long time, almost five years, since he had experienced what death felt like. He had been happy during those years, had not felt the need to feel blood flowing through his fingers, but he had become bored lately. And stressed. He needed something to make him feel powerful, alive.

In the early-morning hours of January 4, 1999, Sean spotted his next victim.

Katherine Hall left the housing project on North Street, where she lived a life of squalor, to begin her nightly walk up and down the street waiting for men to stop. She had spent years trading her body for money to feed her addiction, and this night was no different from any other. The small thirty-year-old black woman felt safe on these streets. She had only been arrested once, back in 1995, for possession of cocaine, and since then, the cops had left her alone. Or she had gotten smarter and better at stashing her supply.

She knew instinctively which johns to get in a car with and which looked too dangerous. This was her home, and she knew most of the people who passed by as she walked.

Tucked into the pocket of her brown jacket, her food stamp card guaranteed she would eat the next day, but on this night she had a habit to feed. When the white man holding up twenty dollars stopped, she didn't hesitate to climb into his car. He looked harmless, grinning the way he was. He seemed nice as he drove her toward River Road. He turned on the radio and talked with her. He told her he wanted oral sex.

When he stopped the car near a deserted property, Katherine simply assumed that she would perform the required act and return home with enough money for a rock or two. Sean had other ideas.

He leaned back in his seat and unzipped his pants, allowing her to service him before he pulled out the nylon zip tie he had brought along, just in case.

Katherine did not realize what was happening until the smiling man wrapped the nylon zip tie around her neck and pulled tight, but not tight enough. The unsuspecting woman began to fight for her life. As she fought, she felt desperately for the door handle. Finding it, she pulled hard and jumped out of the car. She screamed as she ran across the field, praying someone would hear her. No one did.

Sean caught up to her easily. He knocked her to the

ground and began punching and stabbing her. Katherine fought hard, but Sean was stronger.

Sixteen times his blade raked across her skin, through flesh and muscle. His knife cut through her left eye, through her breasts and stomach, through her genitals, until a final slash across her throat robbed Katherine of her life.

Satisfied that she was dead, Sean tore off her jacket and tossed it aside. Then he slowly removed her clothes. He didn't worry about anyone seeing him in this desolate area. It was dark, and he was alone. It was time to enjoy himself.

Like a butcher carving up a piece of meat, Sean went to work. He dug his blade into her arm near the shoulder and viciously pulled it hard, slicing open her entire arm down to her hand. He slashed a circle around her right breast and then cut open the left. He stabbed her stomach and genitals eight times. He cut off one of her eyelids.

Sean turned her over, digging deep with his knife into her left buttock and ripping her skin open, all the way down to her knee. Then he split open her calf. Twenty-one more times he cut her after she had died, reveling in his handiwork.

Finally sated, he picked up the mutilated woman who had given him such pleasure and carried her back to his car.

He retrieved her jacket and arrogantly hung it on the gate. He gathered her clothes to be disposed of later.

With Katherine's body in the front passenger seat, Sean drove to the Splash Car Wash on Gardere Lane, where he would clean her blood from the seat. After he had checked the exterior, he pulled her from the car and laid her on the ground in plain sight while he scrubbed the inside of the vehicle.

No one noticed.

Later that morning, Ledell Blakes was heading to the sixty acres he leased on River Road to check on his thirty-five head of cattle. He fed and watered them each morning. As he approached the gate that led to his field, he noticed something hanging on it that had not been there the day before. He stopped the truck and got out. He saw that it was a small brown leather jacket, and he wondered how it had gotten there. He dug through the pocket and found a food stamp card. The name on it was Katherine Hall.

As he looked around, he spotted a nylon zip tie lying on the ground near the gate, the heavy-duty kind used in many industries. Ledell knew that something wasn't right. He searched the area but didn't find anything else. Worried, he gave the card to his wife to turn in to the welfare office. Then he called the police.

The outskirts of southeastern Baton Rouge, where East Baton Rouge Parish bordered the more rural Ascension Parish, was a haven for those who wanted to escape the traffic and burgeoning crime in the capital city. In 1999, new neighborhoods were springing up each month along country roads lined with pretty camellia bushes and sprawling oak trees. One such neighborhood still under construction, Vignes Lake, offered beautiful new homes at moderate prices, and many of the houses sold before they were even built.

On the morning of January 5, Herbert K. Jones happened to be squirrel hunting in a field near where a new road was being built in the neighborhood. He knew that before long, he would not be able to hunt this area anymore. As he walked toward the 19000 block of Poujeaux, looking for squirrels, he saw something out of place at the end of the road, near an unattended backhoe.

He moved closer. What he saw shocked him.

The nude body of a black woman lay in the street near a dead-end sign.

Herbert hurried to his truck and called 911.

The St. George Fire Department was already on the scene when police arrived. Deputy Mark Sturges was dispatched at 4:54 P.M. and arrived shortly thereafter. Firemen informed the deputy that they had found a nude black female lying in the street, with numerous slash marks across the front of her body.

"She's been here awhile," they informed him. "There was no chance of saving her."

Sturges radioed headquarters for crime scene technicians and homicide detectives.

Police searched, but the crime scene yielded no evidence as to the attacker. Nothing but leaves and dirt surrounded the body. It was obvious from the amount of wounds and the lack of blood on the ground that the murder had happened elsewhere. It was also obvious that the choice of dump site, next to a dead-end sign, was the killer's idea of a joke.

After photographs and fingerprints were taken, Katherine Hall was wrapped in a body bag at 7:20 P.M. and tagged as *0232157*. Her ordeal was over.

Katherine's fingerprints, registered with police at the

time of her arrest years before, identified her. Police soon learned where she had been murdered when they recovered her food stamp card, which had been found on River Road.

Ligature marks on her neck matched the zip tie Ledell had discovered; however, her cause of death was listed as exsanguination from a stab wound to the jugular vein.

Katherine had bled out.

She would soon become a cold case, another forgotten, murdered hooker.

Years later, a pubic hair found between her front teeth would link her murder to a serial killer.

Hardee Moseley Schmidt

It was foggy on the morning of May 30, 1999, when Hardee Moseley Schmidt got out of bed. She threw on her running clothes, even though it looked like it might rain. She always got up early to begin her morning run, before most people were even awake. She liked the peace and quiet, the time she spent alone with her thoughts when she was training for a race.

Hardee was usually training for some race or other. Even at fifty-two, she was in great physical shape. She took care of herself, from her thick blond hair that flipped up on the ends to the body that could have belonged to a twenty-year-old. Running had done that for her, and she loved it. Hardee had participated in the Boston Marathon almost a decade before and had done very well. It had been a highlight for her, one of those moments that made all of the cramped muscles worthwhile.

Hailing from a well-to-do, respected Baton Rouge family, Hardee had a life many people might envy. She had a loving husband, Bob, who was an attorney, and three beautiful children, Estelle, Joelle, and Robert. She had named Joelle after her sister, who was her best friend. Her father, Donald Moseley, was a family court judge, and Hardee looked just like him. She had been raised to be a lady with impeccable manners and taste. She had raised her children the same way. A stay-at-home mom, Hardee devoted herself to her family, but she knew she needed something that was just for her. That something was running.

As she headed out the door that morning, she followed a path that was familiar to her. Pollard Estates, the neighborhood in which she lived, was filled with beautifully landscaped homes lining blacktop roads named Quail Run Drive, Pleasant Ridge Street, Creekwood Drive, and Dawson's Creek Lane, all located just off the heavily traveled Perkins Road. On this day, the magnolias were in bloom, and she was treated to blasts of spring colors and sweet scents as she ran. Cypress, pine, oak, and the occasional palm tree decorated large front yards and created the serene environment that Hardee enjoyed. She could hear the twitter of birds as they began to announce the new day.

She had traveled the same route many times over, but she never tired of it. This was her neighborhood, her home, and she felt safe. She knew all about safety. Her friend Kathleen Callaghan, a Baton Rouge attorney who had published an article about safety for women only days before, kept her informed.

Hardee knew that the most important thing you can do while running is stay in well-traveled residential areas. She knew to avoid isolated areas. She knew that she should not assume she was safe just because it was daylight. She knew it was safest to run when people are home and getting up for work. She knew to be aware of her surroundings, that she should not wear headphones, that a dog could not keep her safe. But she had been running for years, and Pollard Estates was an upper-middle-class neighborhood, where neighbors looked out for each other. She had nothing to worry about.

What she didn't know was that a man had seen her running three weeks before and had come back to the neighborhood on numerous occasions, hoping to spot her again.

Sean Gillis couldn't believe his luck. Terri Lemoine was still at work, and he didn't have to pick her up for almost two hours. He had been driving around, drawn back to the place where he had seen the pretty blond woman. And then he saw her, running down Quail Run Drive. He slowed down for a moment, planning his attack. He didn't think she would stop if he tried to talk to her, and he knew this had to be quick. People would be out and about soon.

Sean got closer, trying to decide what to do. He smiled and licked his lips as he watched her from behind the wheel.

He gunned the engine of his Ford Taurus, a company car with which he had been entrusted by his new employer, Shamrock Office Supply. Hardee did not realize what was happening until the car plowed into her, knocking her into a nearby ditch.

Sean jumped out of the car and ran to her, wrapping a nylon zip tie around her neck. Stunned from the impact of being hit by the car, Hardee did not move. Sean pulled the zip tie tight.

When he was satisfied that she was dead, he picked up the lovely woman's still body and put her in the car.

Before he drove away, he looked around to make sure no one was outside. He was safe. No one had seen anything.

Sean drove down Perkins Road toward Highland Road,

searching for a quiet place where he could spend some time with his victim. The BREC Park (supervised by the Recreation and Park Commission of East Baton Rouge Parish) was perfect for what he had in mind. As he drove past the ball fields, where children played after school each day, he searched for an isolated area. When he saw one, he stopped the car.

He picked up Hardee's body and gently laid her on the ground, unafraid that someone would see him. It was five-thirty on a Sunday morning, much too early for anyone to be in the park. He carefully removed her clothes, admiring the firm lines of her body. She was beautiful.

Sean felt the hunger building inside him and hurriedly pulled down his pants. His mouth watered as he rubbed his penis over her dead body, over her vaginal area. Then he could wait no longer.

Sean raped Hardee, spilling his semen into her lifeless body.

After he finished, he picked her up and placed her naked body in the trunk of his car. He had to hurry. It was almost time to get Terri from work. Unsuspecting, Terri noticed nothing out of the ordinary when Sean arrived at the Circle K.

Bob became very worried when Hardee did not come back from her run. She had a routine and always stuck to it. He got in his car and drove around, hoping to find her talking to a friend on the side of the road. He asked everyone he encountered if they had seen her. It didn't take long before he realized that something was very wrong. He hurried home and called the police to report his wife missing.

* * *

"What is that horrible smell?" Terri said to Sean as she got in the car the next day.

"I ran over a squirrel yesterday. It must have stuck to the tire," Sean replied. "I'll go to the car wash and get rid of it."

"You'd better. It stinks in here."

Sean grinned. "Don't worry, Honey Bunny. I'll take care of it."

Sean dropped Terri off at the house and drove away. Instead of going to a car wash, he drove down Highway 61 toward New Orleans. Although the road from Baton Rouge to New Orleans was heavily traveled, he wasn't worried. He was smart. He had decided to dump the body in a rural parish close by so police in Baton Rouge wouldn't work the murder.

Bordering Ascension Parish, the stretch of Highway 61 that runs through St. James Parish is surrounded by swampland. By May, the swamp is already coming alive as soft green needles cover the cypress, and willows weep sap as snakes wrap stealthily around their branches. Nutria can be spotted from the roadway nibbling on the abundance of plant life to be found there. Bass, bream, and turtles fight to survive in the narrow bayou that runs alongside the road. Alligators thrash their tails in anticipation of another meal of tasty nutria.

Sean had traveled this roadway many times and knew that water would wash away any evidence from the body he carried in the trunk of his car.

He made a U-turn when he found the perfect spot, then slowed his car to a stop. He got out, looking up and down the road for other cars. When he was satisfied no one was coming, he opened his trunk and dragged Hardee's body to the side of the road, tugging and pulling until he reached the edge of the bayou. With a final shove, he rid himself of the woman he had wanted so desperately for almost a month. He wiped his hands on his pants and got back in the car.

Hardee's body would be found the next day.

Kathleen Callaghan, being interviewed by a reporter from WBRZ-TV, channel 2, where Sean's mother had worked years before, was in the middle of discussing her safety tips when a reporter informed her that Hardee's body had been found.

"The instant she came up missing, I knew she was dead. Hardee wouldn't just disappear. It was a shock, horrifying," Kathleen remembered. "To have this happen to someone you know, a friend, it was a tragedy."

Bob Schmidt would soon find himself to be the prime suspect in the murder of his wife, whom he had loved for more than twenty years.

At home alone, in front of his computer, Sean masturbated.

Joyce Williams

By November 1999, Sean Gillis's fantasies were becoming darker, more macabre. He found himself thinking about death and dismemberment every day. Just the thought of a woman's severed arm or leg could get him excited. As his lust for death grew, he felt the urge again; it now controlled his thoughts.

After bringing Terri to work, Sean liked to drive around, searching for the perfect victim. Sometimes he picked up a prostitute, chatted with her for a while, then let her go— the woman unaware that she had just escaped a gruesome end at the hands of the man who seemed so friendly. When he picked up a sixteen-year-old girl one night, he lectured her about making a good life for herself and getting off the streets before deciding she wasn't the one he wanted. He was picky. Most of the victims he chose were around his age or older.

On the night of November 12, Sean headed toward Scotlandville, a small community that had a mostly black population. Home to Southern University, approximately 3,500 people live in this town, located only six miles from

Baton Rouge, near the Mississippi River. Industrial plants are the mainstay of the community, providing wages for the men who toil there in order to feed their families.

Sean drove along Scenic Highway for a while, then turned onto Highway 19. Near the sheriff substation, he saw a black woman walking along the road. She wore what looked like a long, flowing nightgown. Sean noticed that she had pretty legs.

He drove past her, then turned around to take another look. When he passed her the second time, he stopped, smiling as she walked up to his car.

"Hi," she said. "I saw you drive by earlier."

Joyce Williams sensed nothing about this man that seemed dangerous. She had been walking these streets for a long time. She knew when to be afraid. This white boy looked nice.

"I'm going to my home girl's to pick up some smoke," she told him.

"I'll give you ten bucks for a blow job," Sean responded.

Joyce agreed and got in the car.

Sean gave her the money and drove her to her friend's house, waiting as Joyce made her score. He impatiently tapped his fingers on the steering wheel, worried that she wouldn't come back.

Soon Joyce strutted out of the house, feeling better and pleased with the way the night was going.

When she got back in the car, Joyce handed him a beer. Sean tuned the radio to an oldies channel, and the two rode around singing songs from the 1960s.

Joyce had always loved to sing. Born on May 29, 1963, to Hazel and Freddie Watson, Joyce had grown up in Baton Rouge. As a child, she was always smiling, especially when she was with her younger sister, Alfreda. The two were very close, and Joyce, who loved to dance, always learned the latest dance moves as soon as she saw them on *Soul Train*. She would then try to teach them to Alfreda.

She spent the latter part of her high-school years at McKinley Senior High School in Baton Rouge before attending two years of college at Southern University. Although she was smart and had big dreams, Joyce spent most of her twenties working in the fast-food industry. She soon married and had two children, Ken and Kendrika, but then things had become a little too difficult. Like so many women, Joyce turned to drugs to ease her pain and soon found her life spiraling out of control. Gone were the days of laughing and dancing with Alfreda. Instead, Joyce found herself hustling men and living for her next rock of cocaine, but her friendly personality could not be totally repressed by years of life on the street.

As Sean drove toward Airline Highway, Joyce, comfortable with her new friend, talked and talked. Sean listened, smiling. But when he drove over the Mississippi River Bridge, Joyce began to get concerned.

"Dang, you're taking me out of my parish," Joyce said as Sean drove into West Baton Rouge Parish. "If you weren't so nice, I'd be worried."

Sean turned onto Rosedale Road in Port Allen, an area with only a few homes, which were surrounded by miles of sugarcane fields. Although some of the fields had already been chopped and burned, Sean chose one where the cane was still at full height. He turned into a pathway that led through the field, well aware that any sound would be muted by the stalks that provided such sweetness.

"I need to pee," Joyce said, and got out of the vehicle.

Sean needed to relieve himself as well, but he realized that he was in the perfect place to put his carefully laid plan into action.

He pulled out his zip tie and walked up behind Joyce. Sean tried to wrap it around her neck, but it caught on her mouth. Joyce began kicking her feet back at him, trying to get away.

"Be still. Be still," Sean commanded.

He kicked her feet from under her.

Joyce stood up quickly right into the waiting noose, which fell to her neck.

Sean pulled tight and waited for two or three minutes, until she was still—and he knew she was gone. He picked her up and placed her in the passenger seat, careful to secure the seat belt.

As they drove toward Sean's house, Joyce's head fell into his lap. He smiled, anticipation making him drive faster. Terri was working, and it would be hours before he had to get her.

He backed into the driveway, looking this way and that to make sure that no neighbors were outside:

I laid her down in the kitchen by the bar and sink and stroked her body—the usual sick playing with her. She had beautiful legs. I wanted to keep those legs.

I used a sharp knife to cut through the muscle of her leg, but it took a while to get through it. I cut too low. I finally got it off with a hacksaw and went for the next leg. The blade snapped on me when I was about halfway through the femur.

I remember trying to get her arm off next. There was a lot of blood. I sopped it up with paper towels, packing paper, which is very absorbent, 409, and water.

I used one of Terri's knives, a filet knife that was razor sharp. You got to be careful handling it. I tried to get the arm at the elbow, then the wrist. Things were popping out of joint, but I couldn't get it off, even though I twisted it real good.

At that point, I pretty much went for the head.

The knife went through just like that. It was like cutting butter.

With Ms. Bryan, I couldn't get through. When they are alive, the muscles in the neck make it harder.

There was a lot of blood, so I washed her head in the sink.

I inserted my penis into her head, in her throat.

Her spinal cord or something pricked my scrotum. It was very uncomfortable.

I guess I got what I deserved.

It wasn't a sex thing. It was a mind thing. It was more just to see what it was like. I didn't, you know, get off. Then I put my penis in her mouth.

After that, I picked up her leg, holding it with the foot close to my face, severed end down. She had lovely legs, like Terri.

—*Sean Vincent Gillis*

Caught up in the frenzy of his own perversion, Sean reached for his knife again. He performed what he would later call a "nipplectomy" on Joyce, slicing off one nipple, then the other. He held the small pieces of flesh in his hand, looking at them for a moment. He had spent years on the Internet researching dead bodies, sadistic acts, other serial killers. He decided in that moment to elevate his standing among the most perverse of human beings.

He put the nipples in his mouth and ate them.

His desires sated, his fantasy complete, Sean realized it was getting close to the time when he had to get Terri from work.

He folded the leg that remained attached to Joyce's body up over her torso, then crossed her arms in front of her and shoved the mutilated woman into a large garbage bag.

He put the severed leg in another bag and her head in another.

He forced her into a large Xerox packing box, then began scrubbing the floor, erasing the evidence of his perverse sickness.

He carried the body outside and placed it in the back of the station wagon. Body parts were sticking out of the box, so he shoved other boxes and garbage bags, which were in the car, around it to hide them as best he could.

Sean was not at all anxious when Terri slid into the car next to him. He was excited, having the woman he loved in the same car with Joyce's body parts. It made him feel powerful.

"Hi, Honey Bunny," he said, before leaning over to kiss her, the taste of his victim still fresh in his mouth.

Terri smiled. Sean was always so sweet.

He brought her home and told her he would be back in a little while. Sleepy from a long night of waiting on customers, Terri just nodded and went to bed.

Sean left to search for a place to dump Joyce's body. He drove to River Road, which runs parallel to the Mississippi, but there were too many cars around. He then headed to the Plaquemine Ferry, but cars were lining up to cross the river. He turned around and drove south down River Road, farther away from the more traveled areas.

He rode for a while until he was on the east side of Iberville Parish, near the small town of St. Gabriel. The little town, which was founded by the Acadians in the mid-1700s, is located on the east side of the Mississippi, only twelve miles south of Baton Rouge. Sean passed near Bayou Manchac, which separates Iberville from East

Baton Rouge Parish, and drove on past Levee's Edge Horse
Farm to milepost 1340, before stopping to survey his surroundings and to make sure no one was around. Only a few
old shacks interrupted the landscape across the street.
Cows in nearby fields chewed contentedly on their cud.
Just down the road, the Iberville Christian Center Youth
Ministry offered hope for a better life to the young people
in the area. Satisfied that he had chosen the right spot,
Sean drove up the gravel pathway that led to the top of the
levee. A steep concrete wall located on either side of the
levee made it almost impossible to walk to the river.

"I got the box out of the trunk and slung her leg down
first," Sean would later tell police. "Then I slung her head.
It went 'bloomp, bloomp, bloomp' all the way down. The
torso was last, because that was harder."

Pleased with himself, Sean got back in his car and went
home to cuddle with Terri.

I never did get my blow job, he thought. *Damn.*

Body on River Road

Captain Ernest Williams hurried from the Iberville Parish Sheriff's Office (IPSO) on the morning of January 22, 2000. The new millennium had barely begun, and already a report had come in about some bones found on River Road. It was 9:58 A.M. when he reached the spot where David Giurintano and David Peltier had found the bones. The two men had been walking through the woods behind the levee, looking for birds, when they stumbled upon a bone that looked like a human leg.

Detective Kevin Ambeau was the next to arrive. Together, Williams and Ambeau walked with the men to the area where they had seen the leg. After determining that it did look like a human leg, they secured the perimeter and searched the area for thirty meters in all directions. They didn't find any other bones, so they returned to the leg and took pictures before collecting it to send to the lab.

On January 26, while searching the area again, Ambeau and Deputy J. Carter discovered more bones, about fifty-three feet from milepost 1340. They also discovered a woman's jacket. Williams returned to the levee to help search, and discovered a skull and another leg bone. The state police crime lab, the coroner, and forensic anthropologist Mary Manheim, from the Forensic, Anthropology and Computer Enhancement Services (FACES) Laboratory at LSU, were called to the scene.

On February 11, Williams and Ambeau received a call informing them that the remains had been identified. They belonged to Joyce Marie Williams of Scotlandville. Manheim had identified her through dental records provided by Earl K. Long Memorial Hospital in Baton Rouge. As soon as he had gathered information about her family, Captain Williams drove to Scotlandville to notify Joyce's sister, Alfreda, of her death.

Alfreda had last seen Joyce on Oriole Street in Baton Rouge on November 12. She told the captain that Joyce had a son, who was incarcerated at East Baton Rouge Parish Prison. In shock, she answered all of his questions as best she could. She was honest about her sister's lifestyle and related how she had always been worried about something happening to her. Alfreda said she knew something was wrong when Joyce hadn't come home, but she didn't know if Joyce had just taken off or if something had happened to her.

Satisfied with Alfreda's cooperation, Captain Williams called the prison and asked that they notify Joyce's son of her death before the media aired the story.

After Williams left, Alfreda sat down for a moment to collect her thoughts. She now had to figure out a way to tell Joyce's two-year-old daughter that her mommy was never coming home.

With no evidence other than the bones, which had been scavenged by animals, and the jacket, the sheriff's office created an "Information Wanted" poster, hoping someone would come forward to help them solve the case. They faxed the flyer to East and West Baton Rouge Parishes, offering a reward of one thousand dollars from Crime Stoppers for anyone who supplied information leading to an arrest.

Joyce Williams, black, female, D.O.B. 5-29-63, read the caption below a photograph of the victim. The sheriff's office hoped the flyers would get the attention of someone who had seen her the night she had been killed.

They did.

Sean Gillis walked nonchalantly into the Louisiana State Attorney General's Office. Shamrock Office Supply, where Sean was employed, had gotten a call that the agency's copy machine was on the blink and needed servicing. Sean was sent to answer the call. A whiz at machinery, it didn't take long for Sean to fix it. Needing to test his work, he looked around for some blank pieces of paper. Instead, he saw a flyer featuring the picture of Joyce Williams.

Sean could barely contain his glee as he fed the flyer into the copier. He grinned as each new copy was spit out by the machine, reliving his night of pleasure with her. No one noticed anything amiss about the repairman using the flyers of a murder victim to test the machine. No one noticed that he made more than two hundred copies. No one noticed that he was smiling as he lovingly ran his fingers over Joyce's face.

Another Case Goes Cold

It was getting late, about 8:00 P.M. on January 26, 2000, when police, who were still searching the area where Joyce's remains were found, noticed a car parked at the top of the levee. They approached the vehicle, wondering why anyone would be loitering around the crime scene.

"Let me see some identification," Deputy Shoun Waters said to the young man in the car.

Edward Schiele produced his license for the officer and agreed to let him search the car. Inside, Waters found two hatchets, one keyhole saw, one axle, and a hacksaw.

The deputy's heart began pumping a little faster. These were tools that could be used to cut up a body. Waters called headquarters and learned that the man had an extensive arrest record for thefts and burglaries. Schiele, who they would later find out was related to a police officer in Baton Rouge, immediately became the prime suspect.

Schiele told police that he had seen all of their cars on the levee and had become curious to know what they had found. The police did not believe him. Schiele said he would be willing to take a polygraph test. Well aware that

killers sometimes return to the scene of the crime and
inject themselves into the investigation, the police brought
their suspect in for questioning. They hoped the case
would be closed quickly.

It wasn't long, though, before another suspect emerged.

Mike Robertson, Joyce's brother-in-law, informed
police that word on the street was that a woman named
Veda Washington (aka Veda Sterling) had been bragging
that she had witnessed Joyce's murder. Mike said he
had heard that Veda had stolen some drugs and blamed it
on Joyce. When Veda got drunk, Mike continued, she told
the story to anyone who would listen.

Renee Williams, a homeless woman in Scotlandville,
also heard the story, but her version was a little different.
Renee told police that she had been at the Skylark Motel
about two months before when Veda Washington arrived
at her room and wanted to hide inside. Veda was crying,
and although Renee did not let her in, she did ask what
was wrong. It took Veda about five minutes to stop crying
long enough to answer.

"I killed Joyce Williams," Veda said between sniffles.
"Me and this guy was in a van, and me and Joyce was ar-
guing over some dope, and I killed her."

A material witness warrant was drafted, but it took
police a while to find Veda, who had gone into hiding.
When they finally brought her in for questioning, Veda
implicated a man, Charles Brown, in the murder.

Charles stated that he knew Veda, that she had performed oral sex on him a few times the year before, but
that he didn't know Joyce Williams.

The sheriff's office called Richard "Richie" Johnson,
at that time assistant chief of police of the Brusly Police
Department (BPD), in West Baton Rouge Parish. Johnson

was a burly, good-looking man who was known to be tough on criminals. As owner of Louisiana Polygraph Services, Johnson was often called to conduct polygraph tests on suspects in other jurisdictions. He administered a polygraph on Veda to discover if she had killed Joyce or knew anything about what had happened to her. He determined that Veda had not killed Joyce and that she knew nothing about the murder.

Edward Schiele also turned out to be a false lead. Although his car had tools that could have dismembered someone, tests revealed no blood or other evidence on the hatchets and saws. He was soon discounted as a suspect.

The police realized they would have to start over and look in another direction if they wanted to solve this crime. No new leads emerged, and like the others, Joyce's case went cold.

On March 17, a memorial service was held at the First Presbyterian Church for this mother of two who had been so violated by a serial killer. Reverend Herman Pride reminded friends and family members about the young girl who had once been so full of joy. Alfreda read to guests from the Old Testament just before the congregation sang, "What a Friend We Have in Jesus." Sister Margaret Cobbs offered words of comfort from the Scripture. Reverend Gregory White gave the eulogy. After the services were concluded and what remained of Joyce's body had finally been put to rest, everyone gathered at Alfreda's home to reminisce about the beloved woman who had been taken from them. Despite her problems, Joyce had been loved by those who knew her. She did not deserve to become an experiment in a serial killer's ghastly fantasy.

Lillian Robinson

    Lillian Gorham Robinson had once been like other women. She had been raised in a family that loved her, and she had always been very close to her sisters, Patricia Dawson and Virginia Valentine. She once had a job she enjoyed and lived a normal life. With beautiful tan furs decorating her shoulders, Lillian had attended church with her sisters. She had two adult children and a grandchild she loved dearly. But all of that was before life's disappointments became too much for her to bear, and she began to take a little nip of alcohol now and then to ease her pain. When those nips became full-blown alcoholism, Lillian's life changed. Her friends changed. But it wasn't until her first taste of crack cocaine that things really began to go downhill.

    Like so many others, Lillian began to sell her body to feed her addiction to crack, and North Baton Rouge became home to her. She was soon comfortable on those streets, surrounded by women who were like her, who understood her. But this new life was a far cry from the way she had been raised—to live life for the Lord. Although she tried to be like the others on the street, Lillian's breeding stood out. She couldn't hide her sweet smile or the fact that she didn't really belong there.

Virginia, who was an evangelist, tried to save Lillian and prayed every day for her soul.

When Lillian did not return their calls for several days in January 2000, Patricia, who had worked with the East Baton Rouge Parish School System for about twenty years, and Virginia reported their sister missing to the Baton Rouge Police Department. They called every other day to see if a woman fitting her description—petite, black, fifty-two years old—had been found. The answer was always "No." The women did not give up. They knew something was wrong. Even though Lillian was an addict, she always returned their calls.

Only two months had passed since Sean Gillis had killed Joyce, but he already was back on the prowl, roaming the streets of North Baton Rouge looking for petite prostitutes. As he drove, Sean's mind lingered on thoughts of Joyce, of the fun he had with her at his house. She had been something special, a memory he retrieved over and over again. She made him want to kill again, just to have the pleasure of another dead body.

It was the second week of January 2000 when Sean spotted Lillian Robinson walking through his favorite part of Baton Rouge. Lillian was a little different from the other prostitutes Sean had killed. She didn't have the face of a prostitute. Hers was softer; her eyes were gentle. Sean noticed her dark black skin and full lips. He drove by slowly, then turned the car around, checking her out carefully as he approached. He decided she was the one and pulled alongside her.

As he usually did, Sean offered Lillian money for oral

sex. Needing a fix, Lillian saw his kind eyes, his wide smile, and got in the car, reassured that he would not harm her. Sean took her to a secluded area not far from where he had found her and waited until the right moment. He pulled his zip tie out and encircled her neck. Lillian fought, but only for a moment as the pressure increased. Sean smiled as he pushed her off him back into the passenger seat.

He drove toward his house, anticipating what was ahead for him. When he got home, he pulled Lillian from the car and stripped her naked. He propped her against the kitchen cabinets in the same spot he had mutilated Joyce. He looked at his watch and realized that he would not have time to dismember her and get the mess cleaned up before Terri got home. It had taken him a while to find just the right woman on this night.

Sean spent the next hour playing with Lillian's corpse, squeezing her breasts and rubbing her most private area. He inserted his penis in her mouth. He wished he had more time. He wanted to cut on her, saw on her, but he was afraid of the blood that would spill onto the floor from severed arteries. He consoled himself with the feel of her dead body beneath his fingers.

Finally, worried about the time, Sean put her back in the car and drove down Interstate 10, away from Baton Rouge. He drove past Whiskey Bay, which would become a favorite dumping point of another serial killer in just a few years, and continued on toward the Atchafalaya Basin, the largest swamp in the United States. Driving across the eighteen-mile bridge that stretches from Maringouin to Henderson, Louisiana, Sean looked for a spot to dispose of his victim.

The water in the basin used to flow into the Mississippi River, but the U.S. Army Corps of Engineers (USACE)

stopped that water source through the damning of bayous
and the laying of sluices over the years. The water, once
brown, but now black due to lack of aeration, is the perfect hiding place for a body. No one can see into its murky
depths from the bridge that rises high above. Most people
are too busy admiring the beautiful cypress trees, which
rise majestically from the basin, to look too closely into
the water that is home to a plethora of wildlife, including
the predatory alligator that greedily devours the wealth of
food available in this wetland.

Sean saw his spot and pulled the car over onto the side
of the bridge. Checking to make sure no cars were
coming, he hurriedly pulled Lillian from the car. He maneuvered her body up and over the concrete railing put
there to protect travelers from going into the water.

Sean let her go. A second later, he heard the splash,
which told him he was safe. He knew that his victim
would never be found. If the water didn't claim her, an
alligator would. Satisfied, Sean hurried back to Baton
Rouge. It was time to pick Terri up from work.

In March, some fishermen discovered a woman's corpse
floating in the Atchafalaya Basin, near St. Martinville, nine
miles north of New Iberia and miles from where Sean
had dumped her.

The coroner there autopsied her body, collected his evidence, and tried to identify her. Her body was too decomposed to obtain fingerprints, and he learned nothing
from her teeth. As often happens in the case of unidenti-
fiable bodies in Louisiana, the coroner cut off her head
and sent it to LSU for research purposes. Lillian, whose
family was still calling police and asking if they had
found anyone who fit her description, was buried head-
less in a pauper's grave.

Because the body was found in another parish, Baton

Rouge police were not notified. Pat and Virginia waited and wondered what had happened to their sister. It would be months before they learned about the woman who had been found in St. Martinville.

Determined to give their beloved sister a proper burial, they had Lillian's body exhumed and discovered, to their horror, that she had been beheaded by the coroner after being viciously murdered by an unknown assailant. It was almost too much for the sisters to bear.

Marilyn Nevils

Sean was on his way to New Iberia on October 20, 2000, a trip he had made every other weekend for eight years—only this time, he was by himself. His friend John Rosas could not make the trip on this weekend, so Sean decided to go by himself. The two men always traveled together to visit Christine, John's daughter, who lived with John's ex-wife. Christine always looked forward to these visits. She and Sean were very close and would ride around, sometimes smoking a joint together, even though she was only sixteen. John didn't know about that.

John had chosen Sean Gillis to be Christine's godfather, and Sean had been a good one—always making the trip with John to visit his daughter. Sometimes they threw Frisbees to the young girl; sometimes they played games. Other times, they drove around firing tater tots at stop signs. At Easter, Sean would fill plastic eggs with prizes and hide them in his car for Christine to find. She had laughed with delight the year that she saw the one-hundred-dollar bill folded inside one of the eggs. Sean always took care of her.

Christine loved her dad and Sean, but she was especially close to Sean because she felt like she could tell him anything. When she had been molested, it had been Sean who comforted her. When she started smoking weed, it was Sean she told. When she didn't get along with her mother, it was Sean who made it all better. And if he talked a little too much about *Star Trek,* Christine didn't mind. He was her "uncle Sean," someone she could always count on to be there for her.

Sean felt the same way about Christine. He loved the pretty, blond-haired little girl and wanted to be a good uncle to her. He had watched her grow up, and she didn't look at him like he was weird, as others so often did. She was the daughter he'd never had, and he enjoyed the time they spent together. He was looking forward to visiting with her on this day when he pulled off Interstate 10 in Lafayette.

Sean wasn't planning to kill anyone that day, but when he saw Marilyn Nevils walking down Evangeline Thruway, he couldn't help himself. He made eye contact with the thirty-eight-year-old white woman and smiled.

Evangeline Thruway is a heavily populated area of Lafayette, a road where industrial plants and retail stores intermingle. It's not a street where prostitutes would usually hang out—too much traffic, too many police cars. Normally, streetwalkers stayed closer to the Four Corners area between Cameron Street and North University Avenue. Sean couldn't believe his luck.

He stopped at the next traffic light and waited for her to get close. He smiled at the slender woman.

"Come on. I'll give you a ride," he said, smiling broadly as he leaned over to open the door. "Come on, I'll make it worth your while. I've got a big-screen TV at the house."

When she climbed inside, he asked her how much she would charge him for oral sex.

"Ten dollars," Marilyn said.

Sean agreed and drove to Sixth Street, where he saw an empty field. He pulled off the road and handed her the money.

He leaned back in the front seat while Marilyn serviced him. When she was finished, Sean reached for his handy zip tie. He quickly wrapped it around her neck and started to tighten it. It would not lock.

Realizing what was happening, Marilyn fought back. As she thrashed about, kicking and hitting at Sean, her foot hit the windshield, breaking it on the right side.

Desperate, Marilyn managed to wrench open the door. She jumped out of the car and ran as fast as she could across the field. Sean was right behind her.

He spotted a piece of metal rebar and picked it up before resuming his chase. It didn't take him long to catch up to her.

Swinging, he hit her hard in the head with the rebar, over and over, until she stopped resisting. Marilyn fell to the ground, zip tie still tangled around her neck. Sean pulled it tight again, this time making sure that she was dead.

He dragged her back to the car, placing her body on the floorboard on the passenger side. Suddenly Sean remembered the ten dollars he had paid her, and reached into her pocket to retrieve it. *It really wasn't a bad blow job,* he thought, smiling as he put the money in his pants pocket.

Still breathing heavily, Sean drove to a car wash on Louisiana Avenue, about two blocks away. He placed Marilyn on the ground while he washed the blood from the floorboard.

"I used as many quarters as it took to get the red out," Sean would later tell Detective David LeBlanc.

Sean put Marilyn in the trunk of the car, wrapping some rags around her head to keep blood from getting on the carpeting in the trunk. Then he drove to a Texaco on the corner of Jefferson Boulevard and northeastern Evangeline Thruway to get gas.

"Did you get the upper hand?" the male cashier asked him when he saw the blood all over Sean's shirt.

Sean grinned. "You should see the other guy," he said, paying for his gas.

He got back in the car and headed east on Interstate 10 back toward Baton Rouge. He drove across the Atchafalaya Basin quickly, anticipating the evening ahead, his visit to New Iberia forgotten. Terri was at work, and he would have a few hours to spend with his latest conquest.

But he couldn't wait. At the Butte La Rose exit, excited by the prospect of seeing her naked, Sean pulled into a rest area. He opened the trunk, his actions covered by darkness, and checked out the woman he had killed, examining her like she was a choice piece of meat. Eyes gleaming, he closed the trunk and got back in the car.

When he arrived at Burgin Avenue, Sean pulled Marilyn out of the trunk and carried her into the house. He laid her on the floor of the kitchen and removed her clothes. He was surprised when she urinated. When he touched the puddle, it was still warm.

That's odd, he thought. Repulsed by the urine, Sean carried her into the shower, located just off the master bedroom.

He turned on the water before he undressed, then stepped eagerly into the shower with Marilyn's corpse.

Sean had difficulty keeping Marilyn's body upright.

She kept falling over toward him. To the deranged man, it seemed like she was trying to embrace him. He tried to place his penis in her mouth, but her jaw had locked, and he was unsuccessful. Nothing he tried worked, and he finally gave up. He contemplated cutting her like he had the others but realized there wasn't enough time. Terri would get off work soon.

Sean held Marilyn close for a few more minutes before pulling her from the shower.

Hurrying, he wrapped her body in Xerox packing paper and carried her back to the car. He drove toward the levee on River Road. He hoped to dump her in the Mississippi River, but there was too much debris and too many tree limbs near the edge of the gently flowing water. He couldn't get to the river.

Sean left her body, naked, on top of the levee, throwing the bloody packing paper out of the car before he left.

For eleven days, Marilyn's body lay rotting on that levee, not far from where Joyce Williams had been left ten months before. No one but Sean knew she was waiting to be found there, waiting for someone to realize that she was gone. Finally, on Halloween, a man walking his dog discovered Marilyn's decomposed body. He called police, who tried to determine her identity.

No one had reported her missing.

It would be the only case Detective LeBlanc would ever work in which there was no family to contact, no one to tell that she had died. Sean had stumbled upon the perfect victim, one who would not be missed. The only clue was the packing paper found not far from her body, but that was not enough to lead police to a serial killer.

Marilyn's case would soon be forgotten, lost amid the

numerous murders that would occur in the ensuing years in the Baton Rouge area:

> *I act like I'm literally trying to pick them up on a real date. The hookers loved me. I treated them like women, like ladies. Do you understand? That was the smoothness, I guess, to where some of them, they couldn't wait to get into my car. And the money, although, was the immediate motivating factor of them being there. They were wanting to ride with me, to be with me.*
>
> —*Sean Vincent Gillis*

Sean Gillis would not kill again for three years. Instead, he lay low and watched with a grin on his face as police scrambled to find another serial killer who was complicating their investigation into Sean's murders.

This game of chess he was playing with police was getting more and more interesting.

Sean Takes a Backseat

The Baton Rouge Police Department realized they had a problem. Too many women were coming up missing or dead, many of them prostitutes who worked the North Baton Rouge area. In September 1999, thirty-six year-old Florida Edwards was found strangled in an abandoned lounge on North Boulevard. Shirley Mikell's brutalized body was found a month later on Florida Boulevard. She was only thirty-three. In April 2000, Dianna Williams, age thirty-five, was found in North Street Park. She had also been beaten to death. Just days later, the body of Tannis Walker, age thirty-six, was discovered behind a building on Roselawn Drive. She had been strangled. Another body of a woman was found in May. Thirty-nine-year-old Patricia Hawkins had been strangled to death on Plank Road. And in June, Veronica Courtney, age forty-four, was found behind an apartment building on Monet Drive.

The women had all been posed in the same way—naked, with their legs spread wide. The killer wanted to humiliate them. A task force was formed to find the person whom police quickly named "the Prostitute Killer." Keith Bates was named as head of the task force, which would comprise members of a variety of police agencies, including the FBI and the Louisiana State Police (LSP).

Combined with Sean Gillis's murders, prostitutes were dying at an alarming rate on the streets of Baton Rouge. Because Sean left the bodies of his victims in numerous parishes, police remained unaware that they had more than one serial killer on their hands. They pieced together clues and followed every lead, but the Prostitute Killer remained at large, and the public remained oblivious to the fact that Baton Rouge was being plagued by a serial killer because media coverage of the murders was minimal. No one really cared about the deaths of hookers who had chosen to live a high-risk lifestyle.

But soon, media from around the country would be focusing on a series of killings that began with the murder of Gina Wilson Green in September 2001.

Gina, a nurse who lived on Stanford Avenue in Baton Rouge, was found strangled in her home. She was beautiful, talented, and ambitious, and her murder would attract attention. She wasn't like those other women. She was a productive, upstanding member of society.

And when a young LSU student, who lived just across the Mississippi River in the small town of Addis, was beaten and stabbed to death in January of the next year, media coverage was heavy. Because Geralyn Barr De-Soto's husband, Darren, was the prime suspect in that murder, the two murders were not connected.

Then Christine Moore, a lovely LSU student out jogging along River Road, disappeared in June. Her bones would be found weeks later in a ravine along Bayou Manchac, next to the Ebenezer Baptist Church.

But it wasn't until the death of Charlotte Murray Pace, a recent graduate of LSU who had moved from Stanford Avenue only a week before her murder, that police and the media realized that a different kind of killer was on the loose, a killer who targeted beautiful, accomplished women. It was May 2002 when Murray Pace was attacked in her new town house on Sharlo Avenue. She was stabbed eighty-three times with a flathead screwdriver. Suddenly everyone in Baton Rouge realized that a vicious killer was on the loose.

In the small town of Breaux Bridge, just outside Lafayette, another nurse, Diane Alexander, was attacked in her home that July. A burly black man had forced his way in and attempted to rape and strangle her. Fortunately, Diane's son drove up in time to interrupt the attack and save his mother's life. The man escaped out the back door.

A week later, Pam Kinamore, owner of a small antiques store in Denham Springs, located just outside of Baton Rouge, was taken from her home in a safe Baton Rouge neighborhood and brought to Whiskey Bay, where she was raped and slashed to death. Pam was a wife and mother, and her death hit home with the community. DNA found on Pam's body matched the other murders. Police finally realized they were looking for a serial killer.

But the Baton Rouge murders were not the first for this particular killer. In 1992, Connie Lynn Warner, who lived in the small town of Zachary, had been found dead on Sorrel Avenue, near downtown Baton Rouge. She had been beaten to death. And in 1998, Randi Mebruer, who lived in the Oak Shadows subdivision in Zachary, just a block from where Connie had lived, had come up missing as well. Blood found all over her home indicated that she had been murdered. Semen left on a trash can liner would match the DNA of the Baton Rouge killer.

Dubbed "the South Louisiana Serial Killer," this rapist and murderer would take center stage while Sean stayed at home and watched news reports on the other man's killings. Sean kept a file on his computer of all the reports he could find. He admired this killer who had accomplished what Sean had not. His murders had attracted attention, and people were panicking.

The public paid attention to these murders. This killer was vicious, and he attacked women in the place where they felt the safest—in their homes. These weren't prostitutes. These were women who mattered in the community. They were beautiful, intelligent, and well liked.

Women in Baton Rouge began to panic. They enrolled in self-defense classes. They bought pepper spray. They didn't talk to strangers. They stayed home at night. They locked their doors and windows. The friendly culture of the South dissipated as more and more women died and the community became more fearful.

In November 2002, Trineisha Dené Colomb, a beautiful young woman whose mother had passed away only six months before, was taken from her mother's grave site in Grand Coteau, a few miles from Lafayette where she lived. Her body was found in Scott, Louisiana, twenty miles away. She had been raped and beaten. DNA soon connected her murder to the murders in Baton Rouge.

And then on Christmas Eve, Mari Ann Fowler, sixty-five years old, wife of Jerry Fowler, the imprisoned commissioner of elections for the state of Louisiana, disappeared from in front of a Subway fast-food restaurant in Port Allen. When Mari Ann was taken, panic ensued. The killer had no age preference, no race preference. Beauty and intelligence were the only requirements needed to attract certain death at the brutal hands of this killer.

The media finally began publicizing how many women had been murdered in the area over a ten-year span, and women in Baton Rouge and the surrounding areas began to understand the real meaning of fear. Sean laughed as the murders piled up. He couldn't believe he was being upstaged, but he knew that this killer was keeping him safe. While police were focusing on these high-profile murders, they weren't looking for him.

Another LSU student, Carrie Lynn Yoder, was discovered in Whiskey Bay in March 2003. Police had been looking for her for more than a week after her boyfriend had reported her missing. The beautiful young woman had been beaten and strangled to death, then dumped off the bridge on Interstate 10 into the bay.

When a geographical profile was created to predict where this killer lived, the area chosen was the area of town where Sean lived. Police told the public that they were looking for a white man in a white pickup truck, and more than a thousand white males in white pickup trucks were pulled over on the side of the road and swabbed for DNA.

But police were looking in the wrong direction. That became clear when Tony Frudakis, with DNAPrint Genomics in Florida, provided a racial DNA profile of the killer. He informed police that the man for whom they were searching was 85 percent sub-Saharan African and 15 percent Native American. Police were stunned. They were now looking for a black man.

On May 28, 2003, after a nationwide manhunt, Derrick Todd Lee, the South Louisiana Serial Killer, was captured in Atlanta, the city where he had run to hide.

Sean watched the coverage of the event, fascinated.

Women all over South Louisiana breathed a huge sigh of relief.

They were safe again.

But they didn't know about Sean Gillis or the Prostitute Killer. They didn't know the murders would continue. It was almost time for Sean to get back to work—now that he didn't have to share the limelight. Like a snake that had been coiled in the grass, he waited for the perfect moment to strike.

A Rare Breed of Killers

Necrophilia is typically defined as a sexual attraction to corpses. Most commonly, people assume that necrophiliacs work in funeral homes, taking their sexual pleasure from people who await burial. This practice, considered "regular" necrophilia, is looked upon as perverse and repulsive, but some psychologists believe that the practice of necrophilia is more widespread than many people think. The most common form of necrophilia—necrophiliac fantasy—in which the act of sex with a dead person is fantasized about, but not acted upon, cannot be documented because there is simply no way to determine how many people dream about having sex with a corpse.

The third type of necrophilia is more rare, the category under which Sean Gillis falls—necrophiliac homicide, in which murder is used to obtain a corpse for sexual pleasure. Of all known serial killers throughout the world, only a few murder simply for the pleasure of sex with a corpse.

Edmund Kemper was one such killer. Arrested in 1973, after he called police to turn himself in, Kemper had committed his first murders at the age of fifteen when he killed his grandparents. That act preceded a string of murders. Like Sean Gillis, Kemper sometimes dismembered and beheaded his victims before having sex with their heads. Kemper would also sometimes cook and consume flesh from his victims. His final victim—the object of all of his rage—was his mother, whose head he bashed in with a hammer before beheading her.

Ted Bundy, who was infamous for his good looks and ability to talk women into his vehicle before he killed them, was also a necrophiliac who murdered women before having sex with them. By the time he was caught, Bundy had killed thirty women in six states, but some believe he killed more. He would later admit to raping the corpses of the women he killed, although in most states necrophilia is not considered rape. Bundy even revisited some of the bodies he had raped and had sex with them again. However, Bundy did not have Sean's propensity for mutilation of the bodies before having sex with them.

"The Rostov Ripper," Andrei Chikatilo, one of Russia's most prolific serial killers, also fits into the category of necrophiliac homicide. This killer abducted and killed fifty-two people, mostly children, gouging their eyes, biting their genitals, and ripping open their torsos with his bare hands in order to become sexually aroused. After raping them, he sometimes took some of their organs with him for later pleasure. Chikatilo was put to death in 1994.

These deranged men shared several characteristics with Sean Gillis, but unlike these killers, Sean was not motivated by rage. He was colder, sicker, more like Jeffrey Dahmer, in some ways. Dahmer reportedly fell in love with his victims and wanted to keep them, which motivated him to keep their skulls and masturbate over their body parts.

Sean, however, was not in love with his victims. He had

no emotion whatsoever beyond a morbid curiosity about body parts and mutilation, a fascination that was beyond his control. His motivation was purely sexual, and the kill was usually only a means to an end—a pleasurable one, albeit. However, his curiosity would eventually lead him to cannibalism.

Because of the viciousness of some of his attacks—Ann Bryan and Katherine Hall, for example—one could view Sean as a disorganized killer. But Sean's planning, his organization, his brazenness, and his intelligence firmly ensconce him in the organized category. He did make attempts to clean up his crime scenes, but he always left clues for police—footprints, zip ties, wrapping paper, and he gloried in his victories when police could not connect his murders. Like Bundy, Sean was full of his own intelligence and enjoyed outwitting police.

> *I considered it spy versus spy—literally. You use what weapons you have which are superior to mine, and I'll try to subvert those weapons, make them useless . . . totally useless. The only thing I can't do is scramble a human being's DNA or change my own. I'm the chess master. It's about winning at all costs.*
>
> —*Sean Vincent Gillis*

The "Nature vs. Nurture" ideology could explain some of Sean's behavior, considering the mental illness that he apparently inherited from his father. According to this idea, which is accepted by many in the psychiatric world, there must be a gene of psychosis present and some abuse or triggering factor in the killer's childhood to create the lack of empathy necessary to create a serial killer. While Sean grew up in a single-parent household, those who knew his family never saw any abuse. Even Sean said that he was not abused, only punished or whipped occasionally when he broke rules. His friends believed that Yvonne was a hard worker, a loving mother who did nothing more than spoil her son a little too much. Therefore, in Sean's case, the nurture element of the theory is missing. So what turned him from a geek who enjoyed smoking weed with his friends to something that is not quite human?

Perhaps it was the incident when he discovered the pictures of homosexuals in his father's room that triggered the darkness that plagued him. Perhaps he felt abandoned when his mother moved to Atlanta. Perhaps it was the hours he spent on the Internet looking at the naked bodies of dead women. Perhaps it was the picture in Terri's wallet of the man she had killed. Whatever triggered him, at thirty-two, Sean turned into a vicious killer who enjoyed the death, the blood, the mutilation, and the sex.

And while he is not famous like some of the other serial killers of our day, his deeds were just as horrific as some and more evil than most.

If she were still alive, Sean's friend Johnnie Mae Williams could attest to that.

Johnnie Mae Williams

"It's time to eat, kids. Come on. Larry, Lauren, Jena, get in here," Johnnie Mae Williams called.

The kids hurried to the table. Johnnie Mae, a pretty black woman, was famous in the neighborhood for her cooking, and their table was usually filled with aunts and uncles and cousins who lived on the same street—Jake Lane, in the small community of St. Gabriel, located on the east side of the Mississippi River in Iberville Parish. A hands-on mom, Johnnie Mae cooked three meals each day for her children, and the kitchen was a favorite spot for the whole family.

Separated from her husband, Larry Williams Sr., Johnnie Mae earned money through catering community functions out of her kitchen and braiding the hair of the ladies who lived nearby. Everyone on the street liked to come by and talk while she cooked or braided hair. Although money was tight, her children lacked for nothing, especially food. And Larry Sr. was a very involved father, visiting often and making sure the children had everything they needed. Theirs was a happy family, and Johnnie Mae took a lot of pride in being a good mother. She volunteered at school, and the house was always filled with tempting smells when she did her baking for bake sales.

After her divorce, Johnnie Mae met Tony Llorens and fell in love. It wasn't long before she and the children moved to Baton Rouge to live with him. Tony was well-to-do, and Johnnie Mae, Larry Jr., Lauren, and Jena suddenly found themselves living in a huge house with an inground swimming pool. They had five fancy cars at their disposal. For the next few years, life couldn't have been better. Johnnie Mae enjoyed being spoiled, not having to work, wearing fancy diamonds set in platinum, and taking expensive cruises around the world. Her life in St. Gabriel had not been bad, but this life was definitely much better. She loved Tony and thought he loved her.

She tried not to say anything when some of his less than desirable friends came to the house. She just smiled and cooked up a delicious meal. She tried to ignore the whispers about other women. She didn't want anything to disturb her happy life.

"He was cheating on her," Lauren explained, "and she couldn't handle it. She loved him. She turned to drugs to deal with her pain."

Nobody realized it at first. Johnnie Mae did a good job of hiding it from her children, but things began to go downhill quickly. She soon became addicted to crack cocaine. She woke up one day, and her world had crumbled around her. The big house was gone. The cars were gone. Tony was gone.

Johnnie Mae's former husband noticed that something was wrong with her. Although they were divorced, they had remained friends, and Larry Sr. was very concerned. He did not want his children to grow up around drugs. For a while, he and Tony alternated caring for the children, but before long, he came and got them and petitioned the court for custody. He won. His son and two daughters were now his sole responsibility.

Johnnie Mae tried to get them back. Just after school let out for the summer one year, she went to Larry's house and told the girls, "Come on. Y'all are coming to live with me."

Lauren knew that wasn't a good idea. Although her mother hid her drug use, she knew something was wrong and that her father would be upset. Jena, who was younger, said, "I'm going with my mama," and she left. Johnnie Mae kidnapped her and kept her for the summer, until it was time for school to start.

"I need you to come get Jena to get her uniforms for school," Johnnie Mae told Larry on the phone one day.

"No problem," Larry said. "I'll be right over."

Larry took Jena to get the uniforms and then brought her back to his house. There was nothing Johnnie Mae could do. Larry had gotten his youngest daughter back.

Larry and the children eventually moved into a house on Jake Lane, just down the street from their mother's family home, so the children got to see their mother when she wasn't using.

"She tried so hard," Lauren remembered. "She was in and out of rehab. She would always tell me she was going to beat this, that she was going to get clean. And she would for six months or so, but then a crisis would come along, and she'd go back on the crack. When she was on drugs, she would call all the time, but she would never let us see her. She got to where she would tell us she had a problem, and would explain how hard it was and how hard she was trying. She always told me, 'Don't ever take life for granted, Lauren.'"

The children always knew that Johnnie Mae loved

them. Even though she was a drug addict, she never let them forget that. The rough streets of North Baton Rouge were a long way from the elegant home in which she had raised them, but being a good mother had always been very important to her. Even the other crack addicts and prostitutes called her "Mother." As she was walking along, she would often hear one of them call out, "Johnnie Mae! Mother! Lauren called for you." She always rushed to the nearest phone and returned her daughter's calls. She often told her, "Lauren, I don't want you to be like me. I want you to be better than me."

"She made sure to call every month when my cycle came down to see if I needed feminine products, so I wouldn't have to be embarrassed by asking my dad," Lauren said. "She tried to take care of us in small ways."

And when life on the streets got to be too much, Johnnie Mae would check into rehab and come out clean, returning to her home on Jake Lane and cooking scrumptious meals for her children again. The kids spent hours and hours with her during those times. They loved it. This Johnnie Mae was sweet and funny and caring, and they made the most of the time they had with her, trying not to worry about when she would disappear again.

When she grew up, Lauren joined the military. While she was away from home, she always sent money to her mom. "I'd pay her bills, put clothes on her back, get her food. I always knew that one day she would get clean and stay that way. She was my mama, my best friend. I just couldn't give up on her," Lauren said. "I would never give up on her."

Unfortunately, someone else would one day give up on Lauren's mama.

* * *

Johnnie Mae Williams met Sean Gillis through a friend who worked at St. James Place and often went into the Circle K where he worked. Sean told Johnnie's friend that he was looking for someone to clean his house once in a while. Johnnie Mae sometimes cleaned houses to earn money to support her drug habit. Johnnie's friend brought her to the store one day, and Sean and Johnnie hit it off instantly. Sean saw Johnnie as someone who had access to marijuana, and occasionally he bought some from her. She also cleaned his house a few times, and the two became friends.

A few years before her death, Johnnie got off drugs for a while and decided to cook her family a big Thanksgiving dinner. She invited Sean, who enjoyed talking with Johnnie's sister and the rest of the family while they ate. No one thought there was anything strange about the white man who joined them as they thanked God for His many blessings. He looked like a decent young man in his early forties, not at all like the men Johnnie Mae usually hung around with nowadays. They were happy that Johnnie Mae was there with them, that she was smiling and free of drugs, that she was making new kinds of friends. Sean smiled as he thanked the family for the delicious meal before he said his good-byes.

Still serving in the military that year, Lauren wasn't able to join them.

Over the years, Sean and Johnnie saw each other now and then, mostly when Sean was looking for some weed. He would drive to North Baton Rouge and search for her, sometimes finding her walking on the streets in search of a john. That's where he found her on the night of October 9, 2003.

"Hop in, Johnnie. How you been?" Sean said as Johnnie Mae got into his car.

"Good," Johnnie said, but Sean could tell she wasn't doing so well. She was obviously on the crack bad this time. Her normally slender frame had faded away to nothing but skin and bones. Most of her teeth were gone. She barely resembled the woman he had met years before.

"You're on the drugs, aren't you?" Sean said.

Johnnie Mae just nodded. She knew she was not in good shape, knew that it was time to get clean again. She missed her kids and wanted to see them.

She leaned back in the seat as Sean drove through Baton Rouge to Old Jefferson Highway in the southeastern section of the city. Sean watched her as he drove. He thought she looked dead. He thought she needed to be dead. He felt that familiar excitement surging through his veins. He spotted Mason's Grill, a popular restaurant known for its barbecue shrimp and grit cake platter, blackened alligator, and Cajun shrimp burger. It had been a long time since he had killed. It didn't matter that she was his friend. The moment she had gotten into his car, she was already dead. Sean drove down a gravel pathway to a grassy area behind the restaurant. Hidden from the road by the building and surrounded by trees, Sean pulled Johnnie Mae from the car.

He began beating the frail woman who was loved by so many. In her condition, Johnnie Mae could barely fight back. He hit her again and again, in the head, in the stomach, until he was sure she was dead. He removed her jacket, her pants, her shirt, her panties, her tennis shoes.

Then he reached for his knife, his eyes gleaming in the darkness.

Sean turned her over and examined her body, his eyes following the tip of the knife blade. He pulled the blade back and stabbed the back of her leg, enjoying the slight resistance as it sliced through muscle. He pulled down fiercely, ripping open the back of her leg. He punched her left buttock, enjoying the sound of his fist hitting her flesh. He cut through the area he had punched. He hit her again, this time just above the right buttock.

He sliced through the line that ran from her lower back and into the crease between her buttocks. Then he cut open the back of her right leg. He cut her over and over, carving her like the Thanksgiving turkey he had eaten with her years before. He felt nothing but the pure enjoyment of the moment. He was so curious. He loved watching the skin fall away as his knife cut into it. He wanted to see the muscles and veins and tissue that made up her legs.

Sean worked his way down, alternating between striking and cutting Johnnie Mae.

He turned her over, letting his hand follow the curve of her arm. Picking it up, he began slicing violently through her wrist, until he held her detached hand in his own. He reached for her other hand, not quite satisfied with having only one to take with him.

The deranged killer could hear her bones snapping as he worked his way through another wrist. He smiled, liking the sound of his knife sawing its way through.

Sean placed both of Johnnie Mae's hands in a ziplock bag. He gathered most of her clothes and put them in a box, leaving behind only her shirt and tennis shoes. He placed his treasures in the car, before picking up Johnnie Mae's ravaged body and placing her in the front seat.

He turned on the engine, hoping no one would hear it, and backed up until he reached the blacktop parking lot of the restaurant. He turned onto Old Jefferson, heading back toward Airline Highway. He traveled north about ten miles, before taking the exit for Plank Road, near where he had found his friend earlier that night. He drove thirteen more miles until he reached Pride–Port Hudson Road and turned right. He could see the first streaks of morning making the way across the sky as he drove down the winding road, but he could barely make out the narrow dirt road he knew was there. Finally he saw it, and turned his car right, heading into the woods. He drove until he reached the end of the road, then pulled Johnnie Mae's body from the car, dragging her down a trail, which was bordered by a two-foot embankment on either side, to a spot about fifty yards away.

Sean leaned Johnnie Mae over the embankment, tucking her handless arms beneath her with her buttocks in the air. It was getting light out now, and he reached into his pocket for his new camera. He took pictures of the mutilation he had inflicted upon the helpless woman. He would enjoy these at a later time.

Sean left her there, posed and alone, for the insects that would voraciously infest her body.

He walked quickly back to the car, eager to revisit his treasures. He reached for the ziplock bag containing Johnnie Mae's hands—touching them, feeling them on his body, rubbing them up and down. Sean cried out his pleasure.

A Body in the Woods

"Dad, I found a body," Ethan, who had burst through the door at full speed, yelled. "She's dead!"

"What are you talking about, son?" Robert Reames jumped out of his chair.

Robert and his wife, Patti, were about to share a late lunch with the new pastor of their church. Mike Robertson and his wife, Bridget, had felt called to minister to the small village of Pride, Louisiana, and had recently moved to the area. Robert, who was the minister of music at Lanier Baptist Church, had invited them over to welcome them to the community.

Patti was still in the kitchen, putting the finishing touches on the chicken and sausage gumbo and preparing drinks for her guests, when she heard the word "dead" coming from her son. She ran into the living room, worried that the dog had died.

"Ethan, what's wrong?" she said, alarmed when she saw his pale face and his labored breathing.

"He found a body in the woods," Bridget told her.

Patti was stunned for a moment, not quite comprehending what she had heard. Ethan had found a body, a dead person?

Ethan had grown up in the woods surrounding their home off Pride–Port Hudson Road. He and his father had been squirrel hunting in the woods earlier that morning. Ethan had smelled something then, something that had the putrid odor of a rotting animal, but he hadn't mentioned it to his dad.

That afternoon, he had gone back into the woods on his four-wheeler with a friend looking for Sam, his chocolate Lab that had run off. Normally, his two Labs followed him and came back when he did, but Sam had stayed gone.

"Where did you see it?" Robert asked.

Ethan told his father that he had seen the body close to the same trail they had ridden that morning.

"Are you sure?"

"Yes, sir," Ethan said.

"Stay here. We'll check it out," Robert told his son as he and the pastor hurried out the door.

As soon as the men were gone, Patti reached out and hugged her son close. She prayed that this was all a mistake, that her son had not seen a dead person. He was too young.

Patti and Robert had been married for more than twenty years, and theirs was a devoutly Christian family. They had sheltered Ethan and his sister, Ashley, from the harsher realities of life. They had hoped by raising them in a small community, miles away from the crime to be found in Baton Rouge, that they could keep them safer, purer somehow. And now Ethan had discovered a dead body in the woods. She hugged him more tightly, hoping against hope he had misjudged what he saw.

Robert and Mike headed toward the beginning of the

trail that could be seen from Pride–Port Hudson Road. The familiar pathway took them deep into the woods. They followed Ethan's directions, and it wasn't long before the scent of death traveled on the wind to them. They knew they were getting close.

They stopped when they saw it.

Folded on her stomach over the bank of the trail was a completely nude black woman. Robert noticed deep cuts on her back and legs. He stared for a moment, shivering, the knowledge sinking in that his young son had seen what was obviously the body of a woman who had been murdered.

The two men hurried back to the house to call the police.

"It was bad, Patti," he told his wife before leaving to meet the police.

Robert met police officers on the highway at the trail's entrance. He led them single file through the woods, then stood aside and watched as they secured the crime scene. He observed quietly as the police traipsed through the crime scene. He had watched enough *CSI* episodes to know that they weren't supposed to do that, but he didn't say anything.

When the woman was turned over, Robert was shocked to see that she had no hands. Whoever had done this had removed them. Police searched the woods but could not find the hands that had been cut from the woman's arms.

Robert turned away, no longer able to watch. It was too much.

He answered all of their questions, then hurried home to check on Ethan.

He soon learned that within minutes of the police being dispatched, the whole community had learned about the body. It was like that in small towns. The phone was already ringing when he got back to the house.

"I smelled it this morning, Dad," Ethan told his father. "I didn't know what it was. I thought it was maybe an animal. But when we were looking for Sam, my friend said he saw a dead body as we drove by it. I stopped, and there it was. I turned around and got here as soon as I could."

"You did good, son. I'm sorry you had to see that," he said, hugging his child to him.

Later that night, as she tucked Ethan into his bed, Patti knelt next to him, and they said their prayers.

"Are you okay, son?" Patti asked as she pulled his blanket more tightly around him.

"I'm glad I found her, Mama, 'cause if I hadn't, how long would she have been there?" the little boy replied. "I'm just going to give that image to Jesus."

"That will help," Patti told him. "But if you need anything tonight, just call for me, okay?"

"Okay, Mama."

It wasn't long before Ethan became known as "the boy who found the dead body." Everyone at school had questions for him, which he didn't want to answer. He didn't want that kind of attention, but there was nothing he could do to stop it. He hoped whoever had killed the woman would be caught. He couldn't know that his discovery would one day link a series of killings that had occurred around Baton Rouge. A hair found in the woman's arm would link her murder to a serial killer.

Two weeks later, Sam came home, wagging his tail like nothing had happened.

A Cold, Hard Truth

While the Tampa Bay Buccaneers were beating the Oakland Raiders in the Super Bowl in 2003, Jena Williams was in the hospital giving birth to her son, Brian Keith. Just a few weeks before, her mother, Johnnie Mae, had moved with her into an apartment to help her with her babies. The mother and daughter had been staying with Jena's older sister, Lauren, but Johnnie Mae and Lauren had gotten into an argument. Jena and Johnnie Mae moved out.

Jena had always felt especially close to Johnnie Mae. The baby of the family, Jena understood her mama, never held any resentment toward her, and always had a place for Johnnie Mae to stay when life on the streets became too much for her.

"Mama kept everything she did away from us," Jena said. "She loved my babies and always helped me take care of them. We had a very special relationship."

On the morning of January 24, 2003, just days before Jena went into labor, Johnnie Mae rose from her bed and told her daughter that she was going into Baton Rouge. It was the last time Jena would see her mother.

After the baby was born, Jena moved in with the father of four of her children and waited for her mother to come visit the new baby. Johnnie Mae loved children, but Jena knew that she would not come around if she was using. She talked to her a few times over the next months, and Johnnie Mae insisted she was okay. She told Jena she was living in an apartment in Turner Plaza on North Street.

By the middle of October, Jena still had not seen her mother.

One afternoon a few months later, while she was lying on the floor in her living room trying to ease the backache caused by another pregnancy, the phone rang. Jena's mother-in-law handed her the phone.

"Hello," Jena said.

It was her oldest daughter's aunt Jasmine.

"You all right?" Jasmine asked her.

"Yeah. Why?"

"You didn't hear nothin' bad today?"

"No," Jena answered, wondering what Jasmine was trying to tell her.

"Girl, I hate to be the bearer of bad news, but yo' mama dead," Jasmine said.

"What did you say?"

"Yo' mama. She dead."

Jena hung up the phone. She didn't believe Jasmine.

She got her mother-in-law to drive her to Turner Plaza, an old, dilapidated apartment complex in North Baton Rouge. She knocked on the door of Johnnie Mae's apartment. There was no answer. She asked a neighbor if he had seen her mother.

"I saw her a few days ago," the man told her. "She be just fine."

Jena smiled, relief flowing through her body. As she

was leaving, she saw some women sitting outside the building.

"Have you seen Johnnie Mae? Have you seen Mother?"

"She used to do my hair," one of the women said. "I saw her crossing the street to catch the bus the other day."

"She was okay?" Jena asked.

"Yeah. Didn't look like nothin' was wrong with her."

Jena hurried home and called Lauren.

"It wasn't her. It's not her!" she exclaimed. "I just went to her apartment, and people there say they saw her in the last few days. Mama's not dead."

A few days later, Lauren called Jena back.

"Mama is dead," she told her. "A detective told me they have her DNA. It was her. She was murdered."

"I didn't want it to be true," Jena remembered, tears filling her eyes. "I didn't accept it. Even at the funeral, there was no body. They had cremated her, and we weren't even there. We didn't see her. There was just a table full of pictures of my mama at the funeral. Even seeing those pictures there, I still didn't believe it. My mama had always done everything for me and my babies. I couldn't understand that she wouldn't be here anymore, that she wouldn't come home. She always came home."

This time, Johnnie Mae would never come home.

"Terri, check this out," Sean Gillis said. "Look what I found on the Internet."

Terri leaned over his shoulder to look at the computer. What she saw repulsed her. It was a picture of a naked black woman lying on her stomach, with her buttocks in the air. Long slash marks ran down her legs.

"Why are you showing me this?" Terri said. "It's disgusting. Where do you find this stuff?"

"Here and there." Sean shrugged.

"You are so weird," Terri said. "I don't wanna see that."

Sean grinned as he clicked out of the photograph. He didn't need it. He had other photos of Johnnie Mae, some he had hidden in a Norton SystemWorks book he kept on his desk, and he had put some in a bank bag in the glove compartment of his car. He could revisit his adventure with Johnnie Mae anytime he wanted.

Like too many victims before her, Johnnie Mae's case went cold.

Donna Bennett Johnston

In December 2003, Sean Gillis and Terri Lemoine were busily enjoying the holiday season. They loved Christmas, and Sean was like a little kid when it came to unwrapping presents. This year, Terri's daughter Christine had come to spend the holidays with them, which made the season even more special for the family. While Lauren, Larry Jr., and Jena were grieving the loss of their mother, Sean was being silly, placing the Styrofoam that had encased some of his electronic gifts on his head, pretending it was a hat. It was a happy time for his family.

After celebrating the New Year holiday, life went back to normal, but Sean became restless again and bored. He felt his unnatural fascination surfacing and knew it was time to start trolling for his next victim. In the early-morning hours of February 26, 2004, he found her, walking near the corner of Geronimo Street and Prescott Road, a little unsteady on her feet.

Perfect, Sean thought, as he watched the woman stumble along.

* * *

Donna Bennett Johnston was born to Johnnie May and Joseph Bennett on July 9, 1960. She would become the fourth of six children. Born in Monroe, Louisiana, the family moved to Baton Rouge shortly after Donna was born. Her father was a welder, and her mother sometimes worked as a switchboard operator at the old Belmont Hotel or at Woolworth as a cashier. Donna grew up around North Baton Rouge, but back then, it wasn't so crime-ridden. The young girl, with the shiny brown hair, loved gymnastics and other sports and enjoyed going to church with her family on Sundays. But her good Catholic upbringing could not keep her from getting pregnant when she was fifteen. Before she turned sixteen, she gave birth to a son she named Michael.

"I took care of her during her pregnancy," Johnnie recalled. "She lived with me, and I showed her how to become a mom."

In 1981, at the age of twenty-one, Donna married, but that marriage didn't last long. In 1984, she married again, this time to Jimmy Johnston, a tall, slender man, with a strong, weathered face. The couple was happy for a few years, although times were often hard. Jimmy and Donna had two children while they were married: Justin and James Anthony (Tony). As a car salesman, Jimmy sometimes made good money, but he didn't work at other times.

"Their marriage was up and down," Johnnie said. "Jimmy did not provide regular financial support or a home for her at times, and occasionally he wasn't faithful. That was the beginning of Donna's downfall. All she wanted was a decent home for her kids. She was a simple girl."

Donna began to drink, just a little at first. As her marriage started to deteriorate, the drinking became worse.

Then it was pills, a few here and there to help her get through each day. When she got her first taste of crack cocaine, not long after the drug had become popular, the liquor was no longer enough. Crack made her feel good; it made her problems go away.

"About seven or eight years into our marriage, she became addicted," Jimmy said. "I put her in rehab four times. She would do better for six or seven months, but then she was back on crack. I couldn't take it. It was hurting the kids. A counselor told me I was contributing to her problem, that I wasn't helping anything. After ten years of marriage, we got divorced."

But Donna loved Jimmy, and he loved her. The couple continued seeing each other and had two more children after the divorce: Savannah and Jesse (Woody).

Donna lived with her mother and supported the children through prostitution. Often she shoplifted the items she needed or stole cigarettes and beer from nearby stores when she felt like partying a little. Once she was arrested at Walmart after passing out in the dressing room. When store employees went in and found her, clothes and other items that she had stuffed in her purse were hanging out. Donna spent that night in jail.

"Before the crack, she was a good mom," Johnnie said. "She cooked. She cleaned. She believed in God. When the drug use started, she began to stay away from them. The kids have often lived with me, and I took care of them. She would come by to see them and was always there for birthdays and Christmas. And she always made sure I had a food stamp card so they could eat."

Donna tried to get a handle on her life, but her addiction was stronger than she was. Every two or three months, she would sober up and go back to her mom's. She would stay clean for weeks. The children loved her, and she would spend as much time as possible playing with them. Those were the happy times—for her and the children.

"I was a mama's boy," said Justin. "My mom was everything to me. She taught me a lot about life, about how rough it is out there. But I've met a lot of people with good hearts on those streets, and my mom was one of those people. She would help anyone she could to the best of her ability."

People tried to help Donna, too. For a while, she lived at Palmer-Northway Apartments at the Mohican-Prescott Crossover, and her landlord's girlfriend, Tanya Thomason, would bring food and cigarettes by for the too-skinny woman. Tanya liked Donna. She felt sorry for her. She could see that this shell of a woman was living a life filled with pain, shame, and degradation. Sometimes Donna had a bad night with one of the men she picked up on Mohican or Geronimo Streets, and she would come home with black eyes and bruises over her body.

Those were the times when Donna longed for the old days when her kids were young, when she was happy and carefree. This life she lived—the drinking, the drugging, all day, every day—clouded the memories of the gospel songs she had loved to sing as a child. Walking up and down the street, waiting for the next man to stop and offer her money to get into his car, was not what she had meant for her life to be. But there was nothing she could do, although she did try.

"When she came home, she would sleep for a whole week, and then it was like she was never gone. She would play with us and take us to the park. We did a lot of things together when she was home," Justin said.

As the kids grew older, they were sometimes exposed to the life she lived more than they should have been. Sometimes she would ask a female friend of her son, Michael, to take her to "Old Man" Mr. Carter's, a friend who rented her a room, where she would meet men. Mr. Carter would open the door with his robe hanging open and his private parts exposed. Michael's friend would hurry back to the car to wait, while Donna did her business inside with whatever man she was meeting. She would pay Mr. Carter a small fee for the room and the condoms he insisted she buy, and then join Michael's friend in the car, like nothing had happened. For Donna, it was business as usual.

Although she had a police record, that record wasn't as bad as it could have been. In August 1999, she had been arrested for solicitation. She was convicted September 7, 2001. Two days before her conviction, Donna was arrested again. This time for solicitation and possession of cocaine. She did not spend much time in jail, though.

Donna had been a police informant for a while. In exchange for information about drug dealers in the area, the Baton Rouge police did not pursue her as vigorously as they did other prostitutes and crack users in the area. Informants were valuable; they helped narcotics officers bust those who sold the cocaine and other drugs that ruined the lives of so many in North Baton Rouge. Donna was happy to help—sometimes for a little cash, sometimes to stay out of jail.

By 2004, Donna was in bad shape. Her teeth had rotted; her once shiny hair was now dirty and tangled. She stayed with friends here and there, but oftentimes she would go to her ex-husband Jimmy's mechanic shop on Hanks Drive and ask to take a shower.

"Every time she came to the shop, she asked for money for food," Jimmy remembered. "I refused to give her money because she wouldn't get food, she would buy drugs."

On the afternoon of February 25, Donna went to the

shop to ask him for money once again. Jimmy could tell she had been drinking. He worried when she drank because sometimes she became abusive.

"No, Donna. You're drunk. I'm not giving you any money," he told her.

"Can I at least take a shower?" she said.

"No. You can come back when you're not drunk."

Surprisingly, Donna didn't argue this time. Jimmy watched sadly as she walked away from the building. He wondered if she would ever get better.

The Depths of Depravity

Although Donna Bennett Johnston knew most of the people who lived in the run-down shacks along Mohican, Geronimo, and Prescott, she tried to be careful. She had been beaten one too many times, and she knew that, given the opportunity, her friends on the streets would not hesitate to steal from her. She kept her money well hidden in her brassiere or in her socks or shoes. She wasn't about to give up any of the money she earned. Because she worked in the early-morning hours—usually between one and four—Donna knew she had to be extra careful. The streets were more dangerous during those hours. Not only was there danger from the men who approached the hollow-eyed women as they stood on their corners or walked up and down the streets, but prostitutes were very territorial and would not hesitate to cut you if you honed in on one of their johns. But Donna had been working here for years. She was comfortable inside this world. It was her world, one that accepted her and did not look down on her. It was where she belonged.

On the night of February 25, she was feeling a little

antsy. She walked to her friend, Brenda's, house on Mohican Street, hoping that Brenda would go with her to the store to get some booze. She was also in need of a fix, but didn't have the necessary paraphernalia to smoke her crack. Donna had known Brenda for about six years. She sometimes worked the street in front of Brenda's home and would occasionally rest underneath the shade of the banana trees that lined the property. It was about nine o'clock at night when Donna knocked on Brenda's door.

"Walk with me to the store," she said.

Brenda, who was seven months pregnant, realized that Donna was a little drunk and told her that she couldn't go.

"Well, if anything happens to me, tell my kids I love them," Donna said.

Brenda replied, "Okay," but she thought that was an odd statement. Then she noticed Donna was carrying her son's baby blanket. She wondered if Donna was all right. She was used to her comings and goings at all hours of the night. She often saw her under the trees in her yard, and then she would be gone for a couple of hours. Each time she came back, she was a little drunker than before she left.

Later that night, Donna had made some money and needed another drink. She was standing alone in a parking lot near Advanced Auto on Byron Avenue near Plank Road when Willie Banks first saw her. He had been checking on his newborn puppies when he noticed Donna in the parking lot across the street. It was 1:45 A.M. Willie was standing by the kennel when Donna walked up and asked him for a ride to the store. It was a cold night, in the low forties, but Willie still thought it was strange that she was wrapped in a quilt.

"I could smell the alcohol on her breath," he said. "I gave her a ride to the EZ Pac-N-Serv, about a mile away.

She went in and bought gin, chips, and a glass container with a rose in it. I dropped her off on the corner of Winnebago, and she walked away pretty fair."

Donna walked aimlessly for a while, ending up at the corner of Geronimo Street and Prescott Road, just a few blocks from Istrouma High, the school she had attended so many years before. Back then, her thoughts had been happy ones, filled with hopes and dreams for her future. On this night, her thoughts were only to make enough money to feed her addiction, yet again. When the pleasant-looking man in the Chevy Cavalier pulled alongside her at around 3:00 A.M. and rolled down his window, Donna did not hesitate. She got into the passenger seat. The two agreed on a price for oral sex, and Donna leaned back. They didn't talk much, just listened to the radio as the man drove along.

Sean Gillis smiled. He could smell the alcohol and knew this was going to be easy. He navigated his way skillfully through the streets that were home to the woman next to him. He had driven them so many times, always late at night. He drove down Mohican, turned onto Uncas, crossed over Weller Avenue and Gordon Street, and continued making right turns and left turns until he reached East Mason Street. He looked over and saw that the woman was sleeping. He began looking for just the right spot. He couldn't bring her to his house, because Terri was home. He knew she would be mad when he returned, but he didn't care. They fought about the nights he stayed out late, but he knew this night would be worth the argument he would face later.

Sean crossed Scenic Highway and spotted a secluded area near a chemical plant. He drove through the fence and parked the car. He carefully retrieved his ever-handy zip tie and wrapped it around Donna's neck.

He had just begun to pull the zip tie when Donna woke up. Even in her sleepy state, she realized something was very wrong. Her survival instincts were strong. She jumped out of the car, running for her life across the grassy field.

Sean chased her. He caught her from behind when she reached the fence, grabbed the end of the zip tie, and pulled as hard as he could. Donna struggled for a moment.

"I can't breathe," she whispered before succumbing to death at the hands of the last man who would ever betray her trust.

His heartbeat quickening in anticipation, this cold, sick killer carried the frail body of his victim back to his car. He put her in the trunk, and then drove away. Sean headed toward Burbank Drive, hoping to find another secluded area. He knew he wouldn't have the cover of darkness much longer. Making his way to Parkway Drive, he drove down a narrow road that led through the woods. He found a secluded spot at the end of the street and parked.

He opened the trunk and took a few pictures of Donna's corpse. He then pulled her body from the trunk and placed her on the ground before grabbing the tools he needed. He wished Terri weren't home. This would have been much more pleasurable there. He wouldn't have to worry about anyone seeing him.

Partially hidden by the density of the trees, Sean went to work. First he removed her silver-and-black belt, then her jeans and shirt. He pulled Donna's hair and realized she was wearing a hairpiece. He removed it. Then he opened her mouth, running his fingers along her teeth and pulling until he removed her dental plate.

Sean gave her quick inspection and decided he should start with her arm. He began sawing, making several cuts near her elbow until he felt the saw give way. Through bone and muscle and tissue, he pushed the blade, harder and harder, until her arm fell away. It wasn't enough.

Her body was illuminated in the darkness by the remaining stars; Sean looked her up and down. He saw a tattoo on her right thigh, and he reached for his knife. The knife dug into Donna's flesh as he made a circle around the tattoo, then maneuvered the blade deeper to cut out the blue art that had decorated her skin. He rolled the flesh between his fingers, reveling in its soft texture. He carefully set it aside.

Sean leaned over the woman, studying her breasts. The knife, covered in blood, left streaks across her skin as he cruelly sliced through the skin around her right nipple, cutting it off. He then raked his knife across her left breast, noticing how the skin parted easily under his skillful hands. He sliced again, this time her left nipple, expertly removing the small piece of flesh. Sean examined the nipples closely. A feeling of power surged through him. He felt the joy of possession—ownership of these most intimate and feminine of body parts.

Fascinated by his trophies, he couldn't stop the hand that moved to his mouth. He simply had to taste this victim, to take these small pieces of her into his own body.

He put Donna's nipples in his mouth, sucking for a moment. Then chewing.

He didn't particularly like the taste but savored the experience. In that moment, this victim became a part of him. No one could ever take that away from him.

He picked Donna up and placed her back in the trunk. He wrapped the tattoo in a paper towel and put Donna's arm in a blue-and-white dishcloth he'd found in the car. His camera began clicking again as he took more pictures.

His hand caressing Donna's breasts and vagina.

Her mutilated breasts.

What remained of her arm.

The depraved killer took forty-five pictures of his handiwork.

Sean looked her over once again, pleased with the way his night had gone. He tossed Donna's dental plate and hairpiece into the woods.

Sated, he finally closed the trunk and got back in the car.

He drove back down Burbank toward Ben Hur Road, located just a few blocks from his home. Turning right just before the bridge that provided access across the canal, Sean maneuvered the car just past an old gate. He pulled Donna from the car, dragging her body across the debris that lined the canal, leaving small pieces of cartilage and bone along the way.

Sean posed her on her stomach and placed her jacket over her right arm and face, tucking her severed arm beneath her and positioning her buttocks in the air. In a vicious final act, he stomped on her back, leaving a bloody shoe print behind.

Satisfied with the way she looked, Sean got back in the car, heading for Burbank Car Wash, where he cleaned all traces of his victim from his vehicle.

With Donna's arm and tattoo still with him, Sean drove toward River Road, traveling for miles along the winding roadway into Ascension Parish. About a quarter mile from the entrance to the Honeywell Chemicals Plant, Sean turned onto a gravel road that led to the top of the levee, which protected area residents from the possibility of damaging floodwaters of the Mississippi River. He spotted a ditch and stopped the car. Before getting out, he reached for the paper towel that held Donna's tattoo.

A ditch near the roadway was filled with water from a heavy rainfall in the area two days before. Sean shook the paper towel over the ditch, watching as the tattoo hit the water. He stayed long enough to watch it submerge before he returned to the car.

After driving a little farther down River Road, almost to St. John the Baptist Parish, Sean stopped again. This time, he simply pitched Donna's severed arm down the levee, hoping the river would take it away.

On the way back to Baton Rouge, Sean made a final stop on St. Elmo Road, near Bocage Plantation. Located about twenty miles from the capital city, this historic plantation dates back to 1837. Built by the famous architect James Dakin, in the American Greek Revival style, this plantation is considered by many to be the crowning jewel of the River Road plantations. It was here, in a ditch on a road steeped in America's history, that Sean threw the last piece of evidence that tied him to Donna's murder—the dishcloth in which he had wrapped her arm.

Finished with his work for the night, he headed home to Terri Lemoine. He hoped she wouldn't be too mad at him.

The Investigation Begins

Johnnie May Bennett got nervous the moment she saw the police at the door. She knew this couldn't be good.

Detective Jared Ruiz and Detective Eric Strickland introduced themselves and asked if she knew Donna.

"I'm her mother," Johnnie replied, worried that Donna would be arrested again.

"Ma'am, we are sorry to inform you that your daughter is deceased. It was a homicide."

Johnnie stared at them for a moment, then began crying hysterically. It didn't matter what Donna had done in her life, Johnnie had always loved her daughter dearly. That was why she had raised Donna's children, had always allowed her to come home when she was clean.

The detectives led her to a chair, trying to console the distraught woman. They allowed her a few minutes to regain her composure.

"Do you think you can answer a few questions now?" Detective Ruiz asked when Johnnie had quieted.

She nodded. "I'll help you any way I can."

Detective Ruiz asked her about Donna's family history, about her criminal history.

"She used to be married to Jimmy Johnston and has five children. I watch them most of the time," Johnnie said tearfully. "Donna is an alcoholic and has a crack cocaine habit. She's a prostitute. That's how she supports her habit. She tried to get sober all the time. She really did, but she always ended up back on the streets."

The weight of the world settled on Johnnie as she talked, resignation lacing her voice. "I tried to help her, but the crack was too strong. She might have been staying with a man on Pawtucket. Randy is his name. She always hung around Weller, Mohican, Pawtucket, those streets. Or she could have lived on Geronimo with a man named Calvin. Jimmy would know better than me. Or maybe you could talk to her sister, Patricia. She's a prostitute, too, and addicted to crack." Johnnie sighed. "She's usually around the Mobil truck stop on Airline Highway."

Johnnie gave police all the phone numbers she had that could help them and watched as they left. She sank back into her chair, tears once again flowing down her face, wondering how she was going to tell the children. No matter what kind of life Donna had led, those kids loved their mama. She fretted about what she would say—what words she could use to tell the younger ones something this horrible.

The detectives called Jimmy and told him that Donna had been murdered. Although this was what he had feared for a long time, he was still shocked. He asked for details about what had happened to her.

After the detectives told him about finding Donna's body, Jimmy asked them to allow him to tell the children. "I need to be the one to tell them. You don't understand," he said. "We were divorced, but we were still friends. We talked at least once a week, and I've tried to help her with her addictions. They were just too severe for her to overcome."

Jimmy went on to tell the detectives about Donna coming to his shop just a few days before, how she had asked for money and a shower, but he had refused because she was drunk. "I didn't like seeing her when she was like that," he said. "Talk to her sister, Patricia, or her friend Calvin. He lives on Geronimo, and it's the only house with a wheelchair ramp leading to the front door. Her friend Brenda lives there, too."

Later that day, Detective Ruiz and Lieutenant Terry Felton arrived at Randy's house.

"Yes, Donna used to live here, but I asked her to leave after she stole some of my things," he told them. "We were still friends, though. I saw her Tuesday or Wednesday morning. She came over and asked to take a shower. I told her I was sleeping, and she left."

Realizing they weren't getting anywhere, the detectives began to canvass the area. A woman named Carol told them that Donna had come over on Wednesday and asked to take a shower. "I was going to let her in, but my boyfriend wouldn't let me," she said. "Me and Donna were good friends, though."

Another woman, Melissa, told them that she, too, was good friends with Donna. "I saw her a week ago, but I don't know when exactly. This is so sad. The whole neighborhood is sad about this. Everyone knew her."

The detectives made their way to Geronimo Street, where they found Calvin and Brenda's home.

"I knew her well," Calvin told the detectives after they had separated the couple for individual questioning. "We were good friends. She was here Wednesday, the twenty-fifth, around two P.M. She didn't stay long, and I don't know where she went when she left. It's not unusual for people to come and go here at all hours."

"Are you on crack?" Ruiz asked.

"Yes, I have an addiction, and people come here to smoke crack."

Brenda told the detectives the same thing—that Donna had been there that Wednesday. "We used to work together, but I'm no longer a prostitute because I'm pregnant. Donna still worked the same area, though. She was always here or on Plank Road or Scenic Highway."

"Did she have any regular customers?"

"Not that I know of," Brenda said. "We had different customers. If she did have a regular customer, she wouldn't tell anybody. She would have been afraid we'd try to take them from her."

"Have you seen anybody suspicious around, or did she say anyone had scared her lately?" Ruiz asked.

"No, but you can talk to her sister. She might know," Brenda responded.

The detectives decided it was time to talk to Donna's sister, Patricia. They headed to the Mobil truck stop on Airline Highway, hoping to find her there. They got lucky.

"I already know," she told them when they approached her.

"When was the last time you saw her?"

"Two weeks ago, by her husband's shop. We got different friends and don't hang out in the same spots," Patricia told them.

"Do you know if anybody scared her lately?"

"No. She didn't mention anyone. Some of my male customers scare me, though. They make strange requests. I've been beat up a lot, and so was Donna."

Ruiz and Felton spent the rest of the evening watching prostitutes walking the streets of North Baton Rouge.

Almost every one they stopped knew Donna, but no one knew who would have killed her. All of the women told police that they always dealt with strange men who scared them. That was nothing unusual on these streets.

On March 3, just four days after Donna's body had been discovered, a task force, named the Unsolved Homicide Task Force, was formed to look into the deaths of Donna Bennett Johnston, Johnnie Mae Williams, and Katherine Hall, as well as other unsolved homicides that could be similar. Police were beginning to remember that there were other murders in recent years where victims were mutilated and left in remote areas.

The task force was composed of East Baton Rouge Parish Sheriff's Office detectives Max Schiele, Bryan White, Richard Mohr, Jared Ruiz, crime scene technician Nicole Compton, and support personnel Chrystal Andrews; Baton Rouge Police Department detectives Rudy Babin and John Norwood; Louisiana State Police detective Jerry Mitchell; FBI agent Jeff Methvin; and attorney general's office investigators Todd Morris and Jeff Bergeron. Working out of the EBRSO, Max Schiele was responsible for coordinating task force efforts.

Donna Bennett Johnston, who had been liked by so many even though she had lived such a tortured life, would soon help the task force stop a serial killer dead in his tracks.

A Pattern Emerges

The task force immediately began reviewing cases in and around Baton Rouge and in other jurisdictions. Task force members pulled old reports of murders from files long since shelved. They pored over crime scene photographs. It didn't take them long to realize that the murders of Katherine Hall, Johnnie Mae Williams, and Donna Bennett Johnston might be connected. They had each been cut up and left in remote areas. Johnnie Mae and Donna had been dismembered. Katherine had been stabbed numerous times postmortem, as had the other two women. They noticed that the bodies of these victims had been similarly posed. They had all been brought to remote locations away from North Baton Rouge. They had lived similar lifestyles. And each of the victims had ligature marks around their necks.

Investigators finally realized they were once again looking for a serial killer.

DNA soon verified that. Investigators learned that the FACES laboratory at LSU had conducted a thorough exam of Johnnie Mae Williams's body and had extracted a limb hair (a hair from an arm or leg) of a Caucasian male from a wound on Johnnie Mae's wrist, where her hand had been severed. Because the Louisiana State Police Crime Laboratory did not have the capability to extract DNA from hairs without roots, the hair had been submitted to the Acadiana Criminalistics Laboratory in Lafayette for testing. While the Acadiana Crime Lab could extract nuclear DNA, it could not extract mitochondrial DNA, so the hair sample would have to be sent to the FBI Laboratory, or crime lab, in Washington, D.C.

Natasha "Tasha" Poe, an analyst at the Acadiana Crime Lab, informed the task force that a hair with a shaft and root had also been found in Katherine's mouth. She recommended that both hairs be sent to the FBI. Poe told investigators that the nuclear DNA from the hair found on Katherine had been entered into CODIS, but it had not produced any hits. (CODIS is the Combined DNA Index System.)

Meanwhile, the state police crime lab had done a total consumption test on the fingernail scrapings they took from Donna. The nuclear DNA had been compared with the DNA on the hair from Katherine's mouth. The two profiles were the same.

The hair samples from Johnnie Mae and Katherine were turned over to Jeff Methvin, who sent them to the FBI for mitochondrial testing. The FBI determined that a similar male profile existed on both hairs. Swabs taken from the wrist of Donna also produced an identical male profile. Task force members now had a positive scientific link between all three victims.

The task force asked other jurisdictions in Louisiana to send case files on cold cases where the victims had been mutilated or had been prostitutes. They soon added Lillian Gorham Robinson to the growing list of victims with similarities. Joyce Williams's case file was sent over from West Baton Rouge Parish. They reviewed Hardee Moseley Schmidt's case. And Ann Bryan's. They weren't sure if Hardee's and Ann's cases were related because of Ann's age and Hardee's status in the community, but they were not going to dismiss them. Both of these killings had been as brutal as the others.

Investigators followed every clue. They intended to be very thorough. They had learned their lesson about relying on a profile of a serial killer from the Derrick Todd Lee investigation. In that case, the profile had led them to believe they were searching for a white man, and they had not followed up on leads that indicated Lee was the serial killer, because he was black. Police had paid for that mistake dearly and would not make the same mistake twice.

Todd Morris, who worked with the Louisiana State Attorney General's Office, along with Investigator Dannie Mixon, had swabbed Lee for DNA separate and apart from the Multi-Agency Homicide Task Force that had been formed to catch Lee in 2002. Morris and Mixon had been working on the cold cases of Randi Mebruer and Connie Warner in Zachary, and had accumulated enough information about Lee to suspect him of a string of killings in southern Louisiana. Following their hunch, they caught the killer and ended his reign of terror on the women in Baton Rouge and the surrounding areas. However, the two men had had to deal with hard feelings from members of that task force for years because they had taken it upon themselves to go after Lee. This time would be different. Everyone on the Unsolved Homicide Task Force realized what was at stake and had learned that the only way to catch a killer was through cooperation and old-fashioned detective work. Following every lead was crucial.

* * *

Todd Morris had been born to be a detective. His father had worked with the Louisiana State Police, and he had grown up listening to the stories about this bust or that. He had been fascinated. Like his father, Morris felt like he had a calling. Being a detective was his way of helping society in some small way. In March 1984, he went to work for the sheriff's office in East Baton Rouge Parish. Back then, there was no Homicide Division. Detectives investigated a variety of crimes—sex crimes, homicides, street crimes, etc. Morris enjoyed working homicides; however, some of his cases would weigh on his mind for years— especially the case of Susan Scott.

This young mother of two was reported as a missing person in 1988. Morris was assigned the case and spent many years looking for her. He knew she had been the victim of foul play, but there simply weren't enough clues in her case to solve it. Her body has never been found.

"Cases like Susan Scott's stay with you. It has always bothered me that we couldn't find out what happened to her. Occasionally we still go back and look at that case," he explained. "Some cases never go away."

By the time Morris was assigned to the Unsolved Homicide Task Force, he had worked in law enforcement for twenty years. Through the years, he had worked with the sheriff's office and the attorney general's office. He knew that the clue to finding Donna's killer was already in their hands. A minor detail in a picture or a crime scene report could be the clue that solved the case. Morris and the other members of the task force diligently went over and over the crime scene photographs and reports, hoping that detail would jump out at someone.

* * *

By March 12, a suspect had emerged. Investigators learned that a man named Roy Procell and his son, Richard, had been suspects in a 1994 murder that had been committed in West Baton Rouge Parish. They spoke with detectives in West Baton Rouge and discovered that the Procells were still suspects in that murder. They also learned from canvassing the streets of North Baton Rouge that Roy and Donna had been friends and that she had occasionally gone to visit him at his travel trailer on Hollywood Street. Investigators obtained a search warrant to compel Roy to provide DNA. They decided to bring him in for questioning.

Later that afternoon, they found Roy in a wooded area on northern Airline Highway negotiating with a prostitute behind a pawnshop. They brought him to the sheriff's office, and he agreed to speak with Bryan White and Todd Morris.

"How long have you known Donna?" White asked him.

"I've known her for several years," Roy said.

"When was the last time you saw her?"

"I ain't seen her in months."

"People that live by you say she's been there recently. They saw her," White said.

"That's not true," Roy said adamantly.

"Have you ever had sex with her?"

"Once," Roy admitted. "But that was years ago. I don't really know her that well."

The detectives continued questioning Roy, but he stuck to his story. He didn't know what had happened to her. When asked about his son, Roy got defensive and told them that Richard didn't know any prostitutes, and he did not know Donna. He agreed to take a polygraph test and agreed to let detectives search his trailer. Nicole Compton entered the room and took a DNA swab from Roy.

On March 17, Nicole Compton and Van Calhoun photographed and videotaped Roy's home. They used an alternate light source to locate any semen, blood, or other body fluids that might be in the home. They used luminol on the floors, but no blood was detected. They took various items from his home for testing, but no blood or fibers that could link Roy to Donna emerged. When Roy's DNA profile came back, investigators learned that it was not a match to the hairs found on Johnnie or Katherine. They realized they were looking at the wrong suspect and went back to the drawing board—the crime scene photographs.

Numbered pictures showed them the cuts to Donna's left shoulder, a wound on her torso, ligature marks on the back of her neck, bruising on her right elbow, the cut marks on her left arm above where it had been severed, a shoe print on her back, her open chest cavity. Photographs also revealed a tire track located near the point where her body had been dragged down to the ravine. They had checked weather reports and knew that it had rained in the days before Donna had been discovered. They knew the tire track had to be recent. They focused on that track.

"Van Calhoun went to Goodyear to find out the model of the tire that made that track," Todd Morris said. "He discovered it was an Aquatred 3. Captain Max Schiele and I contacted a Goodyear representative at his home and asked him to look at the photograph of the tire. He agreed that it was an Aquatred. We forwarded the photo to the engineers at Goodyear, hoping to ascertain the size. They said it looked like a thirteen-, fourteen-, or fifteen-inch tire. The task force subpoenaed Goodyear for a list of all Aquatred 3 tires sold in the Baton Rouge area. We got a list of more than a thousand tires sold. We took the cast to Jim Churchman, at the Louisiana State Police, and he narrowed the size down to a thirteen-inch tire."

Once Churchman confirmed the actual tire size, that list narrowed to about sixty names of people who had bought that particular tire. Task force members randomly split up the list. They went door-to-door throughout Baton Rouge asking anyone who had bought that tire to submit to DNA swabbing.

Number twenty-six on that list was Sean Vincent Gillis.

Sean Toys with Police

April 28, 2004, began like any other day for Sean Gillis and Terri Lemoine. They got up and began their normal routine—Sean playing on his computer and Terri working around the house. Terri had no idea that her world was about to be turned upside down when she heard a knock on the door.

"Is Sean Gillis home?" Agent Jeff Methvin said when Terri answered the door.

"Sean, the police are here," Terri called to Sean, who was on the back patio. "They want to talk to you."

When Sean came to the door, Methvin explained that there had been a murder on Ben Hur Road and that police were swabbing anyone in the Baton Rouge area who had bought Aquatred 3 tires. Sean asked the agent questions about the murder, then agreed to submit to the swabbing. Detective Jeremy Schiro unsealed a Q-tip and rubbed it along the inside of Sean's cheek.

Methvin asked Sean if he had been on Ben Hur Road recently.

"Yes," Sean said. "I grew up around that area. I'm often over there."

"Did you know Donna Bennett Johnston?"

"No." Sean shook his head, acting a little perplexed by the question.

"What about a woman named Katherine Hall? Did you know her?"

"No. Don't know her, either."

"Johnnie Mae Williams. Did you know her?"

"Yes. She was a friend of mine. She sometimes cleaned my house." Sean seemed very comfortable answering Methvin's questions.

Methvin thanked him for his cooperation and headed back to the sheriff's office. "We need to bring this guy in for an interview," he told task force members. "Something's not right here. This guy placed himself at the crime scene on Ben Hur, and he knew Johnnie Mae Williams."

They discussed Methvin's and Schiro's observations about Sean for a few minutes, then decided that Todd Morris and Jerry Mitchell should go back with Methvin and bring Sean in.

Sean Gillis was in the backyard listening to Rush Limbaugh on the radio when Todd Morris and Jerry Mitchell arrived. At first, Sean was almost jovial, seemingly enjoying learning about some of the circumstances of the murders as he spoke with the investigators.

But when Morris told him, "You need to come with us. We need to talk to you," Sean's demeanor changed. He became more reserved. Sean asked the investigators to go inside his house and explain to Terri why his assistance was needed and where he would be.

"Get a phone number," Sean called to Terri. "If it gets dark and I'm not home, you'll know where to find me."

While Jerry Mitchell gave Terri his business card, Sean stood with Todd Morris. Sean was acting a little agitated as he smoked a cigarette.

When Mitchell returned, Sean dropped the cigarette on the ground, put it out with the heel of his shoe, and then looked at the investigators.

"Let's go get this shit over with," he said.

Mitchell and Morris climbed into Morris's truck, while Jeff Methvin pulled off with Sean in his vehicle. Morris looked over at Mitchell and said, "Did you hear what he just said? You know we've got the right guy."

Mitchell nodded his agreement. It was something in the way Sean had said it, calmly and with resignation in his voice, like he knew he had been caught and there was nothing he could do about it.

At 2:18 P.M., Sean Gillis was placed in an interview room and Mirandized. Bryan White and Jerry Mitchell began to talk to him. Both men knew that it was important to establish a rapport with Sean in order to get him to talk to them. White was a sixteen-year veteran with the sheriff's office and had conducted many such interviews. He informed Sean that they were conducting a murder investigation.

Sean told the investigators that he had an associate degree in computers and that he understood his rights. He did not ask for an attorney.

Sean told them that he had been in that field on Ben Hur Road many times. "That field was a party place on weekends when I was young. I used to do mushrooms there."

He told White and Mitchell that he liked his neighborhood and wanted his house to be his retirement home. "Every now and then, there's a crime wave there, though, but nothing too bad. People will be missing a lawn mower or something like that."

Sean was very comfortable during the interview, laughing and joking now and then, drinking a Dr Pepper.

"When was the last time you were on Ben Hur?" White asked.

"Probably the weekend before the murder," Sean replied. "I had to pee, so I stopped in the field. McDonald's was full, that would put it on a Saturday. I think there was an LSU game, because there was a lot of traffic. My bladder was Cheeching and Chonging. I pulled into the gate and hung left, near some trees and bushes. The gate was busted open. I had to get behind bushes because I didn't want to expose myself. It was between midnight and one. I backed in, hopped out, did my business, shook, looked around to make sure no one saw."

"If I remember correctly, the canal comes across right here," Mitchell said, pointing to a map. "The gate is right here."

"Yes," Sean said. "I pulled in and then backed in. There was some furniture or debris in the way, so I backed just to where the nose of my car couldn't be seen from the road. Then I went to Circle K on Lee Drive to get more beer."

"I don't understand why you didn't just go to your house," White said. Sean lived only a few blocks away.

"Shoot, man. Just one of those things. I wasn't thinking clearly. There were red lights. I didn't want to wait for another light."

"Would it surprise you to know that Donna was found there?" White asked.

"I just know that it was in a ditch," Sean replied. "I'm familiar with the case. I read about it in the paper."

"Would it surprise you to know that she was nude?"

"No," Sean said.

"Do you know why we're talking?" Mitchell questioned.

"The tracks?"

"Yes. From the tracks, it looks like she was removed from that vehicle and thrown in the canal."

"When you contacted me yesterday, that's why I was like, 'Oh God, that's the area,'" Sean said.

"How is it that you know Johnnie Mae Williams?" White asked.

"I used to be a night clerk at the Circle K, near Highland and Lee. She worked at St. James Place. I hired her to clean my house four or five years ago. I'd give her money to buy drugs," Sean said. He told them he had given her a ride about thirty days before her body had been found on Pride–Port Hudson Road. "That time, I'd given her some money to get me some weed."

The detectives kept talking to Sean, asking him about his criminal record. "I got busted a few years ago for possession, but there is nothing in my car. Never, never, never," he told them. "Well, you might find some blood in my car, but that's from my wife, Terri." Sean often referred to Terri Lemoine as his wife. "She has epilepsy and bleeds sometimes when she's having a seizure."

Realizing how damning that statement was, but understanding they would get no pertinent information out of their suspect at this time, Bryan White and Jerry Mitchell decided to let him go and they'd wait for the results of the DNA test. They asked Sean if they could search his vehicle, and he agreed to sign a waiver. Jeff Methvin brought

Sean home. The rest of the task force set up surveillance around his house.

"What's going on? Why did they make you go down there?" Terri asked Sean worriedly when he returned.

"It's that lady that was killed on Ben Hur. I have the same kind of tires that they found there," Sean told her. "Nothing to worry about. I answered their questions, and they let me go."

That evening, Sean and Terri shared a romantic dinner together and went to bed. Terri was surprised when Sean climbed in bed with her. He never went to bed when she did.

"Wow. What's the occasion?" she said.

"I just wanted to spend some time with you," Sean responded.

"Oh, you finally like me?" Terri laughed.

Sean laughed with her. "I do like you," he said.

While they slept, wrapped in each other's arms, the DNA results came back. Sean Vincent Gillis's DNA was a match to the DNA found on Katherine Hall, Johnnie Mae Williams, and Donna Bennett Johnston.

"We were very excited," Todd Morris remembered. "We already knew he was the guy, but now we had scientific evidence. We formulated an operational plan with the sheriff's SWAT team. We had all seen in the photos how violent this guy could be, so we wanted to utilize their expertise."

At one-twenty, on the morning of April 29, police broke through the door of Sean's home on Burgin Avenue.

"All of a sudden, there was a big *bam*," Terri recalled. "I turned the lamp on. Sean looked at me and shrugged his shoulders. He smiled like he was sorry. Then he got out of bed and said he was sorry. I only had my underwear on. The police came in and handcuffed Sean and me. I was so humiliated. Another detective came in and said, 'Take those cuffs off of her and let her get dressed.' I asked why they were arresting Sean. The cop said, 'For murder.'

"I got real calm then, because I knew they had the wrong person. I remember laughing, thinking, 'Boy, do you have the wrong guy.' I always thought of Sean as a chicken, someone who would run away from trouble," Terri said.

"He didn't tell you we were coming?" Max Schiele asked her.

"Who?" Terri said.

"Sean," Schiele replied.

Terri suddenly flashed back to Sean's "I'm sorry" from a few minutes before.

"No, he didn't tell me," she said.

Terri and Sean were brought to the sheriff's office for questioning. Terri remained calm. She wasn't even worried. She knew her fun-loving Sean would never kill anyone. He didn't have it in him. This was all a big mistake.

An Inhuman Confession

"I think I really need a lawyer," Sean Gillis said the next morning, sitting again in the interview room at the East Baton Rouge Parish Sheriff's Office. He had just been Mirandized again and was asked to submit to more questioning.

"We have some outstanding evidence against you, evidence you cannot fight in court," said the detective.

"I really need legal counsel," Sean said again. He had spent the night thinking about it. He was intelligent enough to know that DNA evidence cannot be disputed. He knew he had lost the game he had played with police for so many years, but he wanted an attorney to advise him.

"We want to talk about your accomplishments. How long have you known this day was inevitable?" the detective asked, ignoring Sean's request for an attorney.

Sean's ego won over his common sense, and he began talking. Todd Morris walked into the room and sat down—he and Bryan White on one side of the table, Sean on the other. Morris and White could not believe what they were hearing as Sean began to tell the most gruesome tale they had ever heard in all their years of law enforcement.

Now in his element, with a captive audience, Sean gave up all thoughts of getting a lawyer. He had waited a long time to tell this story, and he was going to savor every detail that had been stored in his memory. He spoke like he was talking with a friend about the weather—no embarrassment, no remorse. He laughed; he joked; he talked as if the detectives would understand exactly why he had done the sick and horrible things he had done.

"You've been appointed an attorney from the public defender's office," the investigators interrupted. "Bert Garraway is your attorney. He called and advised that you make no statements."

"I don't care," Sean said, and continued talking.

"He had a wealth of information about the murders, but that's normal for a serial killer," Morris said. "They remember all the details. As he talked, we couldn't let him know we were shocked, but we were amazed at some of the things he had done to his victims. We had not ever experienced this magnitude of depravity. It was not your normal homicide interrogation. He laughed and joked. He was ready to tell his story."

And tell it, Sean did. He told White and Morris about Johnnie Mae Williams, how they had been friends, how he had picked her up and gotten mad at her because he didn't like that she smoked crack cocaine. He didn't mind if people smoked marijuana, that was okay—but crack was something different, and Sean didn't approve. He told them how he had beaten up the fragile woman and cut her up in the field behind Mason's Grill. Without any shame, he told them he had cut off her hands, had pleasured himself with them. He gave them every detail, relishing his memories, enjoying the telling of his story.

They asked him about Katherine Hall. Sean smiled. He had picked her up in North Baton Rouge. "That's where I found most of them, walking the streets," he said. "Some I let go. Others I didn't." He had stabbed her, he said, in a field near a gate, over and over. "I left her jacket hanging there on the fence," he told the investigators. "And I put her body by a dead-end sign." He laughed.

"I was the chess master then. I watched TV to predict my next move, to judge whether I was winning," he said. "I never had a plan about when I would kill my next victim. It was just whenever the opportunity arose."

Sean went on to tell them about Donna Bennett Johnston, how he had seen her walking on Geronimo. Morris did not let his face show any reaction as Sean described how easy it had been to kill her, to cut off her arm, her tattoo. He described how he had stomped her in the back, how he had raped her after she was dead. It was with Donna that he began to make references to eating human flesh. "I was curious." He shrugged as if that explained everything. "I was fascinated by it all. I cut off her nipples and put them in my mouth. They tasted nasty." He shrugged, feeling like the investigators would empathize with him.

But Donna wasn't the only victim with whom he had practiced cannibalism. There was more to come, and it would get much, much worse.

He told them about Marilyn Nevils. White and Morris had not seen her name in any of the cold case reports they had combed through. He told them he had picked up "Miss Nevils" in Lafayette. He always respectfully called them "Miss"—Miss Johnston, Miss Williams, Miss Hall—right before he described the most inhumane acts the detectives had ever heard.

The detectives got on the phone with the Lafayette

Police Department (LPD) to ask if they had a missing person case on a Marilyn Nevils in 2000. Police there had never heard of her. She had not been reported missing.

Sean went on to describe how he had taken Marilyn home and brought her into the shower in the master bathroom. She was already stiff and didn't cooperate, he said. He explained that he had caressed her for a while, played with her dead body in his shower, before dropping her off on River Road.

Detectives took another look at their cold case files of unsolved homicides and discovered that a Jane Doe had been found on the levee in 2000 who matched the details Sean gave them.

He told them about Ann Bryan's murder ten years before. He explained how he had walked into St. James Place and turned the knob of the first door he happened upon. It was unlocked. He described how he had tried to rape the little old lady.

"I tried to shut her up, but she wouldn't stop screaming. So I started stabbing. I tried to cut through her throat, but all that muscle is there. She was still alive, so that muscle was tensed up. My knife wouldn't go all the way through. It was a bloody mess. I just kept stabbing her," he said nonchalantly. "I cut open her bowels and dropped her from the bed."

Over the next few days, for forty hours, Todd Morris and Bryan White let Sean Gillis talk, prompting him only with a question now and then about what vehicle he had been driving, or where Terri Lemoine had been when he was cutting up a body in his kitchen, or asking for clarification on a small detail now and then. They nodded occasionally when he seemed to need reassurance or encouragement, but for the most part, they just listened as Sean weaved a tale of depravity so sickening that at times bile rose in their throats. They hid that well, knowing they could not let Sean see that he was getting to them. Sean wanted a reaction. He was proud of his deeds and wanted recognition of his cleverness. He got neither praise nor condemnation. They simply listened and quietly encouraged him to go on.

He told them about Hardee Schmidt, how he had seen her jogging and watched for her for weeks. He said he had run over her with his vehicle, then put the zip tie around her neck. "I drove with her to the BREC Park on Highland. I knew no one would be there that early in the morning. I played with her body. I raped her. Then I put her in the trunk and went to pick up Terri." He told Todd and Bryan about leaving Hardee in the trunk until Terri mentioned a horrible smell. "I figured it was time to get rid of her, so I dumped her body by a canal in St. James Parish."

"At one point, he wanted to talk to Mary Ellen O'Toole, the FBI profiler," Morris said. "She flew to Baton Rouge to talk with him, but he just wanted to play mind games with her, to find out what she thought of him. He likes to think he's smarter than everyone."

At the mention of Hardee and Ann, the detectives contacted the Baton Rouge Police Department and told them Sean Gillis had confessed to those murders. As Sean continued talking, more and more police agencies were getting interested in this confession and involved in trying to determine if he was telling the truth.

And then he got to Joyce Williams. The detectives thought they had heard the worst, but Sean was about to shock them. "Basically, with her, I started out looking for a new sexual experience," he said. Sean described driving her out to Rosedale Road and stopping to pee. "I decided right then that if this was going to get done, there was no better place on the face of the earth to do it. I put the zip tie around her neck, but it caught on her mouth. I was pulling, but she fought all the way around the car. She had a jack-o'-lantern grin, I was pulling so tight. Her face stretched. I kept telling her, 'Be still. Be still.'" Sean laughed at the recollection. "She stood up right into it. I said, 'Too bad,' and pulled tight."

Sean wiped his hands and mouth on a napkin. He told the detectives that he had taken her back to his house to spend some time with her. "I'm not sure if I bit into her legs or not," he said before describing her dismemberment in graphic detail. "About halfway through her leg, the blade snaps on me."

"Yeah?" White said.

"Yeah," Sean replied, rolling his eyes like *damn the luck.*

"There must have been a lot of blood," White said.

"There was. I sopped it up with paper towels and packing paper. I don't know how much blood y'all found, but I cleaned and cleaned that place."

Sean's stomach growled. "Excuse me," he said politely. "Must be that bologna sandwich I ate for lunch."

He told Todd and Bryan how he had used one of Terri's knives to try to cut off Joyce's arm. "I doubt she'd want it back if she knew what it was used for." He laughed. "I was twisting that arm. The elbow popped out of place and the wrist. I couldn't get it off, so I went for her head."

"So you totally decapitated her?" White queried.

"Oh yeah." Sean nodded. "I couldn't do it with Miss Bryan, the muscles were too tense because she was alive, but it went through Miss Williams's throat like that." He snapped his fingers. "It sliced like butter."

Then he described trying to masturbate himself with her

head. Not a flicker of an eyelash revealed the disgust Todd
Morris and Bryan White were feeling, not even an invol-
untary flinch of a face muscle. They simply looked interested as Sean Gillis proudly described for them how sick
he was.

"It was a painful experience for me," he said, not even
considering the pain he had inflicted on any of his victims.
"I put my penis up her throat, but I didn't get off. There
was a little piece of spinal cord or something sticking up.
It pricked my scrotum. You can imagine that wasn't pleasant," he said to the detectives, expecting them to laugh
with him. When they didn't, he continued. "I put my penis
in her mouth, then picked up her leg. She had lovely legs,
like Terri. Terri was a dancer, you know. I rubbed my face
and lips on her leg. I put her heel on my chest, right here,
with her toes pointing toward my chin, my right hand
under her calf, my left under her thigh. I held it straight
out, admiring it. It was beautiful"—he chuckled—"not
withstanding the fact that it just came off a dead person.

"Then I did a nipplectomy on her. I put them in my
mouth." He grinned, shrugging. It was the second time
Sean had told them that he had eaten the nipples of his
victims. He acted like his behavior was normal, amusing.
He didn't think of himself as a cannibal and did not expect
others to think of him like that, either. He was simply a
surgeon sampling his work.

"How much time did you spend with her?" White com-
mented, not missing a beat. He knew Sean was trying to
get a reaction, but he wasn't going to let that happen. He
was much too professional for that, but he was also positive that this depraved man was telling the truth. No one
could make this up and tell it with such nonchalance.

"Three or four hours," Sean replied. He described how

he had gotten rid of her. "I put her in a much smaller box than I did Miss Nevils. All these parts were sticking out, but I camouflaged them in the car with other boxes, then went to get Terri from work. It was one of the few times she got to ride in the car with a body."

Sean told them how he had driven around until he found the perfect spot on River Road. "I took her leg and slung it," he said. "I took her head, slung it. The torso was a little harder. Then I went to work. I worked my booty off that day."

"Someone from West Baton Rouge might want to ask you some questions about this case," White told Sean.

"They're probably just glad they didn't find a body in their parish." Sean laughed.

Morris and White then showed Sean a picture of Lillian Robinson, a cold case from 2000 that had never been solved.

"Do you recognize her?"

Sean looked at the picture intently before nodding.

"Oh yes. It was the usual sick playing with her, too," he said. "I found her walking down the street, killed her with a zip tie, and brought her home. I propped her body up against the cabinets in the kitchen and played with her nipples and vagina. I didn't have as much time with her as I wanted because Terri was coming home. I dumped her in the Atchafalaya Basin."

After a few more questions about Lillian, the interview was finally over. After days and days spent listening to the most horrific crimes imaginable, Bryan White and Todd Morris were more than ready to go home to their families and try to forget that such evil existed in the world.

"It made me scared for my children," Morris said. "I thought, 'How can this be occurring in Baton Rouge, in my home, in the place I live and raise my family?' People live in a bubble, for the most part. They don't realize what's out there. They need to be more aware and never place themselves in a place where they could be a potential victim. People can be victims in their own neighborhoods. They need to be aware of their surroundings, wary of strangers, and do everything they can to minimize the danger from people like Sean Gillis. I find I'm harder on my own children now—for their own safety. I worry about them more because of the things I've seen in my years in law enforcement."

Todd Morris was proud of the work that had been done by the Unsolved Homicide Task Force to catch this killer and to make Baton Rouge a safer place to live. "This was a group effort, and everybody on this task force contributed to catch this killer. We all followed the leads and produced positive results for this investigation," he said.

Cannibalistic Serial Killers

While the practice of cannibalism has sporadically been commonplace among many cultures of the world throughout history, cannibalism in America is practiced most often by serial killers who eat human flesh for a variety of reasons. Some killers are aroused by the thought of eating the meat of humans and experience a euphoric state while consuming flesh. Some receive sexual pleasure from this forbidden act, while it makes others feel powerful. And then there are those who want to possess their victims, to keep them with them forever, and eating them is a way to accomplish this. Other cannibals are simply curious.

For serial killer Albert Fish, who was put to death in the electric chair by the state of New York in 1936—his penalty for the murder of twelve-year-old Grace Budd—cannibalism was about the pleasure he gained from the experience. In a letter to the little girl's parents, Fish wrote, *I choked her to death, then cut her in small pieces so I could take my meat to my rooms. Cook and eat it. How sweet and tender her little ass was roasted in the oven. It took me nine days to eat her entire body.*

Edmund Kemper III, who is serving a life sentence in California after being convicted of eight counts of murder, explained in his confession that he had wanted to "possess" at least two of his victims. To that end, he cooked flesh from their legs in a macaroni casserole.

Perhaps the most infamous of all cannibalistic serial killers was Jeffrey Dahmer, whose name still inspires a morbid fascination in most who hear it. Dahmer confessed to killing seventeen young men, between 1978 and 1991. When police entered his apartment, they found a head in the refrigerator, skulls in a closet, and various body parts of victims stored throughout Dahmer's home.

Like Sean, Dahmer particularly enjoyed dismembering his victims, although he cut them into little pieces and boiled their heads. He had practiced dismemberment since he was a young boy by bringing home animals he'd found and cutting them up to see what their insides looked like. While there is no evidence that Sean cut up animals when he was younger, he did have a curiosity to see the insides of the women he dismembered, to feel them, and to have sex with their parts.

Dahmer, too, liked having sex with his victims after they were dead; but for him, it involved only oral and anal sex. He is not known to have actually had intercourse with body parts he cut off, although he often masturbated over them. For Dahmer, though, it was about something more than fascination with the process. He wanted to keep his victims, remember them, love them. In his confession, he told Detective Dennis Murphy that he didn't consider the skulls he kept to be trophies. He wanted to keep them because he felt the skulls represented the true essence of his victims. By keeping them, Dahmer stated, he felt like their lives weren't a total loss.

The first incident of cannibalism occurred with Dahmer's

sixth victim, Raymond Smith, also known as "Cash D."
He picked up this twenty-two-year-old black male by offering him money for sex. They took a cab to his apartment,
where Dahmer drugged, photographed, and killed Smith.
He had oral sex with this victim before dismembering
him. Dahmer ate his heart, later saying, "It tasted kind of
spongy."

Initially Dahmer only admitted to eating the flesh of
one of his victims—victim number eight, Ernest Miller,
whom he had met on the corner of Twenty-seventh Street
and Wisconsin in Milwaukee. After picking him up with
the promise of money, Dahmer took Miller back to his
apartment and gave him a drink laced with sleeping pills.
The two men had sex, and then Miller fell asleep. Dahmer
cut his throat. He photographed his victim's body before
cutting it up, keeping his skull, biceps, and heart. He fil-
leted Miller's heart and put it in the freezer before strip-
ping the flesh from his thigh. "His thigh muscle was so
tough, I could hardly chew it," he related to police.
Dahmer went to the store and purchased meat tenderizer
to use on Miller's bicep. He told police that he fried it up
in Crisco oil and consumed the bicep because "it was big
and I wanted to try it. It tasted like beef or filet mignon."
He said he ate this victim because he really liked him.

He would later admit to eating parts of another man he
met on Twenty-seventh Street, Oliver Lacy, his sixteenth
victim. A model and bodybuilder, the twenty-four-year-
old Lacy agreed to go with Dahmer to be photographed
when Dahmer approached him on the street. After drugging, strangling, and raping this victim anally, Dahmer
dismembered Lacy, putting his head in a box in the refrigerator and his heart in the freezer to be eaten later. He also
kept Lacy's right bicep, which he later cooked. "It tasted

like filet mignon," he told police, adding that he "used salt, pepper, and A.1. sauce on it."

Dahmer explained that he had not wanted to talk about his cannibalistic acts in initial interviews because he did not feel that they were "appealing," and he did not want the police to think less of him.

Unlike Sean, Dahmer was remorseful. He said that he preferred to have sex with his victims while they were alive, but if they wanted to leave and he couldn't have them alive, he would have them dead. In his confession, he said, "It's hard for me to believe that a human being could of done what I've done, but I know that I did it. I want you to understand," he told the detectives, "that my questions regarding Satan and the Devil were not to diffuse guilt from me and blame the Devil for what I've done, because I realize what I've done is my guilt, but I have to question whether or not there is an evil force in the world and whether or not I have been influenced by it."

When Sean Gillis told his story to police, he grinned, laughed, and joked as he relived the details of his murders and what had happened afterward. He seemed almost sheepish as he explained that he ate the nipples of some of his victims, shrugging his shoulders and grinning like he was a little boy who had been caught doing something naughty. Much of the time, his demeanor seemed rather boastful—that of a man proud of his accomplishments. He saw nothing wrong with having sex with women after they were dead, although he knew what he was doing was sick. He described to police several times, "the usual sick playing with her body," but he said it as though it was nothing that would shock anyone. Not once did he say he was remorseful or sorry for his actions. He did not question outside evil forces. He relished the evil that lived inside him, was proud of it, and wanted to relive each moment through the telling of his macabre tale.

In letters written to another inmate, Tammie Purpera, who was a friend of his last victim, Donna Bennett Johnston, Sean wrote, *I don't know what my damage is. I don't even know if there's a name for it. Dr. Blanche, the prison shrink thinks I'm bi-polar. I've never heard of bi-polar people going this far into "never never land," but he's the doctor, not me. I really hated God for a long time. I think that's what did it. But doctors cann't [sic] even conceive such a spritule [sic] reason or cause. I think that is the real cause.*

In another letter to Tammie, Sean wrote, *I have broken all ten commandments [sic] at one time or another. Have been consumed by all seven deadly sins. I turned my back on the Father twenty-six years ago. I do not know why he took from me the person whom I needed most at the time.*

Sean went on to say: *Together with your friend, seven other sweet, innocent sisters-in-Christ have died at my hands. Their names and faces will haunt me the rest of the days and nights of my life.*

In yet another letter, he told Tammie: *My sincerest condolences on the loss of your friend. I cannot express how beyond sorry I am for murdering Donna, Johnnie Mae, Lillian, Marilyn, Joyce, Hardee, Katherine and Ann. I will pay for your friend's life and the others however the Most High and my peers see fit. I hate no one. I really don't know what the hell is wrong with me.* Sean ended this letter with: *Please tell me more about Donna. I think I would have liked her.*

While Sean did express some remorse to Tammie, it was obvious from his last statement that he simply wished to learn more about his victim, to have a way to relive his deeds while he was in prison. Tammie Purpera passed away soon after these letters were written, but not before turning them over to prison officials.

While Jeffrey Dahmer told police he felt evil and "thoroughly corrupted, body and soul, because of the horrible crimes I had committed against people," Sean Gillis bragged about outwitting police and watching the news to plot his next move. Dahmer said that he tried to overcome his feelings of wanting to kill and dismember people, but that they would haunt him and overcome him. Sean never mentioned trying to overcome any of his feelings. Instead, he browsed the Internet looking for photographs of dead women he could use to gratify himself sexually. Eventually the hunger to have one of his own would become too strong, and he would roam the streets at night, always searching for the right one.

Dahmer was attracted to most of his victims, which is why he chose the seventeen men he killed. Sean, on the other hand, was not looking for someone to whom he was attracted. He always looked for women who were small, whom he could overpower easily. One major difference between the two killers was that Dahmer preferred men for his sexual pleasure, and Sean was homophobic due to the discovery of his father's homosexuality when he was a teenager. Terri Lemoine had asked him on more than one occasion if he liked women, and he always emphatically insisted that he did. He didn't explain that he only liked *dead* women, though.

These two serial killers did have similar backgrounds. Both were from families that were not necessarily poor, who lived in decent neighborhoods. Neither was physically, sexually, or emotionally abused. Dahmer's mother once suffered a nervous breakdown and, according to Dahmer, had some psychiatric problems as well as postpartum depression after he was born. Sean's father had a series of breakdowns and spent years in mental hospitals. Dahmer was eighteen when his parents divorced; Sean was a baby when his divorced. However, Sean was eighteen when he discovered his father had homosexual tendencies. Both men came to feel they had been abandoned by their mothers—Dahmer when his mother moved to Chippewa Falls and Sean when his mother moved to Atlanta. They both expressed feelings of being left alone.

Both men drank heavily, although Sean tried to hide his drinking from Terri. Dahmer said he drank to be able to live with all the horrible things he had done. Sean drank because he enjoyed it while smoking weed and partying with his friends. Sometimes, though, when he got the urge to kill, he would drink or smoke weed. That would cause him to go to sleep, and he would lose the urge for the time.

Dahmer kept skulls and body parts from his victims, while Sean did not. There is a simple explanation for this. Dahmer lived with his grandmother for part of the time he was killing and utilized her basement to hide bodies until he disposed of them. Then he moved into his own apartment, which gave him free reign to leave body parts lying around. Sean did not have that luxury. When he killed, he was always in a hurry and had to make the best of the time he had before Terri returned home. Although he did sometimes leave bodies in his trunk for a day or two, he could not risk Terri finding them. He had to dispose of the bodies before they decomposed. It's not difficult to imagine what police would have discovered in his house, had he lived there by himself. Like Dahmer, Sean loved playing with his victims. Had he lived alone, there's no doubt he would have devolved to the same levels of depravity that Dahmer had.

Dahmer stated that he tasted his first victim because he was curious, because his bicep was so big, and he wanted to try it. He also said that he wanted to keep his victims with him. Sean had no such feelings about his victims. He ate their nipples because he was curious, obsessed with dead bodies, and he wanted to feel the sexual arousal that came with the experience. Dahmer stated over and over that he liked his victims and only ate the ones he liked the most. Sean had no such motivation. As he told police and a reporter for *The Advocate,* "They were already dead to me." Sean was simply cold and sick.

As he stated in one of his letters to Tammie, *I was pure evil.*

No One Even Noticed She Was Gone

The case of the Marilyn Nevils murder would become the strangest and saddest case Detective David LeBlanc, with the Lafayette Police Department, had ever worked. Slender, with salt-and-pepper hair and a dark tan, the Cajun detective had been a Crimes Against Persons Division investigator for about eleven years. Since 2001, he had taken the lead role on fifteen homicides, but he had never worked a case like this one.

LeBlanc had moved to Lafayette in 1991 and had gotten involved with police work because he wanted to help people. He had started in street patrol, where he worked for about two years before getting into a serious wreck while chasing a felon. He lost the sight in his right eye as a result and required a cornea transplant. In 1998, he applied to work in investigations, where he hoped to be able to follow up on crimes. He started as a property detective, working burglaries and thefts, but soon worked his way up to homicides. In 2001, he was asked to join a five-member

squad in the Crimes Against Persons Division. It was there
that LeBlanc found his niche.

"That includes anything that affects a person—armed
robbery, rape, stalking, home invasions, and homicides,"
he explained. "The average amount of homicides in
Lafayette is ten per year, although sometimes it's more and
sometimes it's less. There is a system to investigating
homicides. First there is a crime scene and the preserva-
tion of evidence there. The scene is videotaped and photographed, and the victim is identified, if possible. A
supervisor notifies the family. A timeline is established, a
team of detectives is assembled, and assignments are
issued. With Marilyn Nevils, everything was backward.
We had a killer, but we didn't even know we had a
murder."

LeBlanc was very familiar with the areas of Lafayette
that were most ridden with crime—the Four Corners area
between Cameron Street and North University Avenue.
Like in North Baton Rouge, prostitutes and drug dealers
roam these streets, selling their wares, hoping no one will
try to steal the money they earn. Here, cheap motels provide privacy as man after man pay for the bodies of the
women who sell their very souls for crack cocaine.

"They will sell their mama for it, sell the pots and
pans for it," LeBlanc said. "Dealers are very bold and will
conduct open-air drug sales—they will run up to your
car and sell it in broad daylight."

As in North Baton Rouge, police in Lafayette try to get
a handle on the problem, but it's simply too pervasive. The
crack seems to be stronger than everyone, the men and
women who become immediately addicted to it and the
police who try desperately to rid their communities of it.
The fight against crack cocaine is once again lost with
every first hit of a crack pipe, as another person falls in

love with the drug that will eventually tear his or her life apart. While LeBlanc was very familiar with the Four Corners section of Lafayette, he would soon learn that Marilyn Nevils had been picked up miles away from the area where prostitutes usually operate.

"On May 4, 2004, the East Baton Rouge Sheriff's Office called to tell us she was missing, that Sean Gillis had confessed to her murder," LeBlanc said. "Marilyn had a long criminal history of drug and alcohol-related offenses since 1994. That's all we knew about her. And then we have a suspect confessing to a crime we didn't even know had occurred. No one had ever reported her missing. She had been dead almost four years."

LeBlanc knew that he needed to interview Sean to have a starting point for his investigation. He headed for Baton Rouge that afternoon, unaware that he was about to hear a confession that he would never forget.

Sean Gillis, as comfortable as ever, greeted Detective LeBlanc when LeBlanc walked into the room. Sean told him about how he had been on his way to visit his goddaughter and had observed Marilyn on Evangeline Thruway. He told the detective he had brought her to the field on Sixth and Chestnut and paid her ten dollars for oral sex. He described how she had fought him when he tried to put the zip tie around her neck and how he had chased her and beaten her with the piece of rebar. "I got my money back for the blow job." Sean laughed.

LeBlanc could not believe what he was hearing. This was a different kind of killer than he had ever seen before. This killer had ice flowing through his veins.

Sean told LeBlanc that he had brought Marilyn back to his home in Baton Rouge and taken a shower with her.

"She kept falling," Sean said. "Rigor had set in. I tried to place my penis in her mouth, but she had lockjaw. I had to hurry with her because Terri was coming home. I didn't get a chance to cut her up."

"An intelligent person wouldn't have talked to police," LeBlanc would later say of Sean. "He was reliving it all in a psychopathic way through his confession. There was no remorse, no empathy for his victims. He was the classic psychopath, bragging about his crimes. The police in Baton Rouge had already told me about his fascination with zip ties, so when he tried to talk about that, I shut him down. I told him, 'Let's move on, son,' because I didn't want to give him the satisfaction."

LeBlanc had asked Sean in his interview, "At what point, did you make the decision that she was going to die?"

"I just knew she was going to die," Sean responded.

"When he said, 'It wasn't a particularly bad blow job,' that threw me for a loop," LeBlanc said. "I've interviewed all kinds of people, but I've never interviewed anyone like Sean Gillis."

When David LeBlanc got back to Lafayette, he immediately began to try to find Marilyn Nevil's family. He wondered why no one had reported her missing. That was very unusual. He would eventually find and talk to some distant members of her family in Michigan, but no one seemed to care that Marilyn had been murdered. He did learn from them that Marilyn had a daughter named Danielle, who ran with the Goth crowds that hung out on the banks of the Mississippi River in Baton Rouge. LeBlanc searched, but he never found her.

"This was the only case I've ever investigated where

I've had no real contact with the victim's family," LeBlanc said. "To me, that was sad. It was like nobody really cared if this woman was alive or dead. I was frustrated because I never got the satisfaction of talking to her family, of giving them closure."

LeBlanc's investigation did seem to verify Sean Gillis's story. He discovered that Marilyn had been staying at the home of a black man who was in a wheelchair, but that the man had moved to Shreveport prior to her murder. He also learned that on October 20, 2000, Marilyn had caused a disturbance at the home of a man named Alex Perry Jr. Alex had called 911. Marilyn, who, Alex said, was extremely drunk, had left his home around 4:00 A.M.

"In my opinion, I think Marilyn was probably just drunk. I don't think she was really there that night to flag anyone down," Detective LeBlanc said. "Sean Gillis just happened to be there on a night when she was intoxicated."

And sadly, no one ever missed her enough to report her disappearance to the police.

Reunited

June 13, 2004

My Dearest Terri,

Thank you so much for the last eight years. I wish we had eight more +++. I have never loved a woman so much that each day away from you seems like a year. The closer my time draws near the less courage I have. I do not want to die this way. I know there is something wrong with my brain, but no one gives a damn to check it out. Well, it's not over till it's over. I will fight the good fight.

Love U So Much Honey Bunny,
Sean

Terri Lemoine didn't know what to do, where to turn. She had called her daughter Christine before dawn after she got home from the police station. Christine had answered the phone, her voice laced with sleep.

"I don't know how to tell you this," Terri cried.

Christine sat up quickly, realizing that her mother was hysterical and something must be terribly wrong.

"What is it? Are you okay?" Christine asked.

Terri could barely say the words. "Sean's been arrested."

"For what?"

"Murder. They are saying he—he killed some women," Terri stuttered.

"Are you sure?" Christine said, not quite comprehending what she was hearing.

"Yes. They have DNA and tire tracks and everything."

Christine did not understand. Sean wouldn't kill anyone. He was funny and loving. Sean had never even raised his voice to her. He was goofy. He was a computer nerd. He wasn't a killer.

"I was shocked. Everything went blank. I didn't know what to think. I couldn't process it," Christine recalled. "How could anyone understand something so big? When I finally realized it was true, I felt betrayed. It was so weird. You have Christmases and Thanksgivings with this person. You eat with him and laugh with him and hug him. How could the person I knew do this?"

Over the next weeks, bits and pieces of memories came sneaking into her mind—the time Sean had shown her the Web site of the dead women. She had thought that was disgusting but dismissed it as Sean just browsing the Web. And the time he had asked her to go for a ride, driving all around the back roads of the area, but never going anywhere in particular. He had seemed to be looking for something, but Christine didn't know what.

And then there was the last time Christine had visited. She had not wanted to go home, but she didn't know why. It was just a nagging bad feeling. Not long after she had arrived, Sean had informed her that a woman had been killed just up the road. "Did you hear about that?" he had asked. She hadn't, but she remembered wondering why he had been snickering when he asked.

All those thoughts kept coming to her mind, but she still didn't get it. Sean had driven to Alabama where Christine lived with her adoptive parents—a pastor and his wife who had adopted her as a child—to attend her graduation. Sean had hugged her and told her he was proud of her. Sean was full of love. It didn't make sense.

Terri didn't understand it, either. Suddenly, her quiet life had been turned upside down by the man she loved, the man she trusted. Her Sean couldn't do something like this. And things were getting worse. Sean had confessed to her that he had killed eight women. The police had let her talk to him on the phone at the prison.

"Did you do what they are saying, Sean?"

"Everything you've heard is true," he said bluntly.

"How many?"

"Eight."

"Who? What? When? Where? How? How could you? How could you do this?"

"I don't know. I'm sorry. I'm sorry for what this will cost you," Sean said, his voice quavering.

There could be no doubt for Terri now. The man she had loved for almost ten years had betrayed her in a most complete and horrifying way. All she wanted to do was go home and hide. But that wasn't possible.

As the days went by and details about the women Sean had murdered and mutilated came out, the media focused more and more attention on Terri Lemoine. She had made the mistake of telling a reporter that she didn't know what she was going to do now.

"This isn't about you," the reporter said. "It's about the victims."

Terri began to receive unfavorable press. Everyone stared at her when she went anywhere, whispering that she was the woman who lived with the serial killer. They wondered if she had known, if she had participated. A neighbor would routinely stop in front of her house and sprinkle holy water on the lawn. The police were tearing up the floors in her kitchen, digging up her backyard looking for bodies, questioning her constantly. She couldn't take it. She dug up an old address book and picked up the phone.

"Have you seen Louis?" she said to the woman on the other end. "Is he out of prison?"

Terri Lemoine had met Louis Michael Gaar when she worked at the Key Club in the mid-1980s. He had been watching her, learning everything he could about her.

"He just showed up one night and told me he had been watching me for about a week," Terri said. "He knew my name and everything about me, even where I lived. Each time he came back, he knew something else. He was adorable, so cute, and felt like somebody who would take care of me. You don't meet people like that there, you know, responsible people."

Louis began to go to the club every night to see Terri. He was a handsome young man, almost waifish, with big blue eyes, shaggy blond hair, and a slender body. Terri was very attracted to him and couldn't wait for him to ask her out. Finally he did, but he didn't take her on the usual dates of dinner and a movie. Louis showed Terri the Baton Rouge he knew. He took her downtown to places she had never been—the *USS KIDD,* the courthouse, the Old State Capitol.

"The capitol was so pretty. It looked like a castle," Terri said. "I had never been downtown before."

While Louis seemed to know everything about Terri, she knew nothing about him, not even where he lived. She didn't know that Louis had a past, one that he kept carefully hidden.

Louis Gaar had grown up on the streets of Baton Rouge, lured into a life of crime at an early age. When he was just fifteen, the owner of a record store had introduced him to one of the Marcello family members. Carlos Marcello, the head of the New Orleans Mafia, was feared and respected throughout the state and country, and his crime organization ruled the area with an iron fist. He had been deported to Guatemala in the early 1960s, due to the efforts of the United States attorney general Robert Kennedy, but he soon returned to the United States. When President John F. Kennedy was assassinated, Carlos was a prime target of the FBI's investigation. No charges were ever brought against him, but many believe to this day that Carlos was involved in the plot to kill this president who had been determined to stop organized crime.

Louis was hired as a "negotiator" for the family in the late 1970s, mostly because he looked like the boy next door. When he showed up at someone's home or business to collect money that was owed to Carlos or had been stolen from him, people weren't afraid. They trusted him. They opened their doors to him.

But they soon understood that he meant business. It was Louis's job to tell these people what was going to happen if they didn't pay up. "I told them that I was on their side, that they needed to pay the money back now, or the guy who would come behind me wouldn't be so nice," Louis explained. Everyone knew what that meant—a broken arm, busted kneecaps, or worse. Louis collected most of the debts.

But sometimes the criminal element with whom he dealt could be dangerous. Louis had been shot at more than once (and today his neck still bears the scar from one of the bullets that came just a little too close).

But in 1980, just after he turned eighteen, Louis encountered a man who would change his life.

He had been assigned to collect some money from the son of former state representative Risley "Pappy" Triche. The popular politician had begun his political career as the mayor of Napoleonville, Louisiana, and had then served in the Louisiana House of Representatives from 1955 to 1968. He had bitterly opposed desegregation in the state, and was considered a racist. Pappy was elected to serve again, from 1972 to 1976, but by this time, he realized his earlier views were wrong. He set about rectifying many of the mistakes he had made in the 1960s. He also served as the legislative floor leader for Governor Jimmie Davis and Governor Edwin Edwards.

According to Louis, Pappy's son, Risley Jr., owed Carlos Marcello money, and Louis was sent to Risley Jr.'s house near the old Bon Marche Mall on Florida Boulevard to collect. Louis did not expect that there would be any problems with this visit. He had heard that Risley Jr. was studying to be a priest. He knew this would be an easy job and would put a few more bucks in his pocket.

Louis knocked on the door and waited for Risley Jr. to answer. He was unprepared for the quick temper of the man he faced when he explained why he was there. To Louis's surprise, Risley Jr. attacked him right there in the front of the house.

"He jumped on me and began hitting me," Louis

recalled. "I looked around for a weapon, something I could use to defend myself."

Louis spotted a bumper jack lying on the ground and reached for it. As soon as he felt his fingers close around the metal, he swung, hitting Risley Jr. hard in the head.

Risley Jr. fell to the ground, unconscious. Louis ran to his car and drove away.

It was later that Louis learned that Risley Jr. had died. He wondered if anyone had seen him there, if anyone had witnessed the fight. He waited for the police to come knocking on his door.

They never did.

He had gotten away with murder, although he had not really intended to kill anyone.

"I thought he was knocked out, but he was dead," Louis said. "As the years went by, I would think about it from time to time, and it bugged me."

Louis wasn't about to tell Terri this sordid tale. He didn't want to jeopardize his budding relationship with her. Instead, he showed her the sweet side of his personality. He never called her, just showed up unexpectedly, hoping that she would go out with him. She always did.

"The time we spent together was so precious that I didn't mind that he didn't call first," Terri said. She was in love for the first time in her life. She felt that Louis was her soul mate. He was kind, intelligent, and good-looking, just the kind of man she had always wanted.

The couple had been dating for two years and living together for part of that time when Terri discovered she was pregnant. Christine was born June 9, 1984, and Terri couldn't have been happier. She had a beautiful baby girl and a wonderful man in her life.

Her happiness wouldn't last long.

The responsibility of having a family scared the hell out

of Louis. Not long after Christine was born, the couple broke up, and Louis disappeared. He moved to Massachusetts and began a new life. It would be years before Terri talked with him again. Realizing she could not care for her baby by herself, Terri allowed a preacher and his wife, who sometimes babysat Christine, to adopt her when she was two.

Eight years later, Louis returned to Baton Rouge. He had not forgotten about Terri. He still loved her and wanted to see his child. But by this time, Terri had married her second husband, Mazen, and was unavailable.

Soon after, Louis was pulled over by a police officer and cited for a broken tailpipe. Something came over him as he waited for his ticket.

"Y'all are looking for me. I'm the one who killed that guy eight years ago," he told the officer.

The officer had no idea what Louis was talking about, but he figured he'd better arrest him and bring him to the station to get to the bottom of this. When they got there, Louis confessed to the murder of Risley Triche, giving police enough detail to convince them that he was indeed the killer.

Well-known Baton Rouge attorneys Ossie Brown and Bonnie Jackson defended Louis at his trial. He was found guilty of first-degree murder and sentenced to life in prison, plus a day. While serving his time at Washington Correctional Institute in the small town of Angie, Louisiana, Louis went to work in the law library.

One day, Secretary of State Fox McKeithen hosted a seminar for prisoners. The Louisian official told them that all of the books in the law library contained the errors of the law. Louis listened carefully, hanging on every word. He began to study those books every chance he could. He learned that the first-degree murder statute in Louisiana required premeditation and an underlying felony, such as theft or kidnapping. He realized that neither of those requirements was present in his case. He appealed.

This time, the charges were reduced to manslaughter and armed robbery. He received a sentence of thirty years. Louis still wasn't satisfied. He appealed again, and pled guilty to manslaughter in return for a fifteen-year sentence. He would make the most of those years.

"Prison wasn't so bad," he said. "Just about everyone there used their time wisely. We got up at four-thirty A.M., made our beds tight, got in line for breakfast, then went to work in the fields."

Louis spent much of his free time studying law and eventually earned his paralegal certification. He helped other prisoners appeal their sentences and was sometimes successful. He also became the editor of the prison's newspaper, *Chainlink Chronicle*. He covered everything from prison sports to the band he had created—Louisiana Shakedown Band, which was a Stevie Ray Vaughan cover band. He typed his stories on an old Royal typewriter and cut and pasted the text onto large sheets of news roll. *The Daily News* in nearby Bogalusa printed the twenty-four pages he put together each month. Louis created cartoons, designed the graphics, and traveled to the state capital to cover the legislature. He also submitted stories that were published occasionally by *Writer's Digest*.

For fifteen years, he devoted himself to learning as much as he could. Louis would turn forty years old before he was released.

"Two sheriff's officers brought me to a bus station and sent me to Jackson, Mississippi," he remembered. "I got off the bus with ten dollars and two condoms in my pocket. I visited my parents, got a job at a donut shop, and slept outside for a week, until I earned enough money to get a room. I felt lost. I had become institutionalized, and everything had changed. I didn't know how to operate a gas pump. The first time I walked in Walmart, I thought it was ridiculously big. And in prison there were high levels of respect. I came out and discovered that kids no longer have any respect. Society had changed so much."

Disoriented in this new world, Louis was more than ready for a phone call from his long-lost love.

"Hi, Gaar," Terri said. "I bet you never thought you'd hear from me."

"Terri?" Louis responded. "Is it really you?"

"Yes. Don't worry, Christine's fine. Nobody's dead. Well, somebody is, but nobody you know."

"What are you talking about?"

"I guess I should start from the beginning," Terri quietly said.

She told him that she had worked at Circle K for many years and had met Sean Gillis there. She gave him a basic description of their relationship, how they had so much in common, how he had been so funny. And then she told him what had happened, that Sean had been arrested for killing eight women. Louis listened intently, only interrupting to ask a question now and then.

"I need you, Gaar. I love you. I've never stopped loving you."

"I love you, too, Terri. Always have."

"I'm different now. You should know that," Terri said.

"How so?"

"I'm more high maintenance, like a child. I want what I want when I want it. Right now, I want you to come to Baton Rouge and help me deal with this, but you need to know that I've changed."

"So have I," Louis said.

"That's okay."

"I'm on my way."

With tears in her eyes, Terri hung up the phone. Louis was coming. He would take care of everything.

The police were still digging up the yard, looking for bodies, when Louis arrived at Terri and Sean's Burgin Avenue home. "It freaked me out," he said. "They were asking all kinds of questions, and I had just gotten out of prison, for murder of all things. I tried to stay out of their way."

During the most horrific moments of her life, Terri suddenly felt better. She knew that she would be okay with Louis's strong arms wrapped around her. Two weeks after Sean was arrested, Louis moved in.

June 15, 2004

My dearest Terri,

I tried and tried to reach you today but all I got was a busy signal. You know all I live for these days is to talk to you at least once in a while. Saturday I could not call because I got screwed out of my hall time. I hope you can come see me Wednesday, I will put your name down as always. This letter will arrive late in the week due to the fact that mail call is past and does not run on Wed. I miss you sorely. I love you so much my honey bunny.

Sean

A Scattering of Bones

On April 29, 2004, the task force announced that it had a serial killer in custody:

> *A joint investigation by the Homicide Task Force, which consists of members of the East Baton Rouge Sheriff's Office, Louisiana State Police, Baton Rouge Police Department, Attorney General's Office and the FBI, has resulted in the arrest of Sean Vincent Gillis, WM, age 42 of Burgin Street, BR, La., for the murders of Katherine Hall, Johnnie Mae Williams and Donna Bennett Johnston.*
>
> *Gillis was arrested at his home on April 29, 2004 at about 1:20 a.m., with the authority of an arrest warrant prepared by the Homicide Task Force. Members of the East Baton Rouge Sheriff's Office CRT (Critical Response Team) entered the home of Gillis and placed him under arrest. He gave no resistance.*
>
> *Gillis was developed as a suspect based on evidence of tire tracks taken from the scene on Ben Hur*

Road where the body of Donna Bennett Johnston was discovered.

Further investigation by members of the Homicide Task Force led investigators to obtain a voluntary DNA swab from Gillis. LSP Crime Lab in conjunction with the FBI Crime Lab were able to process the DNA evidence from the Hall, Johnston and Williams homicides which matched to the DNA sample taken from Gillis.

Gillis was turned over to the Homicide Task Force who then took him to the East Baton Rouge Parish Prison where he was booked on (3) three counts of First Degree Murder (L.R.S. 14:30) and Ritualistic Acts (L.R.S. 14:107.1 C (1)) at 6:28 this morning.

In a subsequent press release the next day, the task force announced that Sean had been charged with two additional murders: Ann Bryan and Hardee Moseley Schmidt. In Ann's case, Sean was charged with first-degree murder, and in Hardee's case, with first-degree murder, kidnapping, and stalking. The task force announced that the investigation of Sean Gillis and his involvement in other murders in the area was ongoing.

As news of another serial killer's arrest hit the headlines of *The Advocate* and local television stations, many people in Baton Rouge couldn't believe it. They had not quite recovered from the fear that Derrick Todd Lee had instilled in them in the preceding years. They had watched coverage of his two trials and were relieved that they never had to worry about a serial killer again. Then the name Sean Vincent Gillis was flashed across television screens and front pages; and once again, area residents realized they were not safe. They had not even heard of many of the women he'd killed. They knew about Ann Bryan, who had been viciously killed in 1994, and Hardee Moseley Schmidt, who had gone missing in 1999 and had later been found dead. The others, the ones who had lived "high-risk lifestyles," had been mentioned in passing on the news and forgotten.

They also knew that over the past decade, stretching from 1992 until 2002, more than sixty women in the area had been reported missing or murdered. But that had been pushed to the backs of minds weary from the worry, the fear with which they had lived for several of those years. Everyone began to wonder what was going on in Baton Rouge, how two serial killers could have been operating unimpeded at the same time. Everyone knew that the D.C. snipers had killed their first victim in Baton Rouge, had lived there for a time. They wondered what was going on, what had happened to the community, where they always had felt safe.

Despite the Greater Baton Rouge area's population of approximately 774,000 people at the time, the city and its surrounding areas have retained a small-town atmosphere. Until Derrick Todd Lee, many people did not feel the need to lock their doors or take personal safety precautions. All of that changed when woman after woman was attacked in her home. But after his arrest and subsequent convictions, the feeling of safety returned and residents soon forgot that Baton Rouge could be a very dangerous place to live.

Most residents didn't know there had been a third task force formed to look for another prostitute killer, making Baton Rouge the only city in the United States to ever have three serial killers operating independently of each other at the same time.

By 2004, people had begun to set aside their fears

and had gone back to the business of living. Then Sean was arrested. He lived in a nice neighborhood. He had attended good Catholic schools. His mother had worked for WBRZ. He had waited on many residents at Circle K. He didn't look scary. This was a boy who had grown up in the city, attended school with their children, a boy who should have never turned killer. No one understood how this could be happening again.

But it was happening, and the task force was busy collecting as much information from Sean as they could before he stopped talking. Although his first attorney, Bert Garraway, had advised him to be quiet, Sean hadn't listened. He had been waiting a long time for notoriety, and he wanted to make sure investigators had every piece of information he had stored in his memory banks.

On May 3, 2004, Sean agreed to take a ride with task force members to point out the locations where he had left various pieces of evidence.

They drove to River Road in Ascension Parish, where Sean pointed out a gravel road leading up to the levee. He told them that had been where he had thrown the tattoo he had cut from Donna's leg. Investigators continued driving down River Road toward St. John Parish, where Sean told them he had thrown Donna's severed arm, but he could not find the exact location.

After investigators had turned around, Sean said, "I just remembered something else you might be interested in." He told them about the blue-and-white towel in which he had wrapped Donna's arm. "I left that on St. Elmo Road next to Bocage Plantation," he said. Detectives searched the area for the towel, but could not find it.

Around 4:00 P.M., Sean pointed out an area of River

Road, about a mile north of Gardere Lane, where he had disposed of the knife he used to cut off Johnnie Mae's hands. Investigators would search the area thoroughly two days later, but would never find the knife.

They kept driving, this time toward St. James Place. Investigators asked Lieutenant Ike Vavasseur and another officer from the Baton Rouge Police Department to meet them there. Here, Sean pointed out Ann Bryan's apartment and described for the officers how he had gotten into her apartment ten years before.

Sean directed investigators to drive toward Old Jefferson Highway and showed them the spot where he had killed Johnnie Mae Williams behind Mason's Grill. "I threw some of her clothes back there," he said, pointing to a grassy area behind the building. "I think it was white tennis shoes, a shirt, her pants, and panties." Investigators searched the area and found a white shirt covered by grass and dirt. Crime scene technician Nicole Compton photographed the shirt and brought it back to the crime lab for testing. A pair of panties was also found in some gravel near a concrete slab behind the building.

Sean wasn't finished. He remembered where he had left every piece of evidence from all of his murders. He told investigators to head toward Parkway Drive, just off Burbank. He showed them a dead end that was used as a dump site. "I threw Donna's hairpiece and dental plate back here," he said, pointing to a pile of appliances and construction materials. "I photographed her here, too."

Next they drove toward Burbank Car Wash, where Sean told them he had thrown away the chemicals he used to clean his car after Donna's murder. Then it was on to Coy Avenue, where he showed investigators a Dumpster behind Small World Day Care. This was where he disposed of Johnnie Mae's jacket and the box and ziplock bag in which he had put her hands.

Sean then brought investigators to East Mason Street, near the chemical plant where he had killed Donna, and explained again how he had killed her.

Done for the day, investigators brought Sean back to prison. The killer had literally spread evidence and bones all around Baton Rouge. With the exception of Katherine Hall's jacket and food stamp card, no one had ever reported finding any bones or bloody clothing.

That same day, Todd Morris called Ron LeJeune, with the West Baton Rouge Parish Sheriff's Office (WBRSO), and explained that Sean Gillis had confessed to the murder of Joyce Williams. On May 12, LeJeune met with Morris, Detective Blair Favron, and Chief Deputy Stephen Engolio, with the Iberville Parish Sheriff's Office, Detective Bryan Doucet, with the WBRSO, and Detective Jerry Mitchell.

Morris and Mitchell informed them that they had taken Sean's taped confession and that he had described how he had killed Joyce Williams in West Baton Rouge Parish and then dumped her remains in Iberville Parish. Favron confirmed that the remains found in his parish were indeed those of Joyce Williams. The men reviewed photographs and talked about the facts of the case. They determined that Sean had given an accurate description of her murder.

Todd then told them how Sean had picked Williams up in Scotlandville and brought her to Rosedale Road in Port Allen.

The next day, Morris and Mitchell brought Sean to West Baton Rouge Parish, where they met up with LeJeune and

Doucet. Sean led the investigators to Rosedale Road, asking them to stop at an entrance to a sugarcane field near a headland that ran parallel to the road. "I'm sure this is the spot," Sean said. "I remember it well. I came back here the night after the murder because I had left some stuff laying around I didn't want to be found." He was talking about Joyce's nightgown that he had ripped from her body. "This has been widened," he told them, pointing to the headland. "And the sugarcane was closer to the road then, but I'm sure this is it."

That afternoon, LeJeune met with the farmer who leased the property. The farmer confirmed that the headland had been widened and the sugarcane had been shortened about two years before. "The parish laid a water line near the ditch, and I didn't want heavy tractors on the trench when they traveled the headland, so I widened it and shortened the rows," the farmer explained.

There could be no doubt that Sean had been accurate in his depiction of the murder of Joyce Williams, as well as his other victims.

Richie Johnson, now a major with the sheriff's office in West Baton Rouge Parish, had certainly never come across anyone like Sean Gillis in his long career in law enforcement. Johnson had spent years teaching criminal and crime scene investigation to foreign police forces for the Department of Justice (DOJ). Although Port Allen, where he works, is a small town, it has seen its fair share of gruesome murders, and Johnson had interviewed the most hardened of killers. He knew immediately that Sean was different. Johnson also knew how to tell if a criminal was lying. He had spent years in the polygraph business and could tell by a flinch, a drop of sweat, a flicker of an eye, if someone was lying. He knew Sean was telling the truth about each horrible small detail.

"When the sheriff's office went and got him from East Baton Rouge Parish, we videotaped him on silent as he took investigators through the last ride of Joyce Williams's life. He called his zip ties 'objectifiers.' He said he would practice using them at home on kitchen chairs to make sure he became an expert with them," Johnson said.

"It's bone chilling to sit in a room with him. He's crazy—a nutcase. He scares you. He wants you to admire what he did. He's very calm, too calm, scary even for a police officer. He scattered the bones and bodies of innocent women across several parishes and was proud of what he had done."

Putting the Pieces
Together

Sean Gillis's confession had stunned members of the task force, and they were determined that they would prepare a rock-solid case against this killer. They would take no chances. They knew that judges often threw out confessions based on this technicality or that, and they wanted to make sure that when Sean went to trial, he would be found guilty.

On April 29, 2004, Nineteenth Judicial District Court judge Todd W. Hernandez signed a warrant prepared by Todd Morris and Detective Richard Mohr, of the EBRSO, to search the home on Burgin Avenue. The warrant gave the task force permission to remove blood, hair, fingerprints, cutting instruments, photographs, electronic and printed documents, computers, CDs, DVDs, cameras, jewelry, clothing, plastic tie wraps, and body parts.

Terri Lemoine answered the door, signed acknowledgment of the search warrant, and watched as investigators proceeded to go through all of the things she and Sean had spent years collecting. By one-fifteen that afternoon, task force members had loaded down their vehicles with the following: one pocketknife, with a two-inch blade; one black-and-silver belt; one red-and-black machete; a pair of black shoes; one black-handled hacksaw, which was missing the blade; one silver hacksaw, again missing the blade; one Maglite flashlight; a multipurpose tool and its case; fourteen condoms; three pictures of Johnnie Mae Williams; three zip ties; eight books, including *An Unquiet Mind, Cops and Robbers, The Hillside Strangler, Alone with the Devil, Sudden Fury, The Blooding, The Silence of the Lambs,* and *Son of Sam*; a small gray toolbox; a pair of gloves; a box cutter; a large gray toolbox with tools; seven saws; one ax; four Pocket Fox books; six *Playboy Playmate* books; a wooden club; eight printed pages from the newspaper with photos and articles about Carrie Lynn Yoder, a Derrick Todd Lee victim; three white computer towers; three hard drives; one Kodak memory stick; a digital camera.

A cadaver dog was used to search the backyard, but police could find no bodies, no bones, nothing that would indicate that Sean had buried anyone there.

Police also seized a four-door white 2002 Chevrolet Cavalier, with license plate number KUA706. A gray 1999 Mazda van, VIN number JM3LV5210L0220199, was also collected as evidence. Police would later search that vehicle for blood, fibers, DNA, hair. They would find a vital piece of evidence that would eventually link Sean Gillis to the murder of Donna Bennett Johnston. Sean had kept a trophy and hidden it in the van, which had not been moved in years.

On May 4, a warrant was issued for Louisiana State Police Crime Lab personnel that would enable them to search the home for blood, bone, and tissue. Technicians photographed the home and searched for blood under the kitchen flooring and in the molding around cabinets, as well as throughout other rooms.

Terri faced another search of her home on May 5. This time, police took a black NASCAR cooler, a scanner, a bayonet with a fourteen-inch blade, two pieces of shoe molding, and three kitchen knives—a twelve-inch, an eight-inch, and a three-inch.

On May 6, Terri received a call from Todd Morris.

"I talked to Sean yesterday," she told him.

"Yeah? What did he say?"

"He told me that he had used one of my butcher knives on one of the victims," Terri responded. "It was from my Chicago Cutlery set on the counter."

"Can I come get it?"

"Yes," Terri said.

Morris turned the knife set over to Nicole Compton, who submitted it to the state police crime lab.

Sean identified the knife as the one he had used to cut up Joyce Williams.

Police also confiscated thirty-one VHS cassette tapes, an empty VHS case, two adult videos, photographs, and two rolls of film.

Next they obtained a warrant to search Sean's Hotmail accounts, his Yahoo accounts, and all of his computer files.

They discovered his Yahoo profile user name was "locoweed70808." Sean had listed his age as 666. Under favorite quotes, he had listed: "Crush your enemies, see them driven before you, and hear the lamentations of their women," from the movie *Conan the Barbarian.*

On his hard drive, they found a history of Sean's likes and dislikes.

On the computer he had named "Angel," Sean stored music, lots of music, and his taste was quite varied—from

ABBA to Bob Seger and Barry White to Britney Spears and Christina Aguilera to Lil' Kim and Pink. Classic music from Kenny Loggins, Neil Diamond, and Joan Jett and the Blackhearts were among his favorites. He loved Christmas music and had compiled an extensive collection of it, including songs from Mannheim Steamroller and Vince Vance and the Valiants.

The character of Buffy the Vampire Slayer, Britney Spears, and Christina Aguilera comprised many files on the computer. They were his favorite sex objects, and he spent hours each week searching the Internet for sexy pictures of the celebrities. Christina Applegate was possibly his most favorite, as his computer housed an enormous collection of photos of the actress. He also had numerous files with names like "Siami," "Tina," "Sword Girl," "Shana," "Abrianna," "Katarina," and "Natasha"— a prized collection of his favorite porn stars posing in various positions designed to give him the utmost pleasure as he sat in front of his computer.

Not one to discriminate, the girls were included under files marked "Asian," "Negro," "Hispanic," "Caucasian." Still others files were titled "Old Fucks," "Lezbos," "Cute Pussy."

Sean's fascination with death and dismemberment could be found all over his computer. Some of his files were labeled "Kinky" and "Macabre," which is where the "Dead Webs" link was stored. Police discovered files named "Beheadings and Hangings," "Russian Necro World," "Fake Dead," "Various Dead," "Best of Snuff," "B&W Dead," "Extra Dead," "Bondage."

His fascination with other serial killers also emerged. He had collected all the information he could find about the Manson Murders in one file and named another "DTL case," which contained news articles about the murders committed by Derrick Todd Lee. He wanted to learn every detail he could about how Lee's victims were killed. Like a true competitor, he had kept his eye on the competition.

On June 10, 2004, Sean Vincent Gillis was indicted for the first-degree murder of Donna Bennett Johnston. Prem Burns, assistant district attorney (ADA) for East Baton Rouge Parish, filed a notice of intent to seek the death penalty, basing that decision on the facts of the murder, coupled with second-degree kidnapping and armed robbery.

Prison Letters

Hi Honey Bunny,

I'm still on the Klingon asteroid Ruhra-Pente; at least it feels that cold here. As you can see, the body's in prison but the soul is flying high again.

> *Many hugs & kisses,*
> *Love U,*
> *Sean, Admiral Starfleet, Retired 4 now*

Dear Sean,

Yvonne sent you an allowance. I've forwarded it to your account.

How are things at the Hilton? Things quite exploded around here with Katie. She was warned to stop selling her things, she swore she was behaving. I found an old pipe in her nightstand while folding her clothes. It held and was still holding about a gram of illegal substance. I was furious enough to tell her the way out the door. Then I called Jimmy. I gave her 48 hours to move. I had even called Sergeant Reed to find out how long I had to wait after evicting her before I could put her things out. When I gave her a deadline, she had no problem getting someone to help her pack AND move. We are changing storage into her name and I've already gotten all your mom's books back here.

Well that's the news from here. Your mom says you have a court date soon. Please let me know when and I'll be present. No one comes by to tell me what is going on. Please ask Sister Kathy to drop a note or something at least as a courtesy. Maybe I can find my own way to the courthouse!

Please take care of yourself and write often. I got your card. Thank you very much. The same sentiments come from me. Especially "Your thought of often and you mean so very much."

> *All my Heart*
> *Terri*
> *(Honey Bonnie) Scottish!*

Star Date, 0504.25

Greetings Admiral Lemoine,

I'm sorry for upsetting you at your last visit. I promise not to do that again. As far as preaching, I guess it was, and I assure you I will not do that again either. About the text, it is the New King James Ver. with corrections made from the 1611 ed.

As far as ($45) for some test. Do you think I'm out of my fucking mind? I may have said some thing about living on $45 a week here, but I want to see the letter. I would tell some preacher what he could do with his mother and father and both horses they rode in on if they wanted a *thin dime for a test of any kind. I am very glad to be taking these courses, but I assure you that the first mother fucker that asks anything more than a heart-felt thanks is in for a rude awakening. Adm. Sean don't play that. As for us being a "mark," only in my generosity with my food (which sucks) and my help in teaching some of these people how to read and write. Maybe I shouldn't teach writing, but as bad as I am at it, you should see what passes for the written word around here. As for as the "hows" of the end; what the heck do you think? I know no one knows but the God (aka the Father) in heaven.*

Glad to hear about things at the Tiger Express. How are the Finis doing? How's Sharon and Faruq? J.R. still has not come by or written. Nor has John Green. Gee, I would have stuck by them through anything. Oh well, I'll never learn will I? So far you have been the only constant in my strange journey to what ever happens.

I may be the village idiot, but I am not a total fool. If I worry all the time, it only is a waste of something I don't have that much to waste. You are the single best thing to happen on this earth for me in my whole futile life. God is so great to let me spend some time with a wonderful jewel such as you. And the kids also, James, Christine and the other one. Two out of three ain't bad. I'm so sorry that the other will be on a real tuff road for a while unless she "wakes up." I hope and pray for Katie every day, as do I for you and Jimmy and Christine, but a little more tearfully that the rest because I feel responsible for her wildness. I should have been a far better example and not acted like a stupid kid myself. At least the other two didn't pay attention and get as screwed up as her.

I'll remind Sister Kathy when I see her again. She has had a lot of court appearances on the day I can have visits. They have been so good to me. Please mention Kerry,

Beenie, Phil, Ken & Kathy in your prayers too. I miss you so much. I hope she can pick you up soon for a visit.

> *Till then, I Love U always,*
> *Sean V. Gillis, Adm. S.F.C. Ret.?*

P.S. Send plain white typping paper and a spelling book too. HaHa.

Dear Sean,

I received the check (money order) from your mom about an hour after you called so I figured I'd get it in the mail tomorrow.

We just got in from work. Ali gave me $10.00 extra for being there on Mother's Day. Christine called this morning. She was on the way home from Chris' house. She won 2nd place in a horse show Saturday night. I am just so proud of her. I guess she'll always be my baby.

I'll write more after I get some sleep. Take care.

> *Terri*

P.S.
Looks like one of your mom's letters. HaHa.

Hey there Honey Bunny,

I'm sorry if it sounded like was bitchy yesterday, it's just I haven't talked to you in so long that I had so much to say in 15 min. I'm realy glad you came and I hope you didn't take me being O.K. with you and Gaar. I am O.K. with it. I have had 10 months to get that way. I'll always love you! That will never change. Just like I'll always love Jimmy, Katie & Christine. They'll always be my kids in my heart and mind. You and Gaar were cheated 20 years ago, and I am so glad to have stood in for the past 10. Now about the electronic tools: I don't know how I know but I know I'll need them in the not so distant future. Some serious shit is about to go down in the next 5 years, and I will need to be prepared. Everything we know will be forever changed, and staying alive will be on everyones agenda. Keep the faith, and seriously reconsider Jesus. I really want to see you in the kingdom that will come to power in 12 to 13 years. Quite a few muslims in here are returning to Christ. Islam, though pretty as it seems is just one of things warned about 1000 years before it existed. Even Christ 500 years before them alluded to the deceitful fairy tales of men. If only Mohamed had not put himself first after God. I can't stress this enough. Forget all the stupid churches, Catholic, Baptist, etc. Read the Bible yourself and see. Pray for a clean mind and forget all that some priest or preacher filled your head with. There is more there that makes sense without the so-called holy men screwing with it. Pray for the kid's souls. Satan wants them very bad. He almost got Jimmy. He may have Katie. I hope not! In failure to get them he will concentrate his energies on Christine. I'm not kidding. He is pissed off that even with all the control he had over me, I was able with the power of God, through Jesus and the Holy Ghost to redeem my soul before it was too late. I realy am losing a lot of sleep over this. I don't have time or space to tell you all the things I am seeing these days, but I assure you I'm not alone in this. People around here are wakeing up scared near to death and cannot even put into words what they are seeing. I love all you guys, esp. U Honey Bunny. I'll pray and you pray too Gaar.

Sean V. Gillis, Adm. S.F.C. Ret.

Dear Sean,

Surprise! I'll bet you thought we abandoned you. As I'm sure you've already sumized, w lost phone service. No money. Katie actually asked how we can have electricity and not the phone. Can you believe? A Blond Moment. I told her it was simply one or the other. Now Gaar isn't able to put his graphics on the net. He did manage to have some on before we lost service but Pay Pal only pays monthly. We managed to get $45 at the beginning of this month. I can only hope it's more in February.

I was having trouble with my bottom tooth. It was so loose that everytyme I closed my mouth it would bend so far inward that I felt like I was being stabbed on my gums. Gaar got some oragel and ice, numbed it a bit then pulled it with a pair of pliers. A week later the same thing had to be done with the tooth next to it. So there's a big gap on the bottom in front. Cute, let me tell ya. I had to learn how to say anything with an S all over again. Tasking to ssss-say the leassst.

I wrote to Yvonne to tell her we are all still waiting for her. I wrote to Christine to send her all her mail. I am also planning to write Christine Ackal just to make sure we stay in touch. Her view on the whole matter is that you were just sick, so let it just stay that way. I did ask her if I could give you her address and she said O.K. Sorry it's gone, My computer died "almost" and ate my address book. I'll write JR and try and get it from him. I apologize.

I'm working on trying to visit but everything is so Murphy Lawing. Entergy is due on the 26th. It's $133.16. We have $55.00. Hope we don't loose electric too. It's cold.

I sent you stamps and paper. Where's my letter? In case you've used it already, here's a couple more. Write! I don't know anything that's going on with you. Just for reference . . . your representatives talk a lot. Only I never hear them.

Take Care,
Terri

Hi Honey Bunny,

I remember that tooth. I'm glad you had success in removing it. I on the other hand will need some surgery to fix my tooth. It's the same tooth, but on the other side of the mouth from yours. I tried to pull it, it was so loose but a root tore some nerves and now I have pyrea or gangreen of the gums. It smells really gross. Sorry I took so long to return a letter. I was in shock for three days at the Christina Applegate clippings. Please do not do that again. That was a really rare collectors edition of Premiere mag-azine. Didn't the fact that it was covered in plastic convey something to you? Do not loose any part of it. I will live and be free in a few years. Please put it away in safety. That really hurts me Honey Bunny. Please don't let Gaar hurt my stuff. I feel better with all that off my chest. I miss you oh so much. The holidays were a real pain in the ass. I seem to be in charge of morale around here. People start a fight or a loud argument and I end up involved one way or another. Now I know why Jesus had to hide from his fol-lowers some times; I can't shut their pain and fear out. Most folks who are around me really seem to have grown along with me this past year. Most of the friends I initially made have gone on either home or "up the road." The new crop seems to have some severe mental &/or emotional problems. I think God has me in here at "this time" for a reason. I really do. Most of these folks are not bad people, just for some reason they are all on the wrong road, in the wrong direction. Mom should be sending some money soon. Some for the phone and some for my store. I need a haircut bad. It gets me confused with the punks and queens. I think you would like one of the little drag-queens we had here last month. His stage name is "Star." When asked his favorite move, either "Too Wong Foo" or "Rocky Horror Picture Show" all the way. The kids got class, to bad he's so confused about his gender at 16. The list of people I pray for is getting longer by the day. Give Heather a hug for me, and Katie too if she'll have it. Tell Gaar I'm not really mad about the magazine but not to do that again. Try sending one of the "volley-ball" girls. I want to see if they will allow them. Send Lisa, the tanned one with the short hair, no loss if they don't let her in. I love you Honey Bunny.

Sean

P.S. OXOX "hug, kiss – hug, kiss."

Sean,

I wanted to drop you a note to tell you Heather [Sean's cat] *has passed on. She began acting strange last Fri. (26th). She would go to all the rooms and sleep for awhile. She didn't eat at all. On Monday, Jan. 24th 2005 she went to her bed in the kitchen and went to sleep. I noticed about 3:30 in the morning. She went quietly and peacefully. We had a little service for her in the back. She has a little head stone with her toys on it, so she'd have something to play with on her journey.*

We're all thinking about you.

All our hearts,
Terri
Louis

Hope you don't mind Gaar signing and doing the picture on the card for you. He took care of everything for Heather after. Katie thought it was . . . inappropriate for him to sign!

Hi again Honey Bunny,

Well the news about Heather Leah put my last stupid & selfish letter into perspective. Please disregard all but the "miss you and love you" parts. The card and picture is nice. Thank you Honey Bunny. Break the news lightly to Rick. Sometimes I think he loves her more than I do. Tell him I miss him and hope he and his mother Alma and cat Dixie are all right. I will tell Mom when I call her this weekend. Heather was a good cat. God must have need of her somewhere else. Enclosed are letters to Katie and Gaar. I hope to see you soon. I love you more than I can say.

This much—100,000,000 miles apart [Sean explained in the circle of infinity he drew].

Love,
Sean

Dear Sean,

Here are the envelopes you asked for. (20) We are O.K. here. Still cleaning the yard up from hurricane damage. Entergy needs to come and tighten the powerline. It's so low it almost touches the shrine; and it does touch the cable line.

How are you doing? We don't hear from you enough. One would think you have a different family stashed away somewhere. I haven't heard from your mom (personally) for quite some time. I'm sure she is well. Haven't heard from

Katie (surprise surprise) but Christine called last Saturday. Still don't know when she will be able to come down. Gaar & I were in the corner store and a man came in and asked for $85.00 worth of gas!!! Can you imagine? Well, I guess it shouldn't be a worry for me. Don't drive. I suppose I'll worry if we ever get a car. Ken said he would try and make sure I have a ride to whatever court stuff you have. So I reckon I'll see you then unless he gets here for a visit.

Take care Doll,
Terri

P.S. Sorry I couldn't send stamps.

ALERT
STARFLEET
Subspace Memo
S.D. 1104.05

Dear Admiral Honey Bunny,

How are things going on the ranch? It's been too long since our last communication. I'm still looking for the Reagan stamps & the 20 sheets of typing paper. Also, now I am down to four envelopes, soo if you can, send up to 20 of them. I have many 37 cent flag stamps and am getting 3 of these post-paid envelopes and an ink pen a month from an indigent inmate in exchange for a few cigs. So far the smokes are holding out fine, and I am getting to be quite a good Feringi. Who am I kidding, I still can't seem to take advantage of someone worse off than me. I'll learn one way or another, but not too soon. Well, let's see, I've got 2 new disciples in Christ and one more "stalking fan." This guy watched me sleeping for 3 hours the other day. Creepy, huh? Oh well, if he let's me, I'll point him to God

Ann Bryan (center) was a sweet eighty-two-year-old lady who became Sean Gillis's first victim in 1994. Here, she poses during happy times with her sisters, Delores (left) and Doris (right). *(Photo by Rachel Ehricht)*

Rachel Ehricht, Ann Bryan's daughter, sits beneath one of her mother's paintings. Even though she only had one hand, Ann was a talented artist.

(Photo by Susan D. Mustafa)

Yvonne Gillis, Sean's mother, raised him as a single mom. She had no clue that her sweet son would grow up to be a cold, sick killer.
(Photo by Terri Lemoine)

Norman Gillis, Sean's father, spent many years suffering from mental illness. He left his wife and Sean when Sean was just one after putting a gun to his son's head and threatening to kill him.

Terri Lemoine and Sean Vincent Gillis hit it off immediately and soon fell in love. They shared many common interests, and Terri thought Sean was the sweetest man. *(Photo by Christine Lemoine Duke)*

The Tiger Express, once a Circle K, located on Lee Drive across from St. James Place, is where Sean Vincent Gillis and his girlfriend, Terri Lemoine, worked for many years. Sean viciously attacked and killed Ann Bryan at St. James Place. *(Photo by Susan D. Mustafa)*

Sean called this brick structure in the backyard his mother's "shrine." When she moved to Atlanta, Sean was left alone for the first time and could sometimes be heard by neighbors cursing his mother loudly late at night. *(Photo by Susan D. Mustafa)*

Sean had his name put on a bottle of Crown Royal, his favorite alcoholic beverage. Terri Lemoine would often find hidden empty bottles in their home after Sean had promised to stop drinking. *(Photo by Susan D. Mustafa)*

Although some people thought he was a little strange, no one would have guessed that Sean was capable of such vicious acts of violence. *(Mug shot)*

In this photograph, even Sean's eyes look kind. That was one of the reasons women trusted him enough to get into his vehicle. *(Photo by Terri Lemoine)*

Katherine Hall was one of the women who trusted Sean. On January 4, 1999, Sean lured her into his vehicle, took her to a deserted field and stabbed her thirty-seven times. *(Mug shot)*

In this photo taken in his home, Sean's eyes seem crazier and reflect his true personality. *(Photo by Terri Lemoine)*

Sean Gillis stalked Hardee Mosely Schmidt, a beautiful wife and mother, for weeks before running her over with his car while she was jogging and then strangling her on May 30, 1999. Sean took her body to this BREC park and raped her. *(Photo by Susan D. Mustafa)*

Sean dumped Hardee's body in this bayou in St. James Parish, where she would be found the next day. *(Photo by Susan D. Mustafa)*

On November 12, 1999, Sean took Joyce Williams to Rosedale Road in West Baton Rouge Parish and killed her, covered by darkness and surrounded by sugar cane. He then took her to his home, mutilated her body, and committed unspeakable acts. *(Photo by Susan D. Mustafa)*

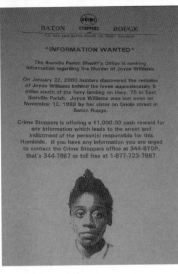

BATON STOPPERS ROUGE

INFORMATION WANTED

The Iberville Parish Sheriff's Office is seeking information regarding the Murder of Joyce Williams

On January 22, 2000 hunters discovered the remains of Joyce Williams behind the levee approximately 5 miles south of the ferry landing on Hwy. 75 in East Iberville Parish. Joyce Williams was last seen on November 12, 1999 by her sister on Oriole street in Baton Rouge.

Crime Stoppers is offering a $1,000.00 cash reward for any information which leads to the arrest and indictment of the person(s) responsible for this Homicide. If you have any information you are urged to contact the Crime Stoppers office at 344-STOP, that's 344-7867 or toll free at 1-877-723-7867.

Crime Stoppers released this Information Wanted poster to the public with the hope that someone would come forward with information about Joyce Williams's murder. Sean Gillis would later make copies of it as he worked on a Xerox machine at the Louisiana Attorney General's Office.

Sean grew up in this house on Burgin Avenue and would later bring his victims there to play with their dead bodies. Joyce Williams was the first woman he brought home. *(Photo by Susan D. Mustafa)*

Terri Lemoine points out the floor in the kitchen of her home where Sean mutilated his victims. *(Photo by Susan D. Mustafa)*

Sean stands in the exact spot in the kitchen where he would later cut up his victims. *(Photo by Terri Lemoine)*

Sean posted this Area 51 warning in the window of his home. *(Photo by Terri Lemoine)*

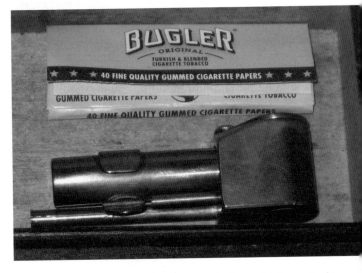

Sean always kept a stash of marijuana in this box at his home. Smoking weed made him feel less stressed and according to him, probably stopped him from killing on numerous occasions. *(Photo by Susan D. Mustafa)*

Richie Johnson, a seasoned detective who is now with the West Baton Rouge District Attorney's Office, conducted lie detector tests on suspects in Joyce Williams's murder. He would later say that Sean Gillis "gave him the creeps." *(Photo by Susan D. Mustafa)*

Sean picked up Marilyn Nevils October 20, 2000, on his way to visit his goddaughter. He strangled and beat her before taking her to his house. *(Mug shot)*

Sean took a shower with the body of Marilyn Nevils in this bathroom in his bedroom. He caressed her dead body before bringing her to River Road and leaving her on top of a levee near the Mississippi River. *(Photo by Susan D. Mustafa)*

Detective David LeBlanc with the Lafayette Police Department worked the Marilyn Nevils case. Police there did not even know she was missing until Sean Gillis confessed to her murder. *(Photo by Susan D. Mustafa)*

Sean Vincent Gillis took a backseat while Derrick Todd Lee, the South Louisiana serial killer, went on a rampage in 2002. Sean created a file on his computer of Lee's victims. *(Mug shot)*

After Lee was caught in 2003, Sean killed Johnnie Mae Williams, a friend he had known for years, and cut off her hands. Here, a young Johnnie Mae poses with her youngest daughter, Jena. *(Photo by James Patterson)*

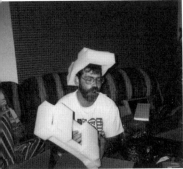

While Johnnie Mae's family grieved, Sean acted silly while he enjoyed Christmas with his family. *(Photo by Terri Lemoine)*

Robert Reames led police to the body of Johnnie Mae Williams in the woods in the small community of Port Hudson-Pride after his young son Ethan discovered her while four-wheeling. *(Photo by Susan D. Mustafa)*

Sean Gillis's last victim, Donna Bennett Johnston, was strangled, mutilated, and left in a ravine near a canal on Ben Hur Road. Her murder would lead police to a serial killer.

A picture of Donna Johnston's son, Justin, lies on the ground near a stone shrine that marks the spot of her murder. *(Photo by Susan D. Mustafa)*

Todd Morris knew immediately that Sean was the serial killer when he went to his house to ask for a DNA swab. Sean would later proudly confess the gruesome and sick details of his crimes to the detective. *(Photo by Susan D. Mustafa)*

Tony Clayton prosecuted Sean Gillis in West Baton Rouge Parish for the murder of Joyce Williams. Sean pled guilty in that case. *(Photo by Susan D. Mustafa)*

Judge Robin Free sentenced Sean Gillis to life in prison. *(Photo by Susan D. Mustafa)*

Prem Burns prosecuted Sean Gillis in East Baton Rouge Parish for the murder of Donna Bennett Johnston. Sean was unexpectedly sentenced to life in prison again, although everyone in the courtroom expected him to get the death penalty. *(Photo by Marie Constantine)*

Johnnie Mae Williams's children (back row), Jena, Larry, and Lauren still grieve for their mother who loved them so much despite her problems. Because of Sean Gillis, Johnnie Mae will never be able to watch her grandchildren (front row), Brian Keith, Laila, LaQuelis, and Steven, grow up. *(Photo by James Patterson)*

Louis Gaar and Terri Lemoine now live together in Sean's house. The horrors that happened there are a distant memory. *(Photo by Susan D. Mustafa)*

Every now and then, a pool of blood raised by cleaning chemicals shows up on the floor to remind them that this house was the playground of a sadistic killer, as when Terri and Louis recently cleaned out a hall closet. *(Photo by Louis Gaar)*

and let him take it from there. I still miss you and the kids every day. My dreams are getting better and stranger by the day. You know, the kind that make me wonder if God is trying to tell me something, or I'm just going more nuts. I hope it's the first one. Love to you and Gaar & the kids if you see or talk to any of them.

> *With Love,*
> *Sean V. Gillis, Adm. S.F.C Retired.*

A Note From . . . Terri

How zit goin? Sorry about the card. It had to be altered (cut down) to meet mail regulations. It was 51/2' by 8'. Hope you like the pics. Happy Christmas.

> *Love ya,*
> *Terri and Gaar*

Greetings,

Hope you like the pics. Couldn't throw you a Starfleet party, so I thought you might like some pictures. Have a merry X-mas. I've celebrated (16) Christmas' in your side of the galaxy. It's like being stuck in the Alpha Quadrant. Keep searching for the wormholes; or maybe the "Q".

> *Bright Blessings,*
> *Gaar*

Hi Honey Bunny,

From all the little Who's in WhoVille, Merry Christmas. "Santa, where are you taking our Christmas tree?" Cindy Loo Who
As I told you on the phone, the real Queen of the

Damned has become a papist. Real stretch, huh? On the political front, there's a book out there that says what I've said for two years; the only viable threat to Sen. Hillary Clinton is Sec. of State, Dr. Condolezza Rice. Step up to the "Dark Side." Did you catch the prez's speech to the cadets yesterday? We plan to win? Better than a plan to lose I guess. Is it, "Merry Christmas" or "Happy Christmas Day?" Two grams of coke . . . and a crack pipe in a pear tree. Ok, I'm back, still looks like jail, but my good humor is catching on around here. Last night, we all sang O Holy Night and The Little Drummer Boy. It was so spontaneous, and had a few tears in more than a few eyes I might add. Much love to you and Louis and the kids where ever they all may be.

> *xoxoxo*
> *Sean, the anti-grinch*

Hi Louis,

I've got what might be a "no-brainer," but I've been thinking a lot about it. Ok, Gloria Copeland says that everyone who has the Holy Spirit in them speaks in tongues. I seem to remember St. Paul saying that there are many "gifts" of the Spirit of which one is speaking in tongues. Don't some interpret tongues, prophesy, heal or have some other super-natural gifts, or none at all? What's the true answer? Thanks for all you've done and are doing Louis. God sent you to us in the nick of time. Love to you, Terri and Christine.

> *Sean, the anti-Grinch*

"They cann't touch me with a 39-1/2 foot pole."

* * *

Dear Sean,

I don't know if you were ever able to receive my last letter. Let me know if you need any stuffs. Things are o.k. here. I'm still working on the "Library." So far I've logged over 800 books. Only 38 of those are paperback so far. There are 7 very large boxes of them still. However, it's looking very nice. I really think your mom will enjoy it whenever she returns home. Any of her books will be at her fingertips. After all it's just something I always wanted to do. You know that. Besides . . . it keeps me busy.

Your mom sent a money order of $100.00 for you. So I'm forwarding it to you. Take care.

Terri

Hi Honey Bunny,

Krishna, Krishna. Glad I got that out of my system. He, he, he. I got Louis' letter today. I've sent him one. He's gonna be more fun than Linda Aldridge to mess with. I needed that too. Oh man did it make me hot! I was cussin' loud enough to be heard at the airport. I take my understanding of all Jesus' lessons very serious. I just wish my spelling would improve. I doubt Louis will see what I mean about having to un-learn the "doctrine of men." Tell me if he blows a gasket when he reads his letter. I hope that it does not piss him off too much. He's a good egg. Just a bit too over the edge though. That wasn't a letter, it was a booklet. Like I said though, I love what it did to me. I haven't been this animated since my last "conversation" with Linda. I'm serious, I gave it to him with both barrels and then re-loaded just for the fun of it. Did you see the novel he wrote me? I'd pay good money to hear him while he's reading mine. You did tell him he's not dealing with a complete imbecile didn't you? I still hope I wasn't too hard on him. I'd put my Life Time in Catholic school against his 12 years J.H.D. any time, and as they say in here, you can believe that. I've told Louis if by some fat chance that total exercise in fun ever comes close to being right, I reserve the right to Na,Na,Na,Na,Na,Na! for the next 1000 years.

I want to share with you something serious. This place is the best kept secret in Baton Rouge. The food's lousy, the room service sucks, but the people in general are real nice and protective. This asshole who caused us some real trouble a few months ago got put back here for a few days. I was that last person he fucked with then and the first when he returned. He's a real goon! Big, rude, ugly, loud, mean and I think a little homosexual too. He started in on me, I shut him down in two min. flat. The next morning he tried to steal another guy's food while the guy was still asleep. That was the last straw. I don't normaly condone violence or throwing of feces, but we shit the mother fucker down till he was screaming to get away. They moved him to the other block on the wing, J1. In less than half an hour he pissed them off and got shit down over there too! Again, not my usual answer to a goon, but in his case I laughed till I could not stand the pain from laughing so hard. In case your wondering, I did not use shit, I hit him with plain toilet water. This guy, so you know, untill this day had the deputies bullied. After this they all got in a few licks, bitch slappin' him to the other side of the prison. So you see, even in this otherwise dismal place, I still can find time to make friends and scorn bullies to tears. It felt good! Without sharing the details, I still pass the time reading the Bible and discussing it over with my line fellows. There's some cool guys here. Some of them saw you on T.V. last year and in the paper. They say you're Fine! I agree with them and thank God for knowing you. I never deserved such a fine woman as you. Tell Louis he'd better remember how special a lady you are and do right by you. I've busted out of every cage in the Alpha Quadrant. This planet doesn't even have a force field in place anywhere. I've revoked my resignation as of this star date: 200505.03. I stand ready to serve as Fleet Commander untill further notice. Klingons, Romulans and Borg beware!

With Love Always,
Admiral Sean V. Gillis S.F.C. S.B.1

Hey Honey Bunny,

It's about 4:00 now, so I guess Sr. Kathy couldn't make it. Oh well, maybe next week. I'll call again on Tuesday. One things for sure, I'm eating better now that all I eat is anything but the stuff that passes as meat around here. Not that I'm becoming some "tree hugging," "Leftist" vegetarian. Still the same old conservative asshole. Just cann't digest the meat here. Ever since I started eating just veggies and fruit a few weeks ago, I've not had the same digestion problems that have plagued me since I came here. Oh, how I'd do anything to eat some of your spagetti and meat sauce again. Even a pizza from Papa John's would be the coolest thing. The best stuff in the store to order are pecan spins and Rock-n-Rolls. Even they don't do it after a while. My spelling and penmanship still sucks, but I think I'm improving somewhat. It's in there, my head, but I just don't seem to access it like or when I need to. It's so frustrating! It's bad enough to find out I'm Darth Vader in the flesh, but an illiterate Sith Lord is really bad. It seems only Mom, Pam and you and Christine are the only ones who see or know something doesn't add up. As I've said before, people like me here. I mean lots of folks that I would never have expected it from, are real nice to me. They keep a distance when I'm a little upset, but otherwise do not seem to have any animosity to me. The nurses love me. At first they were cold, but the past few months they've warmed up to me. I think one of them has a crush on me. I'm not the only one, many inmates and two of the deputies think so too. It's always the quiet ones. I guess I'm lucky one of the deputies or inmates hasn't taken a similar "liking to me." It's so odd the way people come up to me and ask me so many questions such as my take on the war, politics, God and scripture, food, women, computers, family problems they need help with. I mean it really freaks me out how my words can possibly help anyone out, but they keep coming back, thanking me and saying they are praying for me and my family (you, the kids, mom, etc.) It's touching in a way that's hard to describe. I actually feel as if someone other than family and friends gives a shit if I live or die. I cann't even begin to tell you how much I love and appreciate you and even Gaar whom I've never met, but yes, I even love and appreciate him so much too. I cann't bring myself to think about JR or John Green. I cann't even think about Rick without crying. I know it's a shock to every one, but really I never have or would abandon a friend like they have. I'd be hurt and confused as anyone would, but I'd never forsake them. It's funny, I always kept a close-tight group of friends who I would have died for if need be. I cann't even get a "Fuck you" or a "Go to Hell" from them. It hurt. I'm sorry to lay this on you, but you're the only one I trust and feel can understand me. I keep on a happy face for everybody, but I'm so damned sick at heart that only love of and from the Lord,

Mom and you keep me going. I'm so sorry for everyone concerned I was even born. I really don't know how, why or even if, sometimes I don't even care. I know that's not nice to say, but it's not the me that I or you or anybody else knows. I still cry when I read a sad story. I laugh at funny things. I look with wonder on a world that I will never look at the same way again. I cann't be specific, unless someone might get this letter, but there is someone here on the cell-block who should want me dead. I don't know why, I do, but I feel like we are becoming friends. I don't see why he doesn't hate me. We do Bible study together. As you can guess, I'm not to dry eyed now, but it will pass. It always does. I just hate the runny nose that goes with it. It's a waste of good toilet paper and that stuffs like gold around here. One roll a week. I'm real sorry if I bummed you out with this letter, but I hope you understand. I cann't even tell you all I want to and that sucks the most. All I know for sure is that God loves me, Momma loves me, and I'm pretty sure you do too. That's what keeps me going untill I can see and hear you again. I know things have changed. That is the way of the world. You know I would not have it any other way. Be sure, I love you and the kids, and my lost friends too. That will never change. Untill next time.

Hasta La Vista Honey Bunny,
Sean

The Prosecution Begins

The prosecutor slammed the shovel hard, cracking it against the floor, causing the jurors to jump. The sound reverberated through the courtroom. "*That* is how Robbie Daniel crushed in the skull of that young girl," he said.

Defense attorney Jerry D'Aquila jumped to his feet. "Objection!" he yelled. "Mr. Clayton is inflaming the jury. Judge, we don't need this kind of theatrics in the courtroom."

"Overruled," said Judge James Best.

Tony Clayton continued his closing argument, explaining to jurors how paint from that shovel had been embedded into the skull of seventeen-year-old Michelle Sparks, a young girl from Erwinville, Louisiana, who had met Daniel at the fruit stand where she worked. Although he was involved in a homosexual relationship with an older man, Daniel had fallen in love with Sparks; and on the day of her death, the two had smoked a joint together, then gone to Daniel's house. As Sparks leaned down to play with some puppies, Daniel viciously hit her in the head with the shovel, then placed her body in a drainage ditch behind his home. But there was no real motive.

Clayton didn't need one. He had the shovel. He had phone calls placed from Daniel's cell phone in the vicinity, although Daniel had told police he was in the town of Watson, some thirty miles away. He had the paint from the shovel found in Daniel's yard. He had the girl's body discovered two weeks later behind his home in a pond weighted down by bricks, towels, and carpet. Investigators found matching towels in Daniel's backyard. But there was no DNA, no blood on the shovel. The case was not a shoo-in. Clayton's cases rarely were, but that didn't stop him from prosecuting. He liked the hard cases. It made the justice that much sweeter.

Tony Clayton's life as assistant district attorney and chief felony prosecutor for the parishes of Iberville, West Baton Rouge, and Pointe Coupee was filled with the most gruesome aspects of existence. He experienced firsthand the human depravity that most only viewed dispassionately from the comfort of couches as they watched television.

"Cases like this remind me of why I do this job," Clayton explained. "When I was called to the Sparks murder, I watched as the police examined the area while Sparks's battered body lay in that ditch. I watched Sheriff Mike Cazes take off his shirt, then wade in and pull that little girl's maggot-ridden body out. He didn't have to do that, but he couldn't stand to see her like that. To me, he is a hero, and it is in those moments that these cases become personal."

After winning a guilty verdict against Robbie Daniel, Clayton added another victory to his unblemished prosecutorial record. Despite his flamboyance, despite the theatrics, Clayton knew the law and knew how to use it to win justice for the families of victims. But the day-to-day living with the horror was never easy for the prosecutor.

"One of the cases that got to me the most was Edward Tyrone Washington, who killed his ex-wife, her boyfriend, his ex-sister-in-law, and his four-year-old nephew. Washington's five-year-old son was the only eyewitness. A day and a half later, police found the five-year-old drenched in blood and holding the body of his little cousin. The boy told paramedics, 'My daddy made my mommy fall.' That statement was allowed in at the trial and was the only evidence linking Washington to the case. It was gut-wrenching. Washington will spend the rest of his life waiting to die in Angola."

Because of the demographics of the area, many of Clayton's cases involved African-American murderers, and the prosecutor found himself in the position of handling most of those cases. Having a black prosecutor trying black men erases the racial element for the jury, which is one reason many of these cases fall into his able hands. But he didn't see it like that. "Babies don't cry black tears or white tears. They cry tears from pain. Crime causes pain, and my job is to stop the pain—to bring justice to the victims' families. Unfortunately, we live in a world of crime. We, as black people, have come a long way. We are a good race of people, but like all other races, a small percentage of us participate in violent crimes. I'm simply weeding out the bad element. It's a matter of good versus evil. I'm going for good."

But justice wasn't always Tony Clayton's calling. As a young man growing up just outside of Brusly, Louisiana, he simply wanted to attend college, to make something of himself—an attitude instilled into him by his parents, Ernest and Clara. He attended Southern University and graduated Cum Laude in 1991 with a juris doctorate at his disposal. Soon after, he and Paula Hartley went into business together, opening their own law firm in Port Allen.

Tony handled personal injury, while Paula focused on family law. Their relationship blossomed, and the two married.

Clayton's reputation as a personal injury attorney had grown. He sometimes worked with other attorneys to earn huge compensations for clients, including a $21 million verdict for a client in Plaquemine, $11.4 million in a case out of New Orleans, and $8 million for a case in West Baton Rouge Parish.

And Tony Clayton's reputation as a trial lawyer has become even bigger. As the victories kept coming, he became known as the prosecutor who could get the job done, no matter how challenging the case. Because he threw himself wholeheartedly into anything he did, Clayton's life was a busy one. Days sometimes ran into each other as he moved between cases, his family, and civic activities that needed his attention. One of those activities included his role as the chairman of the Board of Supervisors of the Southern University System.

Although ambition was a strong driving force in this prosecutor's life, his successes always revolved around some form of justice. Even the release of the book he cowrote with Susan D. Mustafa and Sue Israel—*I've Been Watching You: The South Louisiana Serial Killer,* which was published again by Kensington Books under the new title *Blood Bath*—was about justice, about letting the world know the monster that was Derrick Todd Lee. That case affected Clayton more than most.

"Geralyn DeSoto (one of Lee's victims) lived just up the street from where I was raised in Addis. That brought her murder home to me. She was so young, and had so much to look forward to in her life. As Sheriff Mike Cazes, my boss, Ricky Ward, and I investigated her case, it became more and more personal. Afterward, so many people were asking me why Derrick Todd Lee did this, how he got into the homes of his victims, why he wasn't caught sooner. I wanted to provide those answers. I wanted people to experience the horror that he inflicted so that they would know how to better protect themselves. I wanted people to feel the loss of the victims. That's what the book is about. It's about surviving in a world filled with human depravity. It's about living in the world I have to deal with every day. It's not a pretty world sometimes, and this book brings that home."

Clayton earned a life sentence for Lee, but many of his trials are death penalty cases, and that has not been easy for the prosecutor. "It's almost like playing God. My job is to convince a jury to sentence someone to life in Angola or to death by lethal injection. That's not an easy thing to do, and each death penalty case must be given the utmost consideration. How do you decide if someone has the right to live? I struggle with that. But when you think about the young men and women who have been murdered in the most gruesome ways, their lives cut short because of the acts of another, you know that justice must prevail. The death penalty is a punishment under the law, and when a murderer commits acts that are sometimes beyond comprehension, I must pursue that sentence. It's the most difficult part of my job."

When Clayton investigated the Lee case, he was horrified by the brutality of Lee's murders, by the rage this killer had inside him. He thought it was the worst case he had ever seen. But that was before the Sean Gillis file hit his desk. Sean had been indicted for the second-degree murder of Joyce Williams on July 14.

"Can you believe this guy?" Tony Clayton said to Richie Johnson one afternoon. The two men had worked together for years—Johnson as investigator and a liaison between the sheriff's office and the district attorney's office, and Clayton as prosecutor. "Did you see that confession? It was unfreakin' believable. This guy is so sick," Clayton continued, wrinkling his nose in distaste and getting that look of determination in his eyes that often came when he was in pursuit of justice. The more horrific the crime, the steelier that look always got. "Are you sure there are no underlying felonies?" Clayton wanted to go for the death penalty.

"No," Johnson responded. "She got into his car willingly. He didn't kidnap her."

"Damn. This guy doesn't deserve to live. Did you see how he cut her up, had sex with her parts? Jesus! Did you see how he said it, like he was proud? This guy is sick," he repeated.

Disgusted, Tony Clayton knew he would have to try Sean Gillis on second-degree murder, which carries a life sentence upon conviction. He knew that Sean would be tried in East Baton Rouge Parish as well, but he also knew, as in the case of Derrick Todd Lee, that if he got Sean life, it would be easier for prosecutors in East Baton Rouge Parish to get him death. He was determined to get Sean to trial as soon as possible.

But that would not happen.

Kerry Cuccia, defense attorney and executive director of the Capital Defense Project of Southeast Louisiana, had taken on the case and would file motion after motion over the next few years to delay the trial and keep Sean Gillis out of Angola and away from death row.

An Unusual Trial Witness

Tony Clayton strode into the courtroom, confident as ever. He was trying Sean Gillis in the West Baton Rouge Parish courtroom in the Eighteenth Judicial District for the murder of Joyce Williams. He had no doubt that he would earn a life sentence for the serial killer, despite the fact that defense attorney Kerry Cuccia had been doing everything possible to delay the trial.

It had been going on for years. Sean had been arrested in 2004, and now it was 2007. Cuccia had filed motions asking that experts be allowed to test all of the evidence, motions that his experts be allowed to test the DNA, motions for a change of venue, motions to suppress evidence, motions that the confession be suppressed. He even had a hearing on whether the lights would be on in the courtroom during the trial. All the while, Cuccia maintained that Sean was innocent.

The confession said otherwise, and Cuccia was determined that no jury would ever hear it. He was confident that it would be thrown out because Sean had asked for an attorney on three occasions. Judge Robin Free saw things differently. "I thought it was admissible. It was a close call, not cut-and-dried," Free said. The judge had watched all forty hours of the videotape. "But he did reinstitute dialogue each time, which is the criteria. He wanted to keep talking." Free ruled that the confession could be used as evidence in the trial, but he sealed it to keep the media from releasing any of the details.

Kerry Cuccia took his fight to the Louisiana Court of Appeal, First Circuit. The court denied his request for review, refusing to even look at it. Cuccia was livid. He knew if a jury saw that confession, his client didn't stand a chance. Frustrated, he filed another motion. He was fighting two jurisdictions and was concerned about how he was going to save his client's life.

Cuccia was being paid by the hour by the state, and he certainly received the most money he could out of representing Sean Gillis. He had done the same thing in East Baton Rouge Parish by dragging the trial of Donna Bennett Johnston through year after year by filing motion after motion in hearing after hearing. Frustrated, Judge Robin Free had finally ordered Cuccia to stop playing games with the court, and a trial date had been set. But Cuccia had one more card up his sleeve. He made a motion that Tony Clayton be recused from the trial. He did not want to go up against the prosecutor who had never lost a murder trial. If he didn't do something drastic, Cuccia knew that Sean would spend the rest of his life in prison.

It was unheard of in West Baton Rouge Parish that a prosecutor could be called to testify as a witness in his own trial, but Clayton was ready. He had no doubt Judge Robin Free would see things his way.

"I call Tony Clayton to the stand," Cuccia said. Clayton smiled his big smile as he took his seat in the witness-box.

The courtroom was packed with staff from the courthouse and detectives who were not about to miss this show. They had heard Clayton was testifying in his own trial, and they knew this would be good.

"Were you a coauthor of the book *I've Been Watching You* (later published as *Blood Bath*) about serial killer Derrick Todd Lee?" Cuccia asked.

"Yes, I was," Clayton said, speaking directly into the microphone.

"And did you make money from that project?"

"Well, not really. I had a big investment in it. I'm still waiting to make my money back." Clayton laughed.

"In that book, did you write a chapter about Sean Gillis?" Cuccia persisted.

"Technically, no. Susan Mustafa wrote that chapter," Clayton said. Twitters of laughter could be heard through the courtroom. Clayton was enjoying himself.

"Where did she get her information?" Cuccia said.

"You'll have to ask her," Clayton responded. "She's just outside in the hall."

"Did you give her that information?"

"No. She gathered it on her own. I didn't know she had written about Sean Gillis until she showed me the rough draft of the manuscript."

"In the book, it states that Sean Gillis is guilty of the murders of eight women. How can you try this man when you have already determined he is guilty, when a book has been written with your name on it that states that?" Cuccia asked.

Clayton smiled. "Well, of course I think he's guilty. I'm a prosecutor. I'm trying him because I think he's guilty. I thought it then, and I think it now. I wouldn't be here if I thought he was innocent. That would be pretty shabby, don't you think, Mr. Cuccia? Let me just tell you something, Mr. Cuccia—your client, Sean Gillis, ice water runs through his veins. Goldfish stop swimming when he walks in a room, Mr. Cuccia. If you think he's innocent, you need to check yourself, Mr. Cuccia."

More laughter spilled through the courtroom. Cuccia continued to badger Clayton, asking the same things over and over again until two hours had passed. At times, Clayton raised his voice, tiring of the questioning that he felt was ridiculous, the look on his face telling observers that he thought Cuccia was a mental midget. There was no conflict of interest. He knew Sean Gillis was guilty, and he was determined to prove it. Finally, Kerry Cuccia said, "No further questions," and Tony Clayton was excused.

Outside the courtroom, Clayton was upset. He had no doubt that he would be able to continue with his case, but he couldn't believe he had been forced to defend himself like that. His animosity toward Cuccia had grown immensely over the past few hours.

"Personally, I didn't like the guy, and I'm sure the feeling was mutual. He was from one side of the tracks, and I was from the other. Just didn't like him, but I do recognize that he's a typical defense lawyer trying his best to save his boy's life," Clayton explained.

Susan Mustafa was called to testify next. A chill ran through her body as she walked toward the stand. Sean Gillis was sitting a few feet away, watching her as she walked. She could feel the evil that sat so close to her. She knew the things he had done better than most. She had researched him for years.

"Did you write this book with Tony Clayton and Sue Israel?" Kerry Cuccia asked, holding up the book.

"Yes, I did."

"And did you write a chapter on Sean Gillis?"

"Yes," Mustafa responded. She was nervous. She had never been on a witness stand in a criminal trial before, had never sat so close to a serial killer. She became more nervous when Cuccia began reading from the book.

"'Joyce Williams also knew that Sean had a dark side. She discovered it in 1999 right before he talked her into removing her hand from between the long zip tie he had wrapped around her neck, assuring her that if she moved it, he would remove the tie. As soon as she did, Sean pulled tight. The sounds of her dying didn't satisfy him. He sawed her leg off at the hip, then had sex with the severed end of it,'" Cuccia read.

Sean Gillis's gaze hardened as he stared at the woman on the stand. Susan Mustafa met his stare for a moment, then looked away.

"Where did you get this information?" Cuccia asked. "It was not in the public record."

Mustafa took a deep breath. She knew what could happen if she didn't answer. She was well aware that other journalists had gone to prison for refusing to answer that question.

"I will not answer that question," she said, taking a deep breath.

"What do you mean, you won't answer? You have to answer," Cuccia said.

"No, sir, I do not," Mustafa said.

"What makes you think you don't have to answer?" Cuccia said.

"Journalistic shield laws, sir. I do not have to reveal my sources."

"Judge, please direct the witness to answer the question," Cuccia said, looking at Free.

"Show me the relevance," Free responded.

"This is relevant to the fact that Tony Clayton should be recused for his participation in this book," Cuccia said.

"Not good enough," Free said. "I need more than that."

Cuccia directed his attention back to Mustafa. "Where did you get this information? Was it from East Baton Rouge Parish?"

"No, sir."

"Was it from West Baton Rouge Parish?"

"No, sir."

"Was it from the attorney general's office?"

"No, sir."

"Was it from the DA's office?"

"No, sir."

"Well, then, where did you get this information? Was it from sheriff's detectives?"

"No, sir. I am not going to tell you where I got the information," Mustafa repeated.

Cuccia was becoming frustrated. "You have to tell me. Judge, please instruct this witness to answer the question," he said loudly.

"I don't think I'm going to do that," Free said. "You have not shown me the relevance."

Mustafa breathed a huge sigh of relief. She knew that if the judge had instructed her to answer the question and she had not, she could have gone to jail until such time that she revealed her source. It had been a close call.

"I have no further questions," Cuccia said.

Susan Mustafa stepped down from the stand, feeling the eyes of a serial killer boring into her as she walked out of the courtroom. As she passed Kerry Cuccia, he grinned at her, almost as if admitting defeat in the battle of wills they had just had.

Judge Free ruled that Tony Clayton did not have to recuse himself from the case.

In August 2007, Sean Gillis pled guilty to the murder of Joyce Williams. He made a Crosby plea bargain, in which he could plead guilty but reserve the right to appeal based on the confession being allowed in as evidence. In return for his plea, Sean received a sentence of life imprisonment at the Louisiana State Penitentiary at Angola. Cuccia was not willing to take a chance against a prosecutor who had a perfect conviction rate, not with the confession in as evidence. That had the potential to bias a jury in East Baton Rouge Parish, where Sean would soon be tried in a death penalty case.

"Cuccia used so many deletory tactics to delay the trial," Tony Clayton remembered. "He's the first lawyer I've gone up against in my years of prosecuting who pled his client out to second-degree murder. He was concerned about the facts of the confession. It seemed hypocritical to me that he had claimed his client's innocence for years and then had him raise his right hand and say he was guilty. Why waste the state's money like that? Why not just have him plead guilty right away? It didn't make sense.

"And what about Joyce's family?" Clayton continued. "He robbed them of their right to know the details about what had happened to their mother, their sister, their daughter. He deprived them of the satisfaction of a trial, the closure it gives. This sure took the air out of my balloon."

A Judge's Perspective

Judge Robin Free has served for fourteen years in the Eighteenth Judicial District Court and has presided over two first-degree murder trials and two serial killer trials. Presiding in a tri-parish district, he serves the citizens of West Baton Rouge Parish, Iberville Parish, and Pointe Coupee Parish. Growing up in the town of Plaquemine—a town surrounded by chemical plants and filled with poor, blue-collar neighborhoods—Free was raised by his grandmother until he was seven years old. He moved back in with his mother then, and grew up the hard way, a poor white boy in a mostly black community. He was raised with the mantra "If you believe in something, you stand up for it," and he would take that mantra and live it through his adult years.

After graduating from LSU with a degree in accounting, Free worked as an accountant for a few years before following his calling and enrolling in Southern University Law School. After graduation in 1989, he worked in the West Baton Rouge District Attorney's Office and in private practice for six years before becoming a judge.

Dressed in his black robe, Free is an imposing figure when he sits on his bench. Tall, with brown hair and clear blue eyes, which inspire confidence, the judge is a handsome man with a strong chin and a forthright manner. Sitting on that bench is his way of putting into practice all he has learned about right and wrong throughout his life.

"When I became a judge, I wanted to change things. I have to try to fix things when I think they are wrong," he explained. "The problem is that it's bigger than I thought. I feel like I'm fighting this battle alone sometimes. I try to always be firm but fair, for the people, by the people. I base everything on criminal activity. I judge on that, not the person at the defense table's soul."

But for Free, that was not always easy. He had been the judge on every first-degree murder case in West Baton Rouge Parish since he became a judge. He had sentenced serial killers like Derrick Todd Lee, whose crimes could make your toes curl. He sentenced Andrew Morgan, a young man in Pointe Coupee Parish who had beaten an old man to death and had slit an old lady's throat. He had seen all of the terrible things that people could do to one another. Sometimes it got to him.

"You eventually just ask yourself, 'Are people just horrible?' At some point, I had a bad feeling about society in general. When people are happy, they don't come through your courtroom. I was jaded for a while," Free said. "I've seen a lot more than I want to see. It makes me worry about my family. The criminal world is different."

But then another criminal was taken off the street and put behind bars, and Free's optimism was restored. Until he dealt with killers like Sean Gillis and Derrick Todd Lee, and then he had to wonder about the state of humanity yet again. Each of these serial murderers killed numerous women, but they were so unlike in every way.

"Lee had more of an animalistic tendency. He was enraged. Fury drove him," the judge pontificated. "Derrick Todd Lee was an animal. Sean Gillis was a sick puppy. Once he got the taste of murder, he couldn't let go. The urge kept coming back. He was someone who was just curious about death. He was killing to see what was what. Lee had anger issues and was just plain mean. Gillis had more opportunity and was, therefore, more dangerous. He was mild-mannered, geekish, nonthreatening. That made women trust him enough to get in his vehicle."

But while Lee had never confessed to his murders, "Gillis wanted to plead guilty and take his medicine early on," Judge Free recalled. "He knew the gig was up. He wanted to 'fess up."

Kerry Cuccia would have none of that. He appealed Sean's plea agreement and subsequent sentence to the Louisiana Supreme Court, and in June 2009, the court refused to review it. In an article written by Steven Ward of *The Advocate,* an irate Cuccia said, *"It's tragic that on the eve of the 65th anniversary of D-Day, when sacrifices were made for people and their rights in the Constitution, that the Louisiana Supreme Court . . . said that the citizen Sean Vincent Gillis is not entitled to his rights under the Constitution."*

For Free, it was validation that he had made the right decision with regard to the confession. The higher court had not even looked at the question raised in the appeal.

The Wages of Sin Is Death

On the night of January 7, 1993, Warrick Dunn was at home watching his five siblings while his mother, Betty Smothers, moonlighted as a security guard for a local Piggly Wiggly food store. Warrick, the oldest child, often helped out around the house because his mother worked so hard to support her six children by herself. Betty, a corporal with the Baton Rouge Police Department, often took on security guard positions to make ends meet. While the children slept, Betty, along with a manager of the store, made her usual run to deposit the store's receipts for the day.

At 12:16 A.M., Betty drove into the drive-through lane at the Citizens Bank on Jefferson Highway in her marked police car. As the manager attempted to insert her key into the night deposit box, several men jumped out of the bushes and attempted to rob her. Angry when the manager refused to turn over the deposit bag, the men started shooting. Both women were hit multiple times as bullets sprayed through the doors of the car.

Betty was killed instantly. The manager, who had been

shot four times, grabbed the wheel, steering the car onto the highway and into the parking lot of a nearby Circle K, where a cashier called police. The robbers ran to a get-away car driven by a third man and escaped.

Warrick Dunn soon received the devastating news. His beloved mother was dead. Still a teenager, Warrick was left alone to raise his brothers and sisters. He did that, using all the morals and values his mother had taught him. The young man would go on to make a name for him-self—first as a running back at Florida State University, and later in the National Football League (NFL) with the Tampa Bay Buccaneers. For the next fifteen years, he would excel at football and parenting, all the while deal-ing with the trials and appeals of his mother's murderers.

Two days after the murder, a man named Eddie Paul called Crime Stoppers and admitted he had been involved in the murder. He implicated three other men—West Paul, who had driven the getaway car, Kevin Brumfield, and Henri Broadway, the triggermen. All were in their early twenties, and all would confess to the shooting. Prosecu-tor Prem Burns would be tasked with bringing Betty's killers to justice. West Paul plea-bargained for a twenty-five-year sentence and testified against his partners. Burns sought the death penalty for Brumfield and Broadway and won. Both men were sentenced to die.

Burns had been with the district attorney's office in Baton Rouge since 1975. In 1977, she became the first woman to try a felony case in East Baton Rouge Parish. At a time when women were not typically cast in the masculine role of the tough prosecutor, Burns's me-thodical approach to attaining justice soon earned her a reputation as being tough and thorough. She became known as "the Black Widow," because of her patient ap-proach. The beautiful, slender woman, her face accented by thick, shoulder-length black hair, slowly weaved a web around criminals—a web of facts and witnesses that made their escape from justice impossible. Her attack in the courtroom was often brutal, and she had no qualms about going for death. To the young prosecutor, the scales of justice had to be kept balanced, and criminals must be punished based on the severity of their crimes. If you killed a police officer on her watch, you were going to die. It was as simple as that.

But Betty Smothers wasn't Burns's first high-profile death penalty case. On February 19, 1986, as he sat in his vehicle, a government drug informant, Adler "Barry" Seal, was murdered in Baton Rouge by three Colombians associated with the Medellín drug cartel. He had been shot six times with a Mac-10 machine gun. Miguel Velez, Luis Carlos Quintero-Cruz, and Bernardo Antonio Vasquez were arrested for the murder.

Seal, a pilot who had earned millions by smuggling cocaine into the United States, was arrested in 1983. Instead of spending the rest of his life in prison, he turned informant, eventually helping federal authorities to arrest and convict numerous cocaine smugglers, as well as leaders of the cartel. Unhappy with this turn of events, the cartel placed a bounty on Seal's head—a half-million dollars to anyone who could keep Seal from testifying against yet another alleged cartel leader. For Jorge Ochoa, Quintero-Cruz (the triggerman), Velez (the driver), and Vasquez (the brains behind the assassination), that amount of money was too attractive to pass up. They traveled to Baton Rouge to murder the informant.

Unafraid, Prem Burns fought the federal government for the right to try the Colombians in her jurisdiction and won. On May 13, 1987, she had her biggest victory to date. All three men were sentenced to die in Louisiana's electric chair. Burns had fought the cartel and won, despite numerous threats to her life during the trial. *Parade* magazine named her one of "America's Toughest Prosecutors," a title usually reserved for men. Prem Burns had arrived!

Throughout her career, this deceptively sweet-looking woman would convict criminal after criminal. Her straightforward approach to dealing with juries, her obsessive attention to detail, her tender handling of victims and their families all contributed to propelling her career upward. Her love of the law and respect for justice kept her from going into private practice, where the monetary rewards for legal advice far outweighed the salary she earned as an assistant district attorney. She didn't care about the money. She cared about the satisfaction she felt when a criminal was put behind bars, when a family member of a murdered victim thanked her for a job well done.

By 2004, operating as section chief of the Special Investigations Division of the Office of the District Attorney for the Nineteenth Judicial District, Burns had become an expert at uncovering that one detail, that one clue that had been overlooked in the cases she tried. Her name was feared by defense attorneys who knew from experience they would have to step it up a notch if they wanted to win an acquittal for their clients. The little woman with the pretty face was a fearsome opponent in a courtroom, and if she went for death, murderers should prepare to die.

But all of that was before Sean Vincent Gillis was handed to her in a case file. Prem Burns was about to fight the longest, hardest battle she had ever fought to convict a killer.

A Barrage of Motions

On May 6, 2004, the Office of the Public Defender, Sean Gillis's court-appointed counsel, filed a motion that the office be withdrawn as counsel in the case. The motion cited several conflicts of interest, among them was the fact that the public defender's office had represented Donna Bennett Johnston on several occasions. At the time of her murder, she was still being represented and had an open case. The office had also represented two suspects in the murders of Hardee Moseley Schmidt and Ann Bryan. The motion stated that the public defender's office currently represented Derrick Todd Lee and, therefore, would be unable to provide an adequate defense for Sean Gillis. The judge agreed there was a conflict of interest and withdrew the court-appointed counsel.

Kerry Cuccia was ready and willing to step up to the plate.

Within weeks of Sean Gillis's arrest, Prem Burns and Kerry Cuccia were dancing a legal mambo, parrying back and forth with motions. Cuccia was an expert at filing motions, his requests detailed and lengthy and sometimes a waste of the court's time. But he had a lot on his hands—a murder indictment in West Baton Rouge Parish, another in Lafayette, and a death penalty case in East Baton Rouge Parish. He had to juggle all three, attending the numerous hearings for which he petitioned in three different cities. His office on Barrone Street in New Orleans was more than an hour's drive from the courthouses in downtown Baton Rouge and Port Allen, and more than two hours from Lafayette.

Cuccia had viewed his client's videotaped confession. He knew how gruesome and despicable his crimes had been. There could be no doubt his client was guilty, but it was Cuccia's job to keep him alive—no matter how many women Sean had killed. He was a specialist in death penalty cases, a firm believer that the state did not have the right to put people to death, and he defended his clients vigorously throughout his career. The notoriety he received from his cases did not hurt, either. But Cuccia genuinely believed that every client—no matter what crimes had been committed—deserved a thorough defense; and it was his job to provide that. Although he had defended many killers throughout his years as an attorney, Sean Gillis was by far the most challenging. South Louisiana was not the place to be a serial killer if you wanted to live after being caught.

Cuccia's strategy was simple—delay the trial as long as possible to keep his client off death row. He worried about the confession; he knew how damning it would be if a jury ever saw it. His job was to make sure that it would never be played for twelve of Gillis's peers. He had tried in West Baton Rouge, but the confession had been allowed in. He could not take that chance in East Baton Rouge Parish, not with Sean's life riding on it.

Motions to quash everything that could convict Sean

Gillis of Donna's murder began to appear regularly on Prem Burns's desk. Cuccia filed a motion to quash the indictment due to the unconstitutionality of the statute, a motion to quash the indictment pursuant to *Jones* v. *United States,* a DNA recovery request, a second request for discovery, disclosure, and inspection for the bill of particulars, a motion to disclose evidence favorable to the defendant under *Brady* v. *Maryland.*

The state refused to quash the indictment against Sean, but the prosecution was then ordered by the court to appear and show cause why the motion to disclose evidence should not be granted. The prosecution and defense would go back and forth over these issues for years.

On July 2, 2004, Prem Burns filed a notice of intent to seek the death penalty.

Soon after, Burns filed a motion for discovery. Kerry Cuccia responded that the defense had not decided which, if any, "books, papers, documents, photographs, tangible objects, copies, or portions thereof it intends to use as evidence at the trial." The defense noted that it could not make a substantive response. The motion also stated that the defense did not have any results of physical or mental exams, scientific tests, or experiments and could not provide those to the prosecution as of November 18, 2004.

In the motion for DNA discovery, Cuccia asked for the complete case file on Sean Gillis, the lab protocols, the chain of custody for all evidence, a list of the software programs used in DNA testing, the data files, the allelic frequency tables used in the testing of DNA, instances for unintended DNA transfer or sample contamination, accreditation of everyone who tested DNA, and background information on lab personnel. He intended to make sure that no evidence had been mishandled and that everyone who performed any kind of DNA testing was qualified. He was looking for anything that could get his client off on a technicality.

A second discovery motion was soon filed, which asked for all waiver-of-rights forms signed by Sean Gillis, the time that the statement Sean gave was ended, reports about Sean's statement prepared by Jeff Methvin, Todd Morris, and Jerry Mitchell, other tire receipts that were obtained from Goodyear, scientific reports that formed the basis of the warrant, diagrams of Ben Hur Road, the FBI's report on the tire tracks, and the search warrant for Goodyear. Cuccia also listed questions in the motion that he wanted answered by the prosecution:

> *What "thing of value" did Sean Gillis take in the armed robbery?*
> *Where was the "thing of value" when Sean Gillis took it? What did the victim do to maintain control of the "thing of value"?*
> *How did Sean Gillis get the "thing of value" in question? Was force used? Was intimidation used?*
> *Give a description of the dangerous weapon that Sean Gillis used to commit the armed robbery.*
> *Does the Law Enforcement Authority have that "dangerous weapon" in their care, custody, or control?*
> *If so, where was it found?*

The list went on:

> *Upon which section or sections under La. R.S. 14:44.1 (B) does the Prosecuting Authority rely? If it is La. R.S. 14:44.1 (B) (1), what was the address*

or location of the victim's seizure? What is the
address of the location where Sean Gillis carried
her?
If it is La. R.S. 14:44.1 (B) (2), where did Sean Gillis
entice the victim to go?
What did Sean Gillis offer as enticement?
If it is La. R.S. 14:44.1 (B) (3), when did Sean Gillis
imprison the victim? Or when was she secreted?
Where was the victim imprisoned or secreted? For
how long was she imprisoned or secreted?
What is the Prosecuting Authority's definition of a
hostage? Or a shield?
If it is La. R.S. 14:44.1 (A) 1, who did Sean Gillis
use the victim to shield himself from?
When did this event occur? Who were the witnesses
to this event?
If it is La. R.S. 14:44.1 (A) 2, then what felony was
the victim used to facilitate? Or what felony was
Sean Gillis fleeing from?
When did this event occur? Who witnessed this event?

The list went on and on, over page after page:

What is the Prosecuting Authority's definition of a
"dangerous weapon"?
What did Sean Gillis do to lead the victim to believe
he had a "dangerous weapon"?
Where did Sean Gillis conceal this "dangerous
weapon"?
If it is La. R.S. 14:44.1 (A) (3), when was the victim
physically injured? How long after this injury did
the victim die? Or when was she sexually abused?
What is the definition of sexually abused? How
long after the abuse did the victim die?

* * *

Prem Burns had just gotten a taste of how tedious the process of trying Sean Gillis would become. Kerry Cuccia was not going to overlook any small detail. But then, neither was Burns. This was a war, and life or death was on the line. Burns carefully prepared her response to all of Cuccia's questions.

In answer, Prem Burns wrote, *Videotaped statements made on April 28, 2004 in the interview room of the East Baton Rouge Parish Sheriff's Office in response to questioning by Jeff Methvin, Special Agent, Federal Bureau of Investigation and East Baton Rouge Parish Sheriff's Office Detective Bryan White and thereafter by Detective Max Schiele, East Baton Rouge Parish Sheriff's Office. The tape begins at 2:18 p.m. and concludes at 7:07 p.m.*

Each question was answered in the same manner, with only the date, time, and names of interviewing detectives changing. Every detail Cuccia needed was in the confession. But then he already knew that. He kept Burns bogged down in paperwork for years.

Three years after his arrest, Sean Gillis still sat in East Baton Rouge Parish Prison, awaiting trial, while the lawyers challenged each other's every move in preliminary hearings.

The next strategy for Kerry Cuccia was to challenge the underlying felonies. Prem Burns had cited two—armed robbery and kidnapping—in the death penalty case. Among the items listed that were stolen were a silver-and-black belt, a blanket, an earring back, Donna's severed arm, and the tattoo Sean cut from her thigh. Cuccia's partner, Steven Lemoine (no relation to Terri

Lemoine), argued in a pretrial hearing that body parts have no monetary value and, therefore, cannot be stolen. He said the other items were simply leftovers from the murder. Prem Burns argued that Sean Gillis didn't take the material things that most robbers take. He wanted body parts and stole them from the victims. She reminded the state judge Bonnie Jackson that the body parts had value to the victims.

Surprising everyone, Jackson ruled that in the state of Louisiana it is not a felony to steal body parts from a dead person, as they have no monetary value. However, the belt and other items did have monetary value; therefore, they could be used as an underlying felony.

Apparently, in Louisiana, a belt is worth more than an arm.

Cuccia had also motioned for the removal of the kidnapping charge. Lemoine argued that we could not possibly know if Gillis had coerced his victim into getting into his vehicle. Burns knew better. She had the letters Sean Gillis had written to Tammie Purpera. "He offered her money for sex, with no intent to have sex with the victim," she told the judge. She argued that Sean had tricked Donna into getting into his vehicle, which is tantamount to kidnapping.

This time, Jackson agreed with the prosecution, and the kidnapping charge stayed part of the indictment. Sean would be tried for first-degree murder and would be eligible for the death penalty if convicted.

Kerry Cuccia's next step was to try to have the confession suppressed. He filed another motion.

Contrary to what had happened in Judge Free's court, Judge Jackson agreed with the defense. Sean Gillis *had* asked for an attorney several times. The confession would not be allowed as evidence. This was a monumental victory for the defense, a staggering blow to the prosecution. If the jury did not see the videotapes, they would never understand the severity of the crimes or understand the pride Sean had taken in his handiwork. They would not be able to comprehend how heinously these women had been treated before and after their deaths. It was time for Prem Burns to regroup. She understood that her job had just gotten a lot harder.

Small Victories for
the Prosecution

Prem Burns would have her victories, though.

The Advocate reporter Josh Noel, who now works for
the *Chicago Tribune,* had refused to testify for the prosecution. Sean Gillis had confessed to Josh on July 12,
2004, in an interview soon after he had been incarcerated.
Josh had reported in *The Advocate* that Gillis had told him
that the women "were already dead to me." He had said
that maybe it was stress that caused him to kill, that he
hadn't killed for five years after Ann's murder because
he was working nights at Circle K, and he was happy then.

In Louisiana, journalists have conditional privilege,
which means that unless ordered to do so by a judge, they
do not have to disclose the identity of a source or information obtained from that source. As a matter of law, reporters can submit an affidavit to the required testimony
instead of testifying in person.

Prem Burns filed a subpoena compelling Josh Noel to
testify. She noted that because the confession had been

ruled inadmissible, Noel's testimony had become that much more important. Burns argued that she could not get this information from any other source; therefore, privilege should not apply.

Judge Jackson agreed and compelled Josh Noel's testimony, limiting its scope, however, to only the information that had been published in the article. Prem Burns had cleared that hurdle and went on to the next.

She filed a Prieur motion in the hopes that evidence from the other cases would be allowed in the penalty phase of the trial to show a pattern of behavior. A Prieur motion allows a prosecutor to use prior bad acts, even if the defendant has not been convicted of those acts, to show a jury that the defendant has committed similar acts before. She hoped that a jury would see Sean Gillis as a methodical killer who planned each murder carefully. She couldn't hope to accomplish that if other murders were not used to establish the pattern.

In her motion, Prem Burns stated that the cause of death in the Katherine Hall case was *exsanguination due to laceration of the internal jugular vein.* She noted that Hall had suffered numerous stab wounds to her body, including lacerations to her left eye. She pointed out that a ligature mark had been discovered on Katherine's neck, and twenty-one postmortem wounds had been listed in the autopsy. *A pubic hair with root was found in Hall's mouth,* Burns wrote.

Burns further explained that the hair yielded a profile consistent with that of Sean Vincent Gillis.

She noted that Sean had confessed that murder to Terri Lemoine and Josh Noel, as well as members of law enforcement.

She moved next to Johnnie Mae Williams, explaining that multiple blunt-force trauma had been listed as the cause of Johnnie Mae's death, and the back of her body, her buttocks, and her legs had sustained "sharp-force postmortem injuries." Burns noted that the body was severely decomposed and her face unrecognizable. Johnnie Mae's hands had been amputated postmortem. *A hair was recovered from a cut on the left distal radius at the LSU FACES lab, which produced DNA consistent with Sean Vincent Gillis,* Burns asserted in the motion.

She then explained what had happened to Donna Bennett Johnston—how the manner in which she was killed, the postmortem dismemberment, and the ligature marks created a signature of a serial killer.

In terms of establishing the killer's identity and further rebutting any proffered claim of mental incapacity, the killer's modus operandi is germane and unique to the point that his homicides of women leading high risk lifestyles may be deemed signature crimes. Indeed, the similarities between the three murders, even prior to the obtaining of a common genetic profile, led law enforcement to believe they were dealing with a serial killer. That Gillis was able to kill the three women over a period of sixty-one months and avoid apprehension is further relevant evidence of his actual mental state, the prosecutor wrote.

Donna Bennett Johnston, Katherine Ann Hall, and Johnnie Mae William each lived a "high-risk lifestyle" engaging in street-level prostitution in order to support alcohol and/or drug addiction habits. Each victim was screened and ultimately selected in part due to small physical size and the inability to resist the physical attack due to alcohol and/or drug impairment. The three victims were further selected as each was believed to be a dispensable human being and less likely to be reported a missing person.

The clothing and property of each victim were in part taken in order to prevent or delay identification, she went on. *Each victim was physically carried to a remote area and therein disposed. Lastly, extensive post-mortem mutilations in the forms of sharp cuttings occurred in each case. Outright amputations occurred in the homicides of Donna Bennett Johnston and Johnnie Mae Williams. It is submitted that the homicides of these three women are the unique signature crimes of one serial killer.*

Burns submitted that it was important that the jury know about the other victims, as to interpose any guilt phase mental defense.

Judge Jackson agreed. The state deemed the motion good and sufficient. The other victims would become part of the trial. Since the confession had been tossed, this was a major victory for the prosecution.

But there had been an error in judgment. The two victims who could have pulled harder at the jury's heartstrings were mysteriously omitted from the Prieur motion. The murders of Ann Bryan, elderly and safely tucked in her bed, and Hardee Moseley Schmidt, beloved wife and mother run down in her own neighborhood, were much more likely to affect a jury than the murders of drug-addicted prostitutes.

The prosecution did not include those murders because there was no DNA evidence to tie those women to Sean. But there was one vital clue that had surfaced in Ann Bryan's case. As investigators for the district attorney combed through the crime scene photos of each victim, a clue that had been overlooked or considered irrelevant back in 1994 was discovered. In a picture of the bedroom where Ann had been so viciously brutalized, investigators noticed a nylon zip tie on the floor. Police back then had no reason to think that clue was anything important, but now they knew it was Sean's weapon of choice. It had become much more significant and could have been used as evidence to link Ann's murders with the others. Had the jury heard about how Ann was murdered, they might have had a little more empathy for the victims.

It was not to be.

As 2008 rolled around, a trial date, February 25, had finally been set. Almost four years had passed, and Prem Burns was more than ready to try this case and put Sean Gillis on death row. She had spent years getting to know the families of the victims. It didn't matter to her that they were prostitutes. They were women—women who had been loved by their families, women who did not deserve to die in such a shocking way simply because a demented man had developed a fascination with the dead.

While her demeanor was rather severe in a courtroom, Burns always had a gentle smile, a caring touch, when she dealt with the families. She knew what they had been through, how their lives had been forever changed. She wanted to give them justice. She would have to wait a few more months.

One of the psychologists, a Yale professor who had been hired to examine and diagnose Sean Gillis for the defense, was suffering from heart problems and had to postpone the examinations.

A new trial date was set.

The Day of Reckoning
Is Upon Us

On July 21, 2008, a sunny day in southern Louisiana, courtroom 601 in the Governmental Building on St. Louis Street, in downtown Baton Rouge, filled up quickly.

Norman Gillis, holding a Bible by his side, head down, hurried to his seat, hoping no one would stop him. Yvonne Gillis, a nervous look on her face, followed. The two had been brought back together in the same room after so many years apart by the crimes of their son. Neither could believe what had happened. Neither understood what had gone wrong. Sean had always been so fun-loving, a good Catholic boy. Each blamed the other. And themselves.

Virginia Valentine and her sister, Patricia Dawson, both dressed to the nines, sat down and looked around. They knew the people in the courtroom would hear about their sister Lillian's lifestyle. They were determined to show that she had come from a good family.

Justin Bennett, his wife, Casie, and their children filed in behind them. Michael Bennett rolled his wheelchair to the end of the churchlike pew, where Justin sat. Michael had been stabbed during an argument in a Burger King parking lot and had been paralyzed. He knew what a knife ripping through skin felt like. For the next week, he would hear every detail about how his mother had been cut up after her death. Those details were hard for him to hear. He knew better than most the fear she must have felt.

Jimmy Johnston stood in the hallway, hands in pockets, lines creasing his brow. He didn't want to be here, either. He and Donna had shared a tumultuous past, but he had cared about her and couldn't stand to watch his children be put through this trial.

Johnnie Mae Williams's children came in next. Lauren looked anxious. She couldn't wait to see, up close and personal, the face of the man who had been her mother's friend. She wanted to confront him, to ask him why he had done this to her family. She was more than ready to do battle for her mother. Her brother, Larry, seemed unsettled. He didn't want to be there, but he had to be. He had to be strong for his family. Jena simply could not attend. She couldn't bear the thought of looking at her mother's killer, of hearing the details about what had happened to her. It was all too much.

A slew of reporters quickly scooped up the remaining seats. Stone Grissom, then news anchor for NBC-TV, channel 33, and an expert in law, had his pen and notebook ready. He wasn't going to miss a moment of this trial. Stone had worked as a legal analyst for Court TV and other news stations across the country. He had covered many high-profile cases, such as "the Green River Killer," aka Gary Ridgway, the capture of Saddam Hussein, and charges against Michael Jackson and Scott Peterson. As an attorney, he had specialized in civil rights litigation, but was particularly interested in criminal defense. Stone couldn't wait for the trial to begin, even if he already knew what the outcome would be. Sean Gillis was the sickest killer he had ever covered, and Stone had no doubt that Gillis would die by lethal injection.

An air of tension permeated the courtroom—anticipation about what would be revealed, fear about what would be revealed. Everyone knew they were about to watch a train wreck, but this time their loved ones had been on the train.

Prem Burns walked in, confident and smartly dressed as always, wearing a beige linen suit and matching shoes. She smiled at family members of the victims as she made her way to the prosecution table at the front of the room. She did not appear nervous as her eyes scanned the papers scattered across the table. As always, Prem was prepared.

Kerry Cuccia, dressed in a blue suit that stretched over his massive frame, paced back and forth, conferring in a whisper with Steven Lemoine. There was no love lost between the two men. Their personalities clashed. Cuccia was more abrasive, whereas Lemoine was soft-spoken, milder. Lemoine had tried to resign from this case, stating that he could not work with Cuccia. In an affidavit, he cited long-standing conflicts with Cuccia, an abusive work environment, and that Cuccia's behavior was erratic. Judge Jackson refused his request.

A few weeks before the trial, Lemoine had filed another motion, asking the judge to reconsider her decision. She refused. Steven Lemoine would have to defend Sean Gillis with Kerry Cuccia, even though the men had experienced "extremely serious work-related differences." Several months before the trial, Steven Lemoine had resigned from the Capital Defense Project, of which Cuccia was executive director, because he could not stand to work with Cuccia. On this day, though, there was no sign of discord between the men, and they whispered to each other about their opening argument.

A door on the right side of the room opened, and Sean Gillis, sporting long sideburns, graying hair, and glasses, dressed in a wrinkled blue suit, was escorted in. As he walked to his seat at the defense table, he smiled and nodded when he saw his mother and father. His eyes scanned the courtroom, looking for Terri. His smile widened when he saw her. "Hi," he mouthed. Terri smiled back.

"All rise. The Nineteenth Judicial Court is now in session. The Honorable Judge Bonnie Jackson presiding."

Judge Jackson, a petite woman whose flawless brown skin and sympathetic eyes were capped by short-cropped hair, took her place behind the bench. From her regal position, she could watch the jury, the witnesses, the defendant. Jackson was known for keeping a tight rein on her courtroom. There would be no theatrics here.

The trial had begun. Kerry Cuccia could do nothing to stop it now.

Cuccia immediately expressed concern about articles and photographs, especially ones of postmortem cuttings, that had run in the newspaper. "The article that ran yesterday talks about Mr. Gillis confessing to the murders of eight women. It says he pleaded guilty in Port Allen. It talks about Johnnie Mae Williams. I feel this makes having an impartial jury impossible. Can we question the jury about whether they saw the articles?"

"Bring in the jury," the judge instructed.

Jackson individually polled the jurors about if they had heard any comments about the trial.

"Yes," said the first juror.

"No."

"No."

"No."

"No."

"No."

"No."

"No."

"No."

"Yes," said the tenth juror.

"No."

"No."

"Were the comments critical?" Judge Jackson asked Mr. Hall, the first juror.

"Matter of fact," Hall responded.

Cuccia stepped in. "How many times were you asked about the trial?"

"Three, maybe four," Hall said.

Mr. Odom, the tenth juror, stood up. "I heard someone say there were seven men and four women. They were talking about it amongst themselves."

"Have you seen anything in the media?" Judge Jackson asked.

"I saw a headline in the newspaper at Walmart in a case by the deli," Odom said. "I remember seeing this gentleman's photograph and something about the supreme court."

Cuccia stood up. "I reurge a motion for a change of venue. I realize these comments of the jurors seem insignificant, but I urge that we move this out of Baton Rouge."

"The remarks overheard were innocuous," Prem Burns retorted. "These jurors were painfully honest to even mention them."

Sean Gillis watched with interest. He had always been fascinated by the legal process.

Judge Jackson agreed with Burns and swore in the jury.

Opening Statements

Bonnie Jackson explained the charges against Sean Gillis. She told jurors that Gillis was charged with the first-degree murder of Donna Bennett Johnston. She defined first-degree murder as the killing of another human being with specific intent and an underlying felony—in this case, armed robbery and second-degree kidnapping.

After further defining the charges, Prem Burns began to tell the story of the last moments of Donna's life. The jury listened carefully as she described how Donna's body had been found on Ben Hur Road, just blocks from Sean Gillis's home. "She was totally nude, her buttocks up in the air, her right arm covered by her jacket, her left arm cut off at the elbow. Flesh was missing from her thigh. Ligature marks were on her neck. Blood and a piece of bone were found near her body. Tire tracks were found nearby.

"The cause of death was asphyxia by ligature strangulation with an object, a zip tie. Strangulation caused hemorrhage to her eyes and neck muscles. There were numerous postmortem wounds," she told the jury.

Burns explained that methamphetamine was found in Donna's blood and that her alcohol level was .22, three times the legal limit.

"She was a forty-three-year-old mother of five children," Burns said. "She was the daughter of Mrs. Johnnie Bennett. She had battled drug and alcohol addiction for years. Donna was a street prostitute and had arrests for cocaine possession and prostitution. On May 4, 2004, she was laid to rest at St. Joseph's."

Burns, sometimes looking at the jury over the top of her fashionable hard-rimmed glasses, explained how on April 28, 2004, Detective Jeremy Schiro, with the Baton Rouge Police Department, had gone to Sean Gillis's house and had learned that Sean had stopped to urinate at the site of the murder a week before Donna was found. She told them that Sean had agreed to a voluntary buccal swab. "He even inquired about employment with the FBI," she said. "Clippings from Donna's fingernails and swabbings from the area of her arm—where it had been severed— had been sent to the Louisiana State Police Crime Lab. Those swabbings and clippings lived on to identify her killer."

She explained how Van Calhoun had focused on a tire track and traced it to its origins. "And in a gray Mazda van behind Sean Gillis's house, we found a silver-and-black belt that belonged to the victim's daughter, Savannah. We found forty-five pictures of the victim that had been deleted from his computer. We found a picture of Donna in the trunk of his car with a nylon zip tie still tightened around her neck. Another picture after it was removed. There was a picture of a blue tattoo on her thigh. Then another of her back in the trunk with her nipples and tattoo removed. There was a picture of a man's hand touching her breast and vagina. Others showed just her vaginal area. In this trunk, police found the backing to her earring and a fingernail. The DNA that Detective Schiro obtained from under that fingernail was consistent with the defendant's."

Burns told the jury that Sean had written three letters to Tammie Purpera while in prison, letters that explained how the murder had been committed. She said that he had confessed to his girlfriend, Terri.

"On February twenty-sixth, between three and four in the morning, Sean Gillis was looking for someone to kill. He found Donna on the corner of Prescott and Geronimo streets. He never intended for her to leave that car alive. When she closed that door, she was already dead.

"In the ninety seconds it took for her to succumb to unconsciousness, she fought and struggled. 'I can't breathe' were her last words," Burns continued, painting a picture of terror for the jury. "He took her valuables, her belt. He photographed her. He took her tattoo, her arm, even her nipples. Then he put her in Ben Hur Canal like a piece of disposable trash."

Burns did not tell the jury that Sean had eaten some of his victim's flesh. She couldn't. That had come out in the confession, and the jury would never be allowed to hear him describe such incomprehensible acts. They would never see him grinning about what he had done.

Prem concluded her twenty-seven minute argument with "The case against Sean Vincent Gillis has been made by Sean Vincent Gillis with his own DNA, in the pictures he deleted, in his own handwriting in those letters. This murder was well planned, well conceived, well executed. In this case, armed robbery and kidnapping are both underlying felonies."

Kerry Cuccia jumped up. "Judge, I move for a mistrial.

This court has previously ruled that you cannot rob body parts."

"Denied," Jackson said.

A juror passed a note to the bailiff. The judge asked the juror to stand.

"I know Jeremy Schiro," a gray-haired female juror said. "He's my husband's first cousin. We see him about once a year at family gatherings. It's been about a year and a half since I've seen him. We have not had any conversations about this case."

"When do you see him?" Cuccia asked.

"Birthdays, Christmas," the juror responded. "I don't think it will affect me."

"If his testimony turns out to be key in this case, is there a chance you would be more apt to believe the testimony?" Cuccia questioned.

"Yes," the juror said.

"Your Honor, I move to excuse this juror."

Jackson excused the juror. The jury was down to twelve members, with no alternates. It was a tenuous situation. If another juror knew any of the witnesses, a mistrial would result.

It was Kerry Cuccia's turn to address the jury.

"We agree that we are all here to follow the law. The one thing we started with is an explanation of five grades of killing. Just because someone kills someone does not mean the crime is first-degree murder. There was no pre-meditation. In Louisiana, we have specific intent, which shares second-degree and first-degree murder," Cuccia explained.

Cuccia displayed a PowerPoint presentation that ex-plained how the killer had to be engaged in the perpetration of second-degree kidnapping and armed robbery, in this case, to be eligible for the death penalty.

"For second-degree murder, the penalty is life without parole. For first-degree murder, the penalty is life or death," he said.

Cuccia smiled at the jury. He wanted jurors to feel like he was their friend. He was an expert at this. In all of his years as an attorney, no client of his had ever been sentenced to death. While Burns's approach was no-nonsense and firm, Cuccia appeared more laid-back, and he tried hard to simplify the law so they could understand the distinctions.

"You are going to hear testimony that Mr. Gillis killed Donna Bennett Johnston. You will hear about after-death cuttings on bodies. Photos you see might shock you, offend you, repulse you. But there is no evidence of first-degree murder. Not one of those photos will be a 'plus factor.' The prosecution has to prove that this was done during a second-degree kidnapping or an armed robbery. You may say, 'What sick mind can do these things?' Don't let these photos cloud your judgment. It's not an element of first-degree murder. Both offenses have to be separate and distinct from the homicide. You may have second-degree murder or homicide, but not first-degree murder," Cuccia said.

The burly lawyer's opening statement was short and sweet, barely ten minutes. He did not want to overstate his case, preferring instead to save his arguments for later.

Sean Gillis had sat quietly, watching intently, not wanting to miss any detail of the proceedings. This was his day in the sun, his time to shine as everyone learned how meticulous he could be when it came to the slaughter of a human being.

Witnesses for the State

A slide projector was turned on, and pictures illuminated on a screen in the courtroom depicted the horror that was the end of Donna Bennett Johnston's life. Those in the courtroom couldn't see because the screen was strategically placed in front of them facing the judge and jury. Sean Gillis could see the screen behind him, and although he had not turned around once during opening statements, he turned around when those pictures were displayed. He looked at every one of them, his face carefully concealing his emotions as he relived his fantasy yet again. He couldn't hide it completely, though. Every now and then, a small smile would appear as the pictures of Donna in his trunk, Donna with her limb removed, Donna's skin underneath his hand, were revealed to the twelve men and women who would determine his fate.

The jurors were not looking at Sean. They were looking at the most horrific images they had ever seen. Several had physical reactions; one male juror fought back tears. Some simply looked away after a first quick glance, the pictures too gruesome to view. These images were the kind that could steal innocence, the kind that would never go away.

Prem Burns knew that if she wanted to win a death penalty verdict, she would have to go on the offense. She would have to make sure that the jury understood the depravity associated with this case. She worried, though, because the victim was a prostitute. From experience, she knew that jurors do not value some lives as much as the lives of others. She was aware that Kerry Cuccia would do everything he could to play up the fact that Donna was on drugs, that she was an alcoholic, a prostitute. She was determined that she would beat him to the punch.

It was like putting a puzzle together. First she had to familiarize the jury with the crime and then let them get to know the victim before adding each individual piece of evidence to create a finished product. In most cases, it's easy to get the jury to sympathize with the victims. That had happened when John Sinquefield, her former boss, had tried Derrick Todd Lee. The victims then had been beautiful, valued members of society. Jurors had felt their loss. With Donna, that would be more difficult. Jurors did not care about hookers. It was simply the way it was.

Burns would do her best to try to make them care.

Van Calhoun was called to the stand. Broad-shouldered, with short brown hair and a reddish complexion, he exuded confidence as he took his seat and raised his right hand.

Burns asked him about his credentials. He explained that he was a crime scene technician for the Allen Police Department in Texas, but he had worked with the East Baton Rouge Parish Sheriff's Office for more than nine years.

"Describe your job for the court," Prem Burns said.

"I document crime scenes and collect and process

evidence," he said. "I walk through the scene detecting evidence, then photograph, videotape, take measurements, and collect evidence for storage and further processing at the Louisiana State Police Crime Lab."

"And did you document the crime scene in Donna Bennett Johnston's murder?"

"Yes. I arrived on Ben Hur Road at nine-seventeen that morning. The weather was cool and clear. It hadn't rained that day. We did a walk-through around the body."

Burns showed the jury photographs of the area. Again, Sean turned around, very interested in the pictures. For a moment, he turned away, but he couldn't help himself. He looked again. This time, the jurors were looking back and forth from the pictures to Sean Gillis.

Calhoun pointed out for the jury where the tire tracks were as Burns showed them pictures, passing them to the jury so they could take a closer look. They took more time with the photographs of the tire tracks than they had with the more grisly pictures of Donna.

"We processed the body at the crime scene," Calhoun explained. "We took buccal swabs of her shoulder, ankles, wrist, buttocks, any contact point where someone would drag you, any area that would be a sexual area."

He went on to describe the positioning of her body and the parts that were missing. Kerry Cuccia fanned himself with some documents, making no objections. Judge Jackson yawned. Sean Gillis listened carefully, his eyes on the witness.

"We made casts of the tire prints with dental stone and pulled impressions from them," Calhoun went on. "The area was full of debris, and any debris in the prints will stay in them. We also did a rape kit and fingerprinted her hand."

"How did you identify the tires?" Burns queried.

"I sent the castings to the crime lab, but I had already

identified what kind they were—watching too much TV. I had seen Aquatred commercials and remembered them."

Burns, questioning Calhoun from her seat, asked him to go through the whole process to convince the jury that all evidence had been properly obtained and documented. Although tedious testimony, it left no room for error.

Cuccia had only a few questions.

"What is your education?" he asked.

Calhoun told him that he had attended LSU and had received training at the state crime lab and with the sheriff's office. He told Cuccia that he had no medical training.

Cuccia focused on the swabbings, and Calhoun explained again which areas he had swabbed. He said that DNA did not come from only blood and bodily fluids, it could also come from skin cells as well.

After a few more questions about how fingernail scrapings are conducted, Cuccia excused Van Calhoun.

Andrew Bergeron, a photographer with the East Baton Rouge Parish District Attorney's Office, then told the court that he had taken aerial photographs of the area around Ben Hur Road. He identified photographs 1 through 7 as the ones he had take from a Louisiana State Police helicopter. "We took photographs from Highland Road and West Lee to south of West Lee to the water tower at Highland and Ben Hur and north to LSU, west to the river and east to the interstate," he said. "We saw the areas that had been photographed by the sheriff's office. We alternated between five hundred and a thousand feet while taking the pictures."

Prem Burns showed the pictures to the jury; then she called Donna's former husband to the stand.

* * *

Jimmy Johnston testified that he had been married to Donna for ten years. "She was addicted to alcohol and cocaine," he said. He told the jury that he could not take being married to her after that, but that they had more children together after their divorce. He said that his daughter, Savannah, lived with him then, but that his son Jesse lived with Donna's mother.

"When did you last see her?" Prem Burns asked.

"It was a Monday. I remember it very well. She came to the shop and asked for money. I refused to give it to her."

"Was Donna a street prostitute?" Burns questioned.

"Yes."

"Did Savannah and Donna share clothes?" Burns asked.

"All the time," Jimmy said.

Burns showed him a black belt with holes lined in silver that had been introduced into evidence.

"Is this your daughter's belt?"

"Yes," Jimmy said. "It was purchased by a girl I was dating. I've seen Donna wearing that belt."

Burns tendered the witness.

"How do you know this belt is Savannah's?" Kerry Cuccia asked.

"I think Savannah's was older and rougher-looking," Jimmy said.

"Is it her belt?" Cuccia persisted.

"It looks like it is." Jimmy didn't sound as sure as before. Cuccia had made his point.

Willie Banks would then testify that he had seen Donna the night before she died, just off Plank Road.

He explained that he had given her a ride and then dropped her off on Winnebago Street. "I was only with her about ten minutes," he said.

Kerry Cuccia established in his cross-examination of Willie that when they stopped at the store, Donna had bought a glass container with a rose in it, which is commonly used to smoke crack cocaine. He would not miss an opportunity to remind the jury that Donna used crack.

Donna's friend, Brenda, was then called. "I knew Donna for six years," she said.

"Did you know her to be a street prostitute?" Prem Burns asked.

"Yes," Brenda said.

"Did she drink a lot?" Burns prompted.

"All day, every day," Brenda said.

"When was the last time you saw her?"

"Around nine, the night of her murder. She was kinda drunk and wanted me to walk to the store with her."

"What was she wearing?"

"Blue jeans, a black belt. She had her son's baby blanket with her. I thought it was weird. She told me, 'Well, if anything happens to me, tell my kids I love them.'"

After excusing Brenda, Burns called Frankie Caruso, a narcotics officer for the Baton Rouge Police Department, to the stand. As he walked to his place near the microphone, it was easy to see that Caruso, who had been with the department for more than twenty years, would be very attractive to the hookers who worked the area he watched, more than any other, in Baton Rouge. Slender and muscular, with wavy brown hair, a moustache, and a goatee, Caruso didn't look like a police officer. It would be easy for this good-looking man to get the prostitutes to approach him just before he busted them.

"I've made many arrests on Mohican and Geronimo Streets," he explained to the jury. "The prostitutes operate on the streets or in houses. I've known Donna for ten or fifteen years, since the early nineties. She had a history of prostitution in North Baton Rouge. She was addicted to crack and a heavy drinker. Most of the prostitutes work after two in the morning when the bars close. We often do sting operations, and sometimes male undercover officers pick up prostitutes, while female officers pick up johns. It's done both ways all the time."

Caruso didn't mention that Donna sometimes worked as an informant, helping officers to arrest drug dealers in the area, and Burns didn't ask.

Instead, she called Jerry Harrison, who was by now retired from the state police crime lab, to the stand. Harrison testified that he had examined Donna's body fluids for controlled dangerous substances. "Her blood alcohol level was .22," he said, explaining that was almost three times the legal limit.

Burns had accomplished what she had set out to do. She had established that Donna was a prostitute, a drug addict, that she drank excessively. She had effectively thwarted any strategy Kerry Cuccia may have had of making the victim look bad. Burns had done it for him. Now she could get on with the business of making the jury understand that murder was murder, no matter what kind of lifestyle the victim had lived.

From her seat near the back of the courtroom, Lynne Marino, mother of Derrick Todd Lee victim Pam Kinamore, felt bad. She knew all too well how the murder of a child affects a mother, a sister, a friend. She didn't want to be there, but she felt she needed to be a victim's advocate. She hoped that her presence would bring some comfort to members of the families whose lives had been so altered by a serial killer. But the trial was bringing back memories, some too painful to bear. She gathered her strength and debated whether she could return the next day. Lynne knew better than most that this kind of pain, these pictures, this testimony, would never go away. It would linger in the hearts and minds of the families, waking them up at night, for many years to come. She said a silent prayer for all of them.

An Explanation of Evil

Over the next few days, a bevy of witnesses for the state would relay to the jury all of the information the state had spent four years collecting. Prem Burns's meticulous attention to detail would lay out a very persuasive argument. Climatologists discussed weather conditions the week of the murder, Department of Motor Vehicles (DMV) personnel verified Sean Gillis's vehicle registrations and license plates, the attorney general's office established that it was an eighth of a mile between Sean's home and Ben Hur Road. Nothing was considered inconsequential. Burns's reputation had been built on her ability to be methodical, and she was determined to win this case. She wanted to make sure that jurors didn't see a normal-looking defendant when they glanced at Sean. She wanted them to see the evil that sat in front of them calmly talking and laughing with his attorney.

Outside the courtroom, before court was in session and during breaks, the atmosphere was thick with tension. Some victims' family members intently watched Yvonne and Norman Gillis, wondering how they could have brought such evil into the world. Norman sat alone, for the most part, reading his Bible and trying to ignore the stares. Lauren Williams talked to Yvonne occasionally, trying to get answers she so desperately needed. Justin Bennett played with his children, wishing the ordeal would be over soon. Lillian Robinson's sisters talked quietly with one another as they sat on a bench. Print and broadcast journalists compared notes and discussed the jury's reactions to the photographs they had seen. Jim Shannon, a reporter with WAFB who had won numerous Associated Press awards for in-depth reporting, watched everyone in the waiting area, taking notes about how the victims' families and Sean's family were dealing with the pressure of the trial.

Yvonne and Norman were allowed occasionally to visit with Sean before the trial resumed each day. They treasured these special moments. Norman was convinced that his son had been placed in prison so that he could minister to other prisoners whose souls needed saving. He was proud that his son had turned his life around, but he was afraid that he would be put to death by the state. Yvonne, too, was petrified that would happen. Sean was still her little boy—no matter what he had done—and no mother wants to know that her child is going to die. She nervously chatted with friends as she waited for the trial to begin each morning. Sometimes Terri Lemoine sat with her, and the two reminisced about old times. Hearing the testimony each day was beyond difficult for both women, but Sean needed them now. More than he ever had before.

Everyone waited anxiously for the door to room 601 to open each day, recognizing as they filed into the courtroom that the nightmare was about to begin once again. And each day, it seemed to get worse.

* * *

On the second day of the trial, James Andernann and Lauren Keller testified. Lauren told jurors how she and James had been out on the morning of February 27, 2004, looking for their dog, when they saw what looked to be a body on the edge of the Ben Hur Canal.

"We backed up and got out of the car. She wasn't moving, and we realized she was real. We called 911."

"Is this what you saw?" Prem Burns asked, showing her a picture of Donna near the canal.

"Yes," Lauren said.

"Did the police check the tires of your Cavalier?"

"Yes, they did," Lauren responded.

Burns called James Andernann to the stand. She asked him to identify the photograph of where the body was found. "Yes, that's it," James verified.

"No questions," Kerry Cuccia said.

The district manager of Goodyear next told the jury that the company kept records for seven years on all tires sold. He said that Sean had bought the tires June 24, 2003.

Max Schiele, coordinator of the task force, described how the list of owners of the Aquatred tires had more than one thousand names, but Goodyear had narrowed it down to less than a hundred after the size of the tire was determined.

"Sean Gillis was on that list," he said. "We divided the list up between task force members and went door-to-door asking people to let us swab them for DNA. The defendant's name was on the list given to Agent Methvin."

Agent Jeff Methvin explained that he had called Sean Gillis and set up a meeting with him. "Me and Jeremy Schiro drove up in a Dodge Durango. We had our weapons at our side, but we did not draw them. Sean was on the back patio. His vehicle was parked in the driveway. We brought up Donna Bennett Johnston and where her body had been found. He related to us that he was there the Saturday or Sunday before we found her. Schiro produced a form for him to sign. He was advised he could refuse. He took the time to read the form before he signed it. Schiro used a buccal swab to obtain DNA. As we were leaving, we talked about the way he plays computer games. He mentioned that he would like to work with the FBI, catching computer hackers. After we left, I delivered the sample to the sheriff's office."

Methvin told the jury that they decided to reinterview Sean based on their conversation and went back to his home and asked him to come with them to the sheriff's office. "I drove him," Methvin said. "He sat in the front passenger side."

Methvin elaborated on the details of the interview, stating that Sean did not seem inebriated or under the influence of any drugs and that he did not ask for an attorney.

Prem Burns then played the video of that interview for the jury. Because Sean Gillis had not yet asked for an attorney and was not under arrest, this part of his interrogation was allowed as evidence. The jury watched as Sean laughed and joked with Bryan White and Jeff Methvin. They observed him; he was relaxed and unconcerned as he smoked a cigarette and drank a Dr Pepper. They listened as he explained, "When you get an urge, it's just one of those things." On the tape, Methvin asked Sean if he would be surprised to learn that Donna's body was found not far from the tire tracks near the canal. "No, it wouldn't. We wouldn't be talking," Sean said.

"What do you mean?" Methvin asked.

"I knew you had my tire tracks, but she was not unloaded from my vehicle."

"You understand the coincidence?" Methvin said.

"I understand. When you called me yesterday, I said, 'Oh God, that's the area,'" Sean responded, taking a drag from his cigarette.

The jury observed Sean's level of comfort, his mannerisms, the ease with which he described urinating near the canal and why he had gone there instead of to his home. Before them on the screen sat a man who seemed to have nothing to hide. They did not see a killer on that tape. They saw a man who had an explanation, although an unusual one, for why his tire tracks were at the scene of a murder. They saw Sean Gillis at the top of his game. What they would never see was what happened in later interviews. Here they saw Sean denying any knowledge of the murder. They would never see him reveling in the details of that same murder.

When the video concluded, Prem Burns decided it was time to remind the jurors that Sean had been so proud of this murder that he had taken pictures. She called Geoff Black to the stand.

Black had been with the attorney general's office for eight years, working as a computer forensic examiner. Black had conducted more than one hundred exams on computers, from child porn cases to theft and fraud. His job was to replicate hard drives and retrieve materials that had been deleted.

"I assisted in searching each room in Sean Gillis's house," he told the jury. "We seized several computers, several loose hard drives, a large number of floppy disks, some CD-ROM discs, and a digital camera."

He explained that he had found pictures of the victims in some unallocated space on one of the computers.

"When a file is deleted, the content of that file is not wiped out," he said. "There were forty-five pictures of Miss Johnston. Typically, when a camera records a picture, it also records details about itself and the settings used. Those details matched Sean Gillis's camera."

Geoff Black then identified each of the photos for the jury. Already becoming desensitized, the jury had little reaction to the photos.

The next witness, however, would bring more of a reaction. After Dr. Edgar Shannon Cooper, the coroner of East Baton Rouge Parish, was called to the stand, Judge Jackson cautioned the jury that the testimony they were about to hear could be graphic.

A graduate of Tulane University, Dr. Cooper had completed his training at Charity Hospital in New Orleans, which operated as a training facility for doctors across the country. He had been on staff at Ochsner Medical Center for twenty-one years, had served as chief of pathology at Baton Rouge General for five years, and then had assumed the coroner's position in 2003.

Cooper explained that a rape kit was done to determine if a sexual assault had taken place. This consisted of swabbings of breasts, rectum, mouth, and vagina, as well as fingernail clippings. He said that clothing was collected for fibers and hair, and a combing of pubic hair was conducted. He stated that he had performed an autopsy on Donna Bennett Johnston the day she was discovered.

"She was sealed in a coroner's bag. Her body was wrapped in a sheet, then a watertight bag," he said. "She died of asphyxia, the blood supply to her brain altered by ligature to her neck. Judging from the appearance of her skin, I believed it to be a large cable tie. She was killed at least a few hours before she was found. The ambient temperature that day was fifty-five degrees, and her body was about that same temperature. Her face and head were reddish in color. Her left arm had been amputated. Her left nipple excised, her right nipple cut, too. A patch of skin had been removed from her right thigh. She had a small abrasion over one eyelid, and blood was coming from her nose.

"She had hemorrhages in the sclera of her eye. The tightened ligature around the neck cuts off blood's ability to get out of the brain, which breaks veins," he continued. "As a person is strangled, loss of consciousness occurs in a matter of minutes. The brain swells. In ligature, the trachea is compressed. When the ligature is tight enough, the carotid arteries are compressed and air supply is cut off. Death can take longer, depending on how tight the ligature is. The maximum time is five minutes. The body just stops. In the early phases, a person can struggle."

Again, Burns displayed photographs on the screen so the jury could see exactly what the doctor was discussing. Sean viewed the photos dispassionately, sometimes closing his eyes as if going back in time.

Dr. Cooper resumed his depiction of Donna's injuries. "She had additional scrapes on her back and shoulders, caused by the dragging of her body across a rough surface. A portion of her thigh had been cut out." Cooper explained that this had been done postmortem, as had the arm and nipple amputations.

"It was a fairly ragged cut on the arm," he said. "The instrument used was not very sharp, maybe an ax or a saw. A knife was used on the thigh. The flesh had been cut out in the shape of a diamond. A sharpened knife blade had been used on her breasts. Her arm was never recovered."

The victim had methamphetamine and alcohol in her

blood, which would have affected her ability to function, Dr. Cooper told the jury.

Kerry Cuccia asked Dr. Cooper if he routinely performed a rape kit.

"It's called a rape kit, but sex could be consensual, right?" Cuccia stated.

"This was clearly a violent homicide. There was a high-risk lifestyle issue. The sheriff's office indicated that's what they believed," Cooper said.

"You don't test them?"

"I don't know the results," Cooper answered.

Cuccia questioned him about the postmortem dismemberment.

"The amputation of the left arm, the flesh of the thigh, the excision of the nipples, all of this happened after death?"

"An incision into a living person will bleed a lot. An incision into someone who is already deceased does not bleed as much," Dr. Cooper said.

"You didn't see bleeding with this victim?"

"No."

"You said she had been dead a few hours?" Cuccia continued.

"The body cools in unpredictable ways. An unclothed body exposed will cool faster than a clothed body wrapped in a blanket. A body that size would take eight to twelve or fourteen hours to cool. There was no decomposition," Cooper said.

"What is your best estimate?"

"Eight to twelve hours to cool."

"It would not have been twenty-four to thirty-six?"

"It could have been thirty-six. The weather was cool so that would slow it," Cooper admitted.

"Did you see insect infestation of the body?"

"No."

"If the ligature is tight enough to cut off blood flow to the brain, would it take a minute?" Cuccia asked.

"Three to four minutes to die. She would lose consciousness in a minute to a minute and a half."

"Can you tell me how tight this ligature was?"

"It was very tight."

"Do you usually get clothes and jewelry with the body?"

"Yes," Dr. Cooper said.

"No further questions."

Nicholas Murphy, a deputy with the sheriff's office who transported prisoners to court, testified next. He told the court that on July 2, 2004, he had been transporting Sean in his Suburban when Sean made an unusual statement.

"He asked me if I was married or had children," the deputy said. "I told him I didn't discuss personal information with prisoners. He asked if I like to hunt or fish. I told him I did. In the cage behind me, there was a flex cuff, a plastic strap we use for larger inmates. Mr. Gillis said, 'That's my weapon of choice.' I said, 'Don't discuss anything else with me. No more conversation.'"

Crime scene technician Nicole Compton then testified that three zip ties, a machete, and two hacksaws had been discovered while searching Sean's home. She went on to describe the kinds of books that had been taken from the house, listing the titles one by one. Through her testimony, the jury learned that Sean Gillis had a fascination with reading about other serial killers.

Nicole identified the three zip ties and the belt she had retrieved from the van behind the house. "The driver's side window of the van was damaged, and debris was stacked around it," she said. "I had to go to the passenger side to get into the vehicle. The van was packed full of stuff. The belt was on the passenger floorboard in plain view. It stuck out because everything else was in boxes and bags. It didn't fit with anything else in the van."

"Objection." Kerry Cuccia asked that the jury be removed so that he could have a conference with the judge. "I want to reurge the motion to suppress the search warrant," he said. "The belt was on the floorboard of the front passenger seat, kinda sticking out by itself. She didn't take it because it looked like it could be used in a crime. The witness clearly stated she took it because it was sticking out of place."

"The body was found in an unclothed condition. The warrant strictly mentioned clothing. In viewing items, the belt seemed out of place. Overruled."

Terri Lemoine, her long hair graying, sat in the courtroom, frowning. She could tell this was not going well, and the trial was taking a toll on her. Although she smiled at Sean whenever he made eye contact with her, she wished this would be over soon. She wanted Louis to be there with her, but Cuccia had told him to leave when he had come with her that first day. He didn't want Judge Jackson to see him sitting next to her. Bonnie Jackson had defended Louis Gaar in his first murder trial, and Kerry Cuccia didn't want her to make the connection between Louis and Terri and Sean and Terri.

From the Pen of a Killer

Jimmy Johnston stood outside of the courtroom, leaning against the wall. Norman Gillis stood on the opposite side of the room, gathering his courage. Something about Jimmy drew him closer. Slowly he walked toward him.

"Excuse me," he said. "I just want to apologize for what my son did." Norman's head was down, shame evident in the lines of his body as he waited for Jimmy's response.

"Thank you," Jimmy said before he reached to shake Norman's hand. "I appreciate that."

The two men talked for a few minutes, unaware that most of the people in the waiting area were watching them.

"I don't want him to die," Norman said. "It would be better if he could live and share the word of God with other prisoners at Angola. I think that's his purpose."

Jimmy just smiled and nodded, not wanting to say anything that would hurt the old man who was so clearly misguided. Before the conversation was over, the two men were talking like old friends.

On the other side of the room, Lauren Williams spoke quietly with Yvonne. Although her son had killed Lauren's mother, Lauren felt sorry for the fragile-looking woman. She felt compelled to comfort her.

Noticeably absent on this third day at trial was Lynne Marino. She had tried, but the testimony proved too much for her. She had sat through two of the Derrick Todd Lee trials and wanted to be there for the victims of Sean Gillis, but the trial had brought the horror of her daughter's death back in vivid detail, and she just couldn't go through it again. It was much safer at home, where she could sift through smiling photos of Pam and remember happier times.

The courtroom door opened. Jimmy held it while Norman passed through to take his place in the third row, directly behind his son.

"All rise."

Court was now in session as the judge took her seat. "Please bring in the jury."

Everyone rose as the jury filed in. Judge Jackson started laughing. "How many times do I have to tell you that you do not have to stand every time the jury goes in and out of the courtroom," she admonished with a grin. "Sit down. Sit down."

Prem Burns, hoping to wrap up her case by the end of the day, called her first witness, David Kimball, who worked for Mills Cable Tie Company. He explained that cable ties are used by the electrical and automotive industries, as well as by law enforcement agencies.

"You can buy them at Home Depot, Lowe's, any wholesale supply company," he said. "They come in different sizes. They have two sides, a smooth side and a rough side. The tie has to be tied on the teeth side."

"Can you reuse them?" Burns asked.

"No. They would have to be cut with wire cutters to get them off something," Kimball replied.

She showed him a variety of sizes, which he identified, before tendering her witness.

"You sell a lot of cable ties across the country?" Kerry Cuccia asked.

"Yes."

"Large and small?"

"Yes."

"So it's not unusual for someone to have cable ties in their homes. No further questions," Cuccia said.

Burns decided it was time to pull out her ace in the hole. She introduced the letters that Sean Gillis had written to Tammie Purpera and passed them out to the jury. Judge Jackson told the jury to study them carefully, as they would not be allowed to view them again during deliberations. The jury, realizing the importance of these letters, took thirty minutes to read them. In the letters, Sean had confessed to his crimes, explaining that even he did not know what made him do the things he did:

For your own sake, Tammie, you must forgive the sinner but you may hate the sin forever. I have no, nor have I ever had any "Satanic Beliefs." This may be so hard to believe, but I am also a Christian. A sick, lost sheep which through the Holy Ghost, Jesus has found. Too late for eight beautiful women who for no other reason were in the wrong place at the worst time. That being when I was there.

In her last moments, Donna was strangled with a device that I have told the police should be out lawed. She was so drunk it only took about a minute and a

*half to succumb to unconsciousness and then death.
Honestly, her last words were "I can't breathe." As far
as the postmortem butcher as you so rightly call it, I
to this day do not know why I did it. Some of the other
women were and were not. I really do not know how
I could have done any of it to these wonderful sisters
in Christ. Your friend like six of the other eight I knew
not. One I knew for ten years and had no reason, dis-
like or cause to kill her either. I do think of all of the
families in my prayers each night. And now their
friends as well. Thank you Tammie for writting me. I
hope to hear more about your friend from you.*

In another letter, Sean gave step-by-step details of how
he had picked up Donna and how he had killed and dismembered her. The jury read how he didn't know what his
damage was. In yet another, he wrote that he had broken
all the Commandments, been consumed by all seven
deadly sins. He talked about how much he loved his
family and how much God loved him. The jury could have
no doubt now that Sean had killed Donna. He had spelled
it out for them in his own handwriting. When the jury finished reading, Burns showed how the letters had been
obtained.

Lieutenant Robert Clement, assistant chief of security
at East Baton Rouge Parish Prison, testified that Tammie
Purpera had been arrested on June 4, 2004, for prostitution and possession of Schedule II narcotics, as well as intentional exposure to the AIDS virus and bench warrants.
He explained that inmates are allowed to write to each
other, and the mail is transported by prison staff to the
mail room, where it is screened.

Melanie Decou, Tammie's sister, told the court that Tammie had passed away from breast cancer on August 8, 2005. She said that Tammie lived with their parents and was addicted to drugs and alcohol. "She was also a prostitute at times," Melanie said, tears streaming down her face.

Kerry Cuccia brought her a tissue.

"Tammie often wrote cards and letters to family and friends," Melanie continued. "She had a very distinct handwriting. She loved to write all over cards."

Corporal Sherry Leader, with the East Baton Rouge Parish Sheriff's Office, testified that it was her job to provide transportation for prisoners to and from court. She said that deputies always shake down prisoners before they enter a courtroom by doing a pat search. On July 6, 2004, she searched Tammie and found a letter in her front pocket.

"We usually don't take paperwork, because it may be court documents, but Tammie told me what the letter was. She asked me to do something with it," Sherry said.

Betty Jo McGinnis, a judicial assistant in Judge Louis Daniel's courtroom, said that she opened the letter and read it after it was turned over to her, date stamped it, and forwarded it to the law clerk, who brought it to Judge Daniel. He told the clerk to make a copy for reference and give it to the district attorney's office.

Linda Martin, at the East Baton Rouge Parish DA's Office, received the letter and gave it to Prem Burns. Alan Dougherty, a criminal investigator for Burns, testified that he was present when she received the letter.

FBI handwriting analyst Hector Hecbormalbonaeo was next in the string of witness after witness who had handled the letter. But by then, Tammie Purpera had turned over two more letters from Sean Gillis. He compared them to Sean's known handwriting and determined that, based on the distinct way in which Sean wrote his *k*'s, *r*'s, *n*'s, *t*'s and *o*'s, he did write the letters. He forwarded them to the Latent Fingerprint Division at the FBI.

Special Agent Gary L. Lucas had been with the FBI for thirty-two years, working as a fingerprint specialist at Quantico. He explained that he applied chemicals and powder to develop the prints. "During the course of my career, I have developed millions of prints," he said. "A latent fingerprint is a reproduction of ridges or friction on the palm side. Latent means hidden. There are three characteristics—ending ridges, dividing ridges, and dot (a ridge as long as it is wide). It has been determined that no two people have ever been found to have the same fingerprints, not even identical twins. I look for characteristics from the latent and ink print, side by side, with a large magnifying glass. One hundred seventy prints were developed in all three letters that matched the defendant's prints," the FBI analyst continued. "I found ten similar characteristics in these prints."

When Special Agent Lucas was excused, it was Terri Lemoine's turn to testify. The courtroom quieted as she walked toward the stand. She was dressed in a sweatshirt, jeans, and tennis shoes. Everyone wanted to hear what she had to say.

"Describe your relationship to Sean Gillis," Burns said.

"I was his common-law wife for ten years," Terri said.

"Tell me about your relationship."

"We had a lot in common. We were big *Star Trek* fans," Terri explained. "We liked to collect things together."

"Did Sean tell you these charges were true?"

"Yes, ma'am," Terri said, "when I saw him at the prison."

"Did you know about the letters he wrote to Tammie Purpera?"

"Yes. He said he wanted to say he was sorry."

"Did he ever show you Web sites with pictures of dead women?" Burns asked.

"Yes, twice, I believe," Terri said.

"Have you ever seen this belt?" Burns said, handing Terri the belt Donna Bennett Johnston was wearing the night she was murdered.

Terri shook her head. "No."

"No further questions."

Kerry Cuccia's partner, Steven Lemoine, stood up.

"Do you know if we're related?" he asked, jokingly.

"We might be distant cousins or something," Terri said. "I don't know."

"Did you love Sean Gillis?" he asked.

"Yes," Terri said.

"Do you still love Sean Gillis?"

"Yes," Terri said, smiling at Sean. He smiled back, a big, happy smile. "I didn't believe he did it. That's not Sean. This was not the person I knew. This is someone who had a cat named Heather."

"Would you trust Sean Gillis with your children?"

"Yes," Terri said, no traces of doubt in her voice. As she walked down from the stand, she again smiled at Sean. Oblivious to the fact that he was in a trial, fighting for his life, he smiled back, his happiness evident at having her love for him confirmed on the stand.

Adam Bechnel, a forensic scientist with the Louisiana State Police Crime Laboratory, was called to testify. The burly man, with a military-cropped hairstyle, had been with the crime lab for ten years as part of the Physical

Evidence Unit. He had photographed Sean Gillis's car and found photographs in the trunk.

Prosecutor Burns displayed the photographs for the jury to see. One was a photograph of Donna in the trunk, with a partial view of Sean's license plate. Sean tried not to look, but his need overcame him. He turned around to view the picture.

Bechnel told the jury that he had also found the backing to an earring and a fingernail in the trunk of the Cavalier. The items were moved into evidence.

Although Burns had hoped to finish presenting her case, the judge called a recess until the following morning. Everyone filed out of the courtroom.

Betrayed by DNA

The fourth day of the trial would feature technical testimony, the kind that wrapped everything up in neat little numbers that would hopefully seal the fate of a killer. Prem Burns, looking as smart as ever in her tailored suit and her hair waving softly around her face, called Julia Wilson, who worked with the state police crime lab, to the stand.

Wilson relayed to the jury that she had compared Sean Gillis's DNA to Donna Bennett Johnston's fingernail clippings and wrist swabbing.

"I called Nicole Compton to let her know it was a match," she said. "It's just a series of numbers from thirteen areas that we take from the blood samples." Wilson tried to keep the explanation simple for the jury. It was enough for Burns.

Kerry Cuccia began to question Wilson. He had to try to confuse the jury somehow.

"How much DNA do you need for an accurate sample?" he asked.

"There's a level at which there has to be enough there to test," Wilson said.

"Where do you get profiles?" Cuccia continued. "What type of surfaces can you get DNA from?"

"I have gotten just as many profiles off clothing as a table," Wilson responded. "The surface has more to do with how long they touched it and how much fluid was on their hand."

"Let's assume there's no bodily fluid. When I touch something, my skin cells are left behind. Is that correct?"

"Yes," Wilson said.

"You don't know the person whose DNA you are testing? When you got Mr. Gillis, Sean's profile, you don't know whose it is?"

"No. We don't know whose it is."

"No further questions."

Natasha Poe, a forensic DNA analyst with the state police, was called to the stand.

"I have tested a couple thousand samples of DNA," she said. "When evidence comes in, the first piece is assigned a unique number that tracks it all the way through and keeps all of the evidence in the case organized. It is maintained in a locked vault or locked refrigerator. Each analyst has a refrigerator and freezer locker that only they can access. I won't accept anything that is not sealed properly."

"Did you receive a blood sample card for Donna Bennett Johnston?" Burns asked.

"Yes, I was the first one to break the seal. I began testing evidence in this case March 9, 2004. We start with the most probative piece of evidence, usually the sexual assault kit. We analyze all evidence before we begin building a profile. We look at seminal fluids, do smears for sperm, et cetera. The oral swab was presumptive for blood, but the pubic hair did not indicate seminal fluid. The fingernail scrapings were examined and went straight to DNA analysis."

"What did you find?" Burns asked.

"We got a mixture of DNA. If you see more than two numbers at any location, it's a mixture. In this case, one was male and one was female. One was the DNA of Donna Bennett Johnston."

Poe then described that if you touch something for ten seconds or more, you leave your DNA behind. "We got a male and female profile from the right wrist swabbings that was consistent with, but not an exact match to, the profile from the fingernails."

Poe said that she was out of the office when the state police received Sean's profile. "Another analyst compared them. I then retested them, and they matched. The chance that it was someone other than Sean Gillis was one in 3.8 trillion."

"How many people are in the world?" Burns queried.

"Seven billion," Poe responded.

"Did you test the back of the earring?"

"Yes. We extracted a DNA profile that was consistent with coming from Donna. It matched Sean's profile. The chance that it could be someone other than Sean Gillis was one in 3.88 trillion people," Poe explained.

"Did you test the belt?"

"Yes. A partial profile was obtained consistent with being a mixture of two people. Sean Gillis could not be excluded as one of those people."

"What about the fingernail scrapings?"

"The fingernail scrapings were consistent with Donna, and Sean could not be excluded. It is 12.2 million times more likely to be Donna and Sean's DNA than Donna's and any other individual."

"Thank you," Burns said.

"I want to direct your attention to the earring back," Kerry Cuccia said. "Your DNA profile is single source?"

"Correct," Poe said.

"You said that was consistent with Donna Johnston?"

"Yes."

"Consistent with Sean?"

"Yes."

"The fingernail, consistent with Sean?"

"Yes."

"The belt and wrist swabs. Mixtures?"

"Yes."

"The mixture from [the] swab from the wrist. You found profile with Mrs. Johnston and Sean?"

"Correct."

"The scrapings?"

"Correct."

"The belt was a partial? Not a complete program?"

"The belt excluded others who had been submitted, but included Sean."

"That's a rough material. Is a rough material more inclined to catch skin cells?"

"Objection," Burns said. "He's asking the same questions over and over and asking too many in one question."

"Sustained."

"Did the belt have Mrs. Johnston's DNA on it?"

"The belt excluded Donna Bennett Johnston completely. Her DNA is not on the belt," Poe said.

"And there is no indication of Mr. Gillis in the oral, vaginal, and anal swab?"

"No," Poe said.

"No further questions of this witness." Cuccia sat down.

Norman Gillis, his head bowed into his Bible, wiped his eyes with a napkin.

Burns called her final witness. Savannah Johnston's blond ponytail swung back and forth as she walked to the witness-box. Her eyes were wide with fear.

"My family calls me Vanna," she told ADA Burns. "I'm going into the ninth grade."

"What's your favorite subject?" the ADA asked, trying to make the young girl as comfortable as possible.

"Math," Savannah responded.

"Do you know what it means to tell the truth?" Burns asked.

"Yes." Savannah nodded.

Burns showed her the belt.

"Yes, that's my belt," the girl said.

Savannah told the court that she lived with her grandmother, but that she had lived with her father's ex-girlfriend when she got the belt.

"When did you last see it?" Burns asked.

"I saw it on the last day I saw my mother, before I went to school. It was in my closet. My mom was my size, and she borrowed or took my clothes."

"Do you have any doubt that this is your belt?"

"No," Savannah reiterated. "That's my belt."

Burns excused the witness.

"No questions," said Cuccia.

"The state rests," Burns stated.

It was Cuccia's turn.

* * *

Cuccia introduced Donna Bennett Johnston's arrest reports into evidence. He distributed a copy to each member of the jury, waiting as they read through them. When they were finished, he walked back to the defense table.

"The defense rests," he said.

The audience in the courtroom was shocked.

Cuccia's only defense was Donna's history of arrests for drugs and prostitution. It was an appalling commentary on the value of her life.

It was just after noon.

"We will recess until tomorrow," Judge Jackson said. "Closing arguments will begin in the morning. There is a constitutional issue that must be addressed before I can give the jury instructions."

The state had appealed Judge Bonnie Jackson's decision regarding whether the strangulation was a separate act apart from the kidnapping. The judge had to wait until the next morning to get the decision.

Closing Arguments

A nervous tension filled the waiting area outside of room 601 on the morning of July 25, 2008. This was the day everyone would find out if the jury believed Sean intended to kill Donna, that he had stolen from her, kidnapped her. It could mean the difference between life and death. For the families waiting in the hallway lined with benches, it was the day they would learn if justice could prevail for a woman who had such a sordid past.

Justin Bennett's brown eyes reflected his worry, his pain, his hope that his mother's killer would be found guilty of the crime of murder in the first degree. Norman Gillis nervously clenched his Bible, while Yvonne sat quietly beside him. Virginia Valentine and Patricia Dawson knew that Sean would never be tried for the murder of their sister, so they prayed as they waited that justice for them would come through Donna. Lauren and Larry Williams fretted along with the rest. Terri Lemoine stood alone in a corner, worrying about what would happen to the man she still loved.

The line to get through the door went faster on that morning.

Prem Burns began by reading the statute about first-degree murder. She explained again that armed robbery is the taking of anything of value. She reiterated that second-degree kidnapping included forcible seizure and carrying, enticing or persuading, or imprisoning or forcibly seizing, while armed with a dangerous weapon.

She told the jury that she had presented one hundred ninety-eight physical exhibits, ten of which actually proved the crime:

1. The letter dated June 16, 2004, in which Sean Gillis discussed how he had committed the murder
2. The digital camera
3. The picture of Donna taken after the murder showing ligature marks on her neck, with the partial license plate in view
4. The photo of Donna with the dangerous weapon around her neck
5. The picture of Donna in the trunk wearing the black-and-silver belt
6. The black-and-silver belt
7. The earring backing, which contained DNA
8. The fingernail
9. The photo of the injury to her left eye
10. The photo of Donna by the car door

"Donna Bennett Johnston's friend, Brenda, testified that Ms. Johnston asked her to go to the store," Prem Burns said, standing in front of the jury and looking from person to person as she spoke. "She recalled that she was wearing jeans and a black belt. Willie Banks saw Ms. Johnston in a parking lot. He recalled a quilted cover. He gave her a ride to the store. She had some money and purchased chips, gin, and a glass tubing, which can be used for cocaine. When he left her on Winnebago at approximately two A.M., he thought she was okay on her feet. She had change in her pocket.

"Across town, around three that morning, Sean Gillis was in the Burgin Avenue area. Terri Lemoine worked the night shift. After she left, Sean drove six and a half miles into the Istrouma area to kill somebody. We know that from the letter. 'I found her on the corner of Prescott and Geronimo.' He knew a victim would be present in that area because a prostitute is someone who by trade will take a lift. A prostitute will ask few questions. They are gullible, available, and at the hands of the person they do business with. They are purchasable. Ms. Johnston was impaired in movements and judgment. He wanted someone who would get into that car.

"If she is lured by the offer of a job, if the job was offered to her . . . 'Sex was not my intent,' we know from the second page of that letter. 'I was pure evil that night.' It could have been anyone else. It happened to be a person in the wrong place at the wrong time.

"Mr. Gillis was negotiating the act of prostitution. He lured and enticed her into that car. We know because he came fully prepared with a dangerous weapon. In this case, it was a very ingenious, well-thought-out, well-planned instrument of death—a zip tie. Unlike a gun, it's cheap, untraceable, and you don't have to hide it. No one would question it, like they would a gun. Not the police. Not a significant other. It doesn't make the noise a gun would make. It would not attract attention. It's not even something a victim would pay attention to. If a prostitute saw a gun or knife, she'd run away.

"He told Deputy Nicholas Murphy, 'It's my weapon of

choice.' Listen to that." Burns held up a zip tie and pulled it tight. "That's the life being sucked out of them. David Kimball talked about how you cannot get out of them. It was brutal.

"Opposing counsel would have you believe he had a Swiss Army knife. Dr. Cooper said the cuts were rough. We know about a very beautiful tattoo of a butterfly, a beautiful work of art on her body. It was cut out. Her left arm was taken along with her identifying left hand. We don't know the full motive for removing her body parts. We don't know what kind of injuries were done. The tattoo was removed smoothly. There were two instruments, not a Swiss Army knife. He brought the instruments he needed to do the job.

"Sean Vincent Gillis, who enjoys going to Web sites to look at dead bodies. He brought a camera to take forty-five pictures to put on his computer so he could relive his moments with Donna Bennett Johnston. He knew that's what he was going to do. He wanted a visual souvenir. He also wanted another visible, tangible souvenir—the belt, a trophy, the way a hunter mounts the head of a deer. He took a very unique belt that fifteen-year-old Savannah testified was her belt. She had pictures of herself wearing it. She hasn't seen it since the day her mom died. Jury, pay close attention, you can see the buckle of the belt in the trunk."

Sean Gillis watched with interest as Prem Burns once again showed the photos.

"You can commit robbery after death. He wanted to take a trophy, a remembrance, a souvenir," Burns continued, warming up to her argument.

"The letter in this case proves the crime. 'I found her driving around searching.' He knew she'd get into the car, but sex was never his intent. Did she know he was pure evil? Did he lure her into his car? Yes.

"Once she got in that car, was she restricted and prohibited? Yes, because he was a man, and he had his weapon. A dent resulted in the top of her head. She was restricted before the ligature. There was a struggle. She got his DNA under her fingernails. It took ninety seconds for her to die.

"I submit to you that he had money. He talked about buying Coors beer. He dropped her off on the way to his house. He missed an earring back. His car was very neat, very clean. He told police, 'No, that body never came out of my car.'

"We see all this religion in the letter, but I submit to you that it's false. A lot of people get religion when they are facing what he is. He didn't have religion when he was shoving, killing, evil, brutal, methodical, planning, cunning, and luring.

"I ask that you find Sean Vincent Gillis guilty as charged of first-degree murder."

Cuccia Fights Back

"Thank you for your time, ladies and gentlemen," Kerry Cuccia said, smiling his wide smile at the jury. "The prosecution gets to speak first and last, because they have the burden of proof. The state has to prove that Mr. Gillis killed Donna Bennett Johnston beyond a shadow of a doubt.

"We all talk about what we are here to do, which is follow the law. There is not and never has been dispute that Sean Gillis committed this murder. He wrote those letters. He confessed to his girlfriend. He let the FBI swab him. There is no dispute. The dispute is what do his actions constitute under the law? Many people believe a killing done intentionally is first-degree murder. An intentional killing, no matter how brutal, shocking, offensive, bad, is not first-degree murder. Under the law of Louisiana, a first-degree murder is specific intent—killing, of course—but it has to be coupled with a 'plus factor,' and the 'plus factor' is that the killing was done while perpetrating a kidnapping and armed robbery," Cuccia explained, wanting the jury to fully understand the law.

"This means the killing was done while committing

another crime. The state put up one hundred ninety-eight pieces of evidence, most of which were focused on the murder.

"Let's talk about the armed robbery. This has to be a separate and distinct act combined with murder. Armed robbery is the taking of anything of value by use of force and armed with a dangerous weapon. If I ask you what an armed robbery is, you would say someone taking a gun or knife and taking my wallet. Give me your wallet. *Boom!* Now, that robbery has become first-degree murder.

"The state says Mr. Gillis committed armed robbery. Ms. Burns used a lot of statements like, 'We don't know. That's speculation. It's not beyond a reasonable doubt.' That very phrase is doubt. Ms. Burns said, 'What did he rob her of? Item 107, a belt.' You've all had a chance to look at it. Assuming you accept and are convinced that the belt is the belt worn by Donna, that someone would kill someone for this belt, is not common sense. The subsequent treatment of the belt afterward, it's not so precious. Detective Ruiz found the belt in a broken-down van outside the house." Cuccia showed the photo of the belt in the van to the jury.

"It's inside a van used for storage, thrown on the floorboard. Ms. Burns said it was a trophy. If that's the case, why is this trophy laying haphazardly on the floorboard of a van? If you believe this is the belt, the belt itself tells you this was no trophy. He didn't take a picture of the belt in the van. It is not the trophy, not the object of an armed robbery. If we accept that it's her belt, it may have been a remnant."

Cuccia showed the jury state's exhibit 139, a photo of the trunk of Sean Gillis's car. The jury paid close attention.

"Remember where the earring was, under the wheel well? The earring backing shows she was there. Does the earring backing seem like a trophy in the wheel well? You've seen other pictures of the body with clothing underneath. Isn't it likely that it was simply left behind? He threw it over here with all the other stuff," Cuccia said, pointing at the clothing in the photograph. "The state cannot prove to you that he robbed her to get this belt. When you look at the way it was later treated, it's not logical that he robbed this woman to get this belt. And that is only if this belt is *the* belt owned by Ms. Johnston.

"The state tried to prove that it was her belt through the testimony of Jimmy Johnston. You saw when I asked him, when I said I don't see any distinguishing marks, he said, 'That's not her belt.' I thought he had said it was her belt. He was disturbed. At first, he thought his daughter's belt was more worn than this one. Then he said, 'Oh, no, that's the belt. That's the belt.'

"Then they put young Savannah Johnston on last to identify the belt. They said, 'You've seen that before in my office.' She said she had one like it, not because 'I remember this little dent,' not because 'I put my initials in it.' Nothing particularly, but 'I had one like it.' Does she believe it was her belt? Yes. Is the evidence strong enough that beyond a reasonable doubt? Because if it's not her belt, it's not the object of a robbery. There's a dent in the middle of the tip of the belt, white lettering on the inside of the belt. It was a present from someone she holds dear. She would remember the dent and the white lettering.

"These are the things that the absence of must convince you beyond a reasonable doubt. The full strength of the state's case is that this belt is Savannah Johnston's worn by Donna because Vanna believes the belt is hers. She's a child. It's not her job to prove the state's case. It's the state's.

"But there's more." Cuccia was on a roll. "Ms. Poe told you about DNA on a rough surface. 'I've certainly got more DNA from clothing,' she said. 'I swabbed that whole belt looking for DNA, blood, body fluids. I swabbed the buckle, rivets.' She found a mixture of DNA. She found Mr. Gillis could be included as one of two people in that mixture. Donna Bennett Johnston's DNA was excluded. They found DNA but not Donna's. If Donna Bennett Johnston was the last person to wear this belt and put this belt on, wouldn't she have had to play with the buckle? Her hands would have touched the buckle. Where's the DNA? Everything tells us DNA should be on this belt. They knew they had the man responsible. They thought they were gonna get Mr. Gillis with Ms. Johnston's belt. It's not there. The absence of her DNA should tell you she wasn't wearing it. If she wasn't wearing it, the crime of armed robbery couldn't be committed.

"Donna's friend, Brenda. It was Brenda who would have been the last one to see it. Mr. Banks saw her in the early-morning hours. Brenda saw her about eight or nine that night. What was she wearing that night? Brenda said she was wearing jeans and a black belt. Ladies and gentlemen, it's a black belt with silver rivets. That would have caught your eye. Would you describe this as a black belt? Brenda's testimony does not support that this is the belt because it is too vague. At the least, that description does not support that this is the belt. I submit it supports that this is not the belt. The evidence cannot prove this is the belt beyond a reasonable doubt.

"Savannah believes it's her belt because she had one like it," Cuccia went on, driving his point home. "Her daddy says she had one like it. Brenda says a black belt. The fact that it's just sitting over here in this pile with the other stuff—but more powerfully, the DNA. No DNA on this belt. Natasha Poe thoroughly swabbed that belt.

Donna Johnston's DNA was not on this belt. That alone gives you reasonable doubt."

Cuccia moved on to the second-degree kidnapping statute.

"This is an awkward statute. It's oddly constructed. It's odd and clumsy and difficult to deal with, because this is the reduced version. Wherein the victim is physically injured or kidnapped or imprisoned, physically injured in the commission of a murder. All of the acts constitute second-degree murder. They must be separate and distinct acts. You cannot find a second-degree kidnapping because Ms. Johnston was killed.

"On the other hand, imprisonment with a dangerous weapon cannot be when the zip tie was wrapped around her neck. That's the murder. You've got the killing and the 'plus factor.' He's got to be killing, and then this separate act has to be separate and distinct over here from the act of killing. Otherwise, you don't have that combination. Obviously, she was physically injured."

"Objection." Prem Burns jumped up. "He's expanded on the court's instructions, as I understand them. He's instructing the jury."

"That's not my understanding of what he said," Judge Jackson said. "Overruled."

Cuccia continued his argument. "The physical injury cannot be an element in the same way the dangerous weapon has to be used in a different way than when it was used to kill Ms. Johnston. You cannot base it on the use in the killing act.

"With that in mind, I want to talk to you about the evidence. I want to go right to the physical evidence. The state's [exhibit] 41 was shown to Dr. Cooper. He talked about injuries in his report. All injuries postmortem, no matter how shocking, they occurred after she was dead. They were not physical injuries, because she was already dead.

"The doctor talked about abrasions, said it looked like it might have been made before, might have occurred that night before she died. Doesn't mean it didn't happen during the killing act. That's if you are convinced it happened while she was alive."

Cuccia went on and on attacking each statement Dr. Cooper had made in his testimony. He wasn't leaving anything out. He had the jury look at pictures of Donna's mouth, her eyes, her forehead, trying his best to discredit the doctor. Then he moved back to the weapon.

"Where's the evidence of imprisonment with a dangerous weapon? No evidence whatsoever that the zip tie was used in the course of the kidnapping. There is speculation that if she was sitting on the left side, maybe she grabbed for the zip tie. There has to be evidence so strong, so powerful, that you have no doubt.

"The letters say he was out searching, he was not out for sex. Terri said, 'Why would you do that?' He said, 'I wanted to let them know I was sorry.' They are answering specific questions from Ms. Purpera. That certainly seems like he was sorry. Does it mean you tempt somebody to go somewhere they do want to go? Maybe the enticement was on the other hand. We don't know. We do know Ms. Johnston was a prostitute at times. According to Lieutenant Caruso, they often flag a person down to attract them. We know from Mr. Banks that Ms. Johnston walked right up and asked him for a ride to get some gin and a glass pipe. We also know that Ms. Johnston had a habit of flagging down people for prostitution."

Cuccia then read from an arrest report. "'Ten forty-four p.m. Undercover officers were flagged down by a white female. She got in and rode south on Plank Street. She told them this is what would happen.'

"Here's the other. 'August 7, 1999, 12:05 a.m. Officer working undercover when he was flagged down by the subject in the 7900 block of Airline. She approached and asked officer if he was looking for a date. She said, "I'll give you a blow job." He said yes. She got in.'

"Evidence of habit is valid evidence corroborated or uncorroborated. If you accept what you know about Ms. Johnston, then you can accept that she instigated contact and behavior. It's something you need to know.

"Even if you find enticement or persuading, you cannot find physical injury other than the act of death. You cannot find Mr. Gillis was guilty of second-degree kidnapping through enticing. You cannot find him guilty of the physical injury. There is no second-degree kidnapping. The dangerous weapon and restraint occurred during the act of murder.

"Ladies and gentlemen, we're going to finish where we started. First-degree murder is when the killer has specific intent to do bodily harm and while a second-degree kidnapping or armed robbery has taken place. When you take that out, you have a specific-intent killing, a killing for the sake of killing. In the state of Louisiana, that is second-degree murder."

Kerry Cuccia sat down, pleased with his argument. The families in the courtroom began to worry. He had sounded convincing. They prayed the jury would not fall for it.

Rebuttal

Prem Burns was not concerned. She had a solid grasp on the laws of the state of Louisiana, and she wasn't about to let Kerry Cuccia twist them and confuse the jury.

"May it please the court, ladies and gentlemen, we never ask jurors to leave common sense and reason outside the courtroom. During the prosecution of Sean Gillis, opposing counsel said that he did not want to read the letters, but he did. He enjoyed it."

"Objection," Cuccia said. "She can't say I enjoyed reading the letters. She's focusing her argument on me. Rebuttal argument is about what I said. It suggests that I enjoyed showing them. She shouldn't make personal comments like that."

"In my instructions to the jury, I'm going to ask them to disregard that remark," Judge Jackson said.

"The focus of the argument has changed to put the victim on trial," Burns continued. "She has been accused of facilitating her own death. The tenure of the argument is that her own daughter and her ex-husband gave testimony that is not believable. The evidence in this case is overwhelming.

"Counsel argued that this is not her belt, but if it is, disregard it as a remnant. There was the insinuation that this belt was not even tagged. That belt was found in that van. It seemed out of place, unusual. It was the only item of female clothing in the van. There were garden items and storage bins in there.

"Donna's friend, Brenda, was not the last person that Wednesday night to see Donna alive. The next morning at one forty-five A.M., Mr. Banks saw her, which is consistent with Ms. Johnston being dead about twenty-seven hours when she was found on Friday morning.

"The one thing counsel did not mention is state exhibit 105, the photo of Ms. Johnston wearing the belt in the photograph taken in the trunk. The proof is in the pudding. How many people take forty-five pictures when they go off to kill?

"One of the instruments had to be an ax or a hacksaw. We know he had intent to have knives and a zip tie. Once again, the camera was in the car. All of these things were in the car. His intent was to preserve this kill with this tangible, physical reminder. State exhibit 122 shows the hand of Sean touching the leg of Donna. We didn't have to swab Cheryl Green (Jimmy Johnston's girlfriend) or Vanna Johnston for DNA for the belt. That belt is shown in that picture. We know he took it. It has value and was taken as a trophy.

"Yes, the earring back was inadvertent. This was deliberate. Clean Mr. Gillis. Do you remember my question to Terri Lemoine? There was no danger of her accessing the computer. That wasn't happening because his live-in didn't know how to use a computer. She never went into the front of the van. It meant something to him. It was a treasure, a trophy. Use your common sense, your reason. This man intended to kill. It could have been any woman. He knew where to find someone. He goes across town. He lures her. He lures her," Burns repeated.

"Do not make her more of a victim than she is, someone who was easy because of the sadness in her life. That's why he picked her. They know they are easy prey."

"Objection," Cuccia said.

Judge Jackson asked that the jury be removed.

"This is the straw that broke the camel's back. This case is about what Sean Gillis did. The last few minutes have been about 'they' who kill them, taking away from the specifics of the case. Many people in that station of life have been killed. This is broadening the prejudice the media has created. I move for a mistrial."

Cuccia wasn't finished. "Ms. Burns said, 'It's her belt, I can assure you beyond a reasonable doubt.' It's a personal argument and forbidden. She said, 'They suffer during strangling. We can't allow that sort of thing to happen.'"

"I did not say that about them," Burns argued.

"Ms. Burns gave a personal assurance based on her analysis of testimony and witnesses. It's not as if she was relaying any information that she had not submitted in testimony," Judge Jackson told Cuccia before admonishing Burns.

"I think you are skirting close to the line," she told her. "Please be more circumspect and choose your words more carefully. The motion is denied. Please bring the jury back in."

The audience in the courtroom stood up as the jury took their seats. Judge Jackson watched and shook her head. Not once had they listened to her.

The prosecutor continued her rebuttal. "Ms. Johnston was chosen for her weakness because she was impaired, inebriated, and under the influence of drugs. Counsel discussed two issues of flagging. Sean Gillis wrote, 'I found her driving around searching. I found her at the corner of Prescott and Geronimo.' He intended as part of that killing to take something that belonged to her. The bait that was put on the fishing pole was the promise of money for sex. He had no intention of having sex. If you find in any manner that he restricted her from leaving that vehicle, then restraint is separate from the murder.

"Dr. Cooper testified to an abrasion, while she was alive, on her head, hand, knuckle. If you find any kind of restraint or physical injury occurred before she was killed, the act of second-degree kidnapping has been completed.

"In this life," Burns concluded, "we know we are going to die and pay taxes. We hope it will be when we are older, at a later date in our life. We hope we can say good-bye. Maybe our last words will be 'I love you.' We have a lady who was only forty-two and had five children. She had a sad life. She didn't get to look in the face of a loved one and say, 'I love you.' What she saw was the face of a killer sucking away her life for sixty seconds with a zip tie, and I'm going to ask that you count off those sixty seconds with me."

The courtroom was silent as Prem Burns picked up a zip tie and pulled it tight. "One, two, three, four, five, six, seven, eight, nine, ten . . ." It seemed to take forever for Burns to get to sixty.

"The state of Louisiana asks this jury to return a verdict of guilty."

A Constitutional Issue

Judge Bonnie Jackson read her instructions to the jury. She informed them that the act of kidnapping did indeed have to be separate and apart from the act of strangulation. When she was almost finished reading the instructions, she was handed a note. She stopped, looked at it, and continued reading her instructions to the jury. The jury was sent to deliberate at 1:50 P.M.

What she had not told them was that the First Circuit Court of Appeal had just reversed her decision on the definition of second-degree kidnapping. The law had changed in the middle of her instructions. The higher court had ruled that strangulation was a part of kidnapping, that it did not have to be a separate and distinct act. During jury deliberations, that could be the difference between a first- or second-degree guilty verdict, the difference between life and death.

After the jury left the room, she announced to the court, "This court has been reversed. The First Circuit Court's writ has instructed the court to only read first-degree murder and second-degree kidnapping."

"Again, I ask for a mistrial on the latter part of her (Prem Burns's) argument," Kerry Cuccia said. "She said, 'We all know that we are going to die.' She's personalizing each reference to appeal to the prejudice of the jury, like somehow that elevates this case. She said, 'We all want,' making herself one with the jury."

"We are human beings. She was speaking in a generic sense," the judge replied. "The motion is denied, and I note your objection."

Cuccia hit himself in the head.

"Then I move for a mistrial on the basis of the new ruling."

"This would ensure that we would have to reargue the case," Burns said. "It hurts me, not them. It's over. Done. Double jeopardy has attached. In my heart, I'm willing to take the chance that the jury will find the kidnapping separate from the murder."

Cuccia's motion was denied.

At 4:15 P.M., the jury asked for the definition of second-degree kidnapping and armed robbery again. Judge Bonnie Jackson brought them back in and read the definition. This time, she read the new definition, even though she did not feel it was the right one. She was bound by the ruling of the higher court. The jurors didn't realize the definition had changed, and she didn't tell them.

At 5:15 P.M., the verdict was returned. Family members clasped their hands nervously as it was read. Lauren Williams was visibly shaking.

"We, the jury, find Sean Vincent Gillis guilty of first-degree murder."

Kerry Cuccia and Steven Lemoine stood up and asked the judge to poll the jury. The judge instructed that jurors be given a sheet of paper on which they could indicate their vote. She read them to the court:

"'Guilty.'

"'Guilty.'

"'Guilty.'

"'Guilty.'

"'Guilty.'

"'Guilty.'

"'Guilty.'

"'Guilty.'

"'Guilty.'

"'Guilty.'

"'Guilty.'

"'Guilty.'"

It had been unanimous.

"Thank you, Jesus," Virginia Valentine said, crying. Lauren Williams rocked back and forth, crying. Sean Gillis stood up and looked around, unsure what to do, how to feel. Prem Burns hugged Lillian Robinson's family members. Justin Bennett and Jimmy Johnston hugged each other. All of the families in the courtroom began hugging and kissing. It was a victory for all of Sean's victims.

"This verdict is the only correct verdict," Prem Burns said to television reporters on the steps of the governmental building, exuberant from her victory. "I knew when I finished my case, I had done my very best. We will resubmit evidence in the penalty phase, but we will also be submitting two additional murders and a whole new arena of evidence."

Kerry Cuccia was not so happy. "It's always a disappointment when you lose a case like this," he told reporters. "It's a sad thing to me, tragic. I do not believe it was first-degree murder. It was second degree. There's always two sides to the story. That's now part of the appeal."

"What would you have done differently?" a reporter asked.

"I'd have prayed a little more," he said, before informing the media that Steven Lemoine would be handling the penalty phase.

Judge Bonnie Jackson had informed the court that the penalty phase would begin the next morning. Burns and Cuccia hurried home to prepare.

The families of the victims thanked God it was over. But it wasn't. Worse—much worse—was still to come.

Thou Shalt Not Kill

At one in the afternoon on July 26, 2004, family members, friends, and reporters filed back into the courtroom to watch the drama of the second part of the trial unfold. Many in the courtroom hoped that Sean Gillis would be·put to death. Others prayed he would be spared. Terri Lemoine, her fatigue covered by makeup, did not want Sean to die. She still didn't believe Sean was capable of the things she had heard during the trial. It didn't seem real to her. In her mind, Sean was the man who laughed and played with her children, who had lain on the couch and watched *Star Trek* with her.

Sitting on a cushion now, Norman Gillis held on to his Bible and said his prayers. He prayed for deliverance for his son. Yvonne Gillis flitted about nervously. Her son could not be put to death. He just couldn't.

Lauren Williams knew that she would be called to testify. She couldn't wait. Justice for her mama was long overdue, and she would see to it personally, if she had to, that Sean would be put to death.

Virginia Valentine and Patricia Dawson were there as

well, determined to see this thing through for their sister. Dressed as always in their Sunday best, they sat erect, dignified, in their seats as they waited for the opening arguments to commence. Lillian would not be a part of this trial; there simply wasn't enough evidence. But justice was justice. It didn't matter how it was obtained.

Reporters filled the empty seats, readying their notebooks for what was sure to be an interesting few days. After sitting through the guilt phase of the trial and hearing the gruesome details—many for the first time—they had no doubts that Sean would soon join Derrick Todd Lee on Louisiana's death row. His crimes were simply too horrific for any other sentence.

The courtroom was silent as Judge Bonnie Jackson began to speak.

"As you have been told, this is a two-part trial. Having found the defendant, Sean Vincent Gillis, guilty of first-degree murder, you must now decide between life and death. You must weigh carefully the characteristics and propensities of his crimes, the impact on the victims' families. You must consider the existence of aggravating and mitigating circumstances," she said to the jury.

Prem Burns stood up and faced the panel of jurors. "Whoever commits the crime of first-degree murder shall be sent to death or life at hard labor," she began. "Not all first-degree murders are the same. There are degrees. Article 905.2 of the criminal code states that 'A sentencing hearing shall focus on the characteristics of the crime. The sentence of death shall not be imposed without at least one aggravating circumstance.' In this case, there are two—armed robbery and second-degree kidnapping. During the guilt phase, you heard about Donna Bennett Johnston, the mother of five children. You will now hear about two other victims.

"On January 4, 1999, Ledell Blakes kept cattle on his leased property [on] River Road. He noticed an unfamiliar jacket, a food stamp card, and a zip tie. He made arrangements to turn them over to authorities. On January 5, 1999, Herbert K. Jones found the body of Katherine Hall [on] Cujo Street, off Hoo Shoo Too Road. Her body was positioned near a dead-end sign—totally nude, face-down, no identification, no valuables. Although she had pierced ears, no earrings. She was five feet two inches tall and weighed one hundred forty pounds. She was thirty years old, a street prostitute and drug addict. She had been attacked, beaten. She had sixteen stab wounds. She died from exsanguination due to ligature of her jugular vein. She had postmortem stab wounds. A pubic hair with the root attached was found in her upper front teeth. Ledell Blakes contacted police about her food stamp card, but this remained a cold case.

"The Louisiana State Police Crime Lab tested the zip tie, and it was consistent with Katherine Hall's DNA. It also contained male DNA. The case remained dormant for three years. In the spring of 2004, the crime lab asked to compare that DNA with DNA that had been found on Donna. When they matched, they realized there was a serial killer in Baton Rouge.

"On April 28, 2004, Sean Gillis's DNA was obtained. It matched. There was a one in 3.2 trillion chance that DNA belonged to anyone other than Sean Gillis."

Prem Burns paused for a moment to let that information sink in.

"On October 11, 2003, four years and nine months after Katherine Hall's body was discovered, a fourteen-year-old boy was out searching for his dog in the woods off

Pride–Port Hudson Road. He found the body of a female and went home to tell his father. Robert Reames found her lying facedown, her body so small, in an advanced state of decomposition. She was totally nude, beaten and stabbed, both her hands amputated. There were multiple blunt-force trauma wounds to her head, thorax, chest, buttocks, legs. There were numerous sharp-force injuries to her body. She was five feet tall and weighed no more than a hundred and ten pounds. Her daughter reported her missing, but she remained a Jane Doe.

"Finally she was identified. Her name was Johnnie Mae Williams. She was forty-five, a street prostitute. A deep cut found in her left arm produced a body hair. It was sent to the Acadiana Crime Lab and then to Quantico. The DNA on that hair matched Sean Vincent Gillis. At the time of his arrest, three photographs of Johnnie Mae were found on his computer. In his 2002 Cavalier's glove box, another picture was found. In the course of five years and two months, he took three lives from this earth. He did it with premeditation.

"You'll hear Mr. Gillis has a brain abnormality, that he's psychotic, that ants move in and out of his brain through an implant in his brain put there by aliens. You'll hear he has migraines, that he sleepwalks, that he's chased by vampires and ghosts. You'll hear the man who spoke in that video underwent extensive testing—MRIs, CAT scans. Four impartial doctors found them to be perfectly normal.

"Pure evil is what he is, a sociopath preying on women, hoping they would not be missed. Sean gave an interview to police and admitted to the murders of Katherine, Johnnie, and Donna. He'd known Johnnie for ten years. He expressed contempt for each of the women. 'It was like they were already dead to me,' he told a reporter.

"In spite of her addictions, Donna's family loved her. None of her grandchildren will ever meet their grand-mother. During the nine months she carried each of those children, she managed to stay drug and alcohol free, out of love and respect for them. She aspired to be a good mother.

"For five years and two months, this man managed to outsmart the smartest police and went on with his life. He went back to Burgin Avenue to be with Terri Lemoine. She was never alerted as to what he was doing.

"Sean Vincent Gillis is pure evil. Sean Vincent Gillis deserves the maximum penalty recognized by Louisiana law," Burns concluded.

What she couldn't say was that Sean had confessed to the murders and mutilations of five more women and that his killing spree had lasted more than ten years. By sup-pressing his confession, Judge Jackson had robbed the jury of the truth to protect the rights of a serial killer, rights that a higher court in West Baton Rouge Parish would eventually rule that Sean did not have.

It was time for the jury to hear from Steven Lemoine. Kerry Cuccia had decided that Lemoine's warm, friendly personality and soft-spoken voice were better suited to win over the jury than his own sometimes abrasive manner.

"Ladies and gentlemen, this is what I ask of you. I ask that you consider that while you have determined Sean Gillis is guilty and killed two other women, your minds are still open to the possibility of a life sentence. He is not just a person who killed Donna Bennett Johnston, Kather-ine Hall, and Johnnie Mae Williams. He is also still one of our own fellow human beings.

"Yvonne and Norman Gillis met in the early sixties at LSU. Norman, a mentally ill man, abandoned his wife and young son for fifteen years. Sean only met his father when his grandfather died. The next time he saw him was at his grandfather's funeral. Yvonne struggled to provide for Sean. She will describe how difficult that was. She knew she didn't do great with Sean.

"I'll ask you to listen to Robert Bumm, Sean's teacher at Redemptorist. He taught Sean history in his sophomore year. Terri Lemoine will describe more about her life with Sean. Then I'll ask you to consider if he is mentally ill. John Rosas will describe Sean as kind and helpful. Christine Rosas will describe how kind Sean was to her. John Green, a childhood friend, will tell you Sean has a kind and generous nature.

"I'll ask you then to consider if that is a man who is pure evil.

"Dr. Ruben Gur will describe to you how the human brain functions. Dr. Dorothy Lewis, a psychiatrist, will explain why some people who commit murder seem normal.

"I ask you to consider that the things you already know and the things you will hear about Sean Vincent Gillis, those crimes speak for themselves. They were done by a person who is pure evil or by a person who has a mental illness. These are not crimes committed for personal gain. These crimes are incomprehensible. They are, in themselves, signs of psychological damage. Norman Gillis suffered from mental illness, until he was able to find a way to get better. He is a flawed man, but a brave man for coming here. Four and a half years in a mental hospital, he tried to kill himself. Sean Vincent Gillis did not go to a mental hospital. He struggled and struggled and tried to suppress the urges. You will see through the letters, when he talked to Josh Noel, he said, 'I couldn't help myself.'

Does that represent a man with a mental defect? Are these lies, what he says when he confesses?

"Does pure evil confess? No. Pure evil conceals itself. Mental illness reveals itself eventually. Yet it's too late. But he's still a fellow human being. Look and think with inquiring minds as to why this happened. Try to understand. Not to wipe away or forgive. Thank you."

Steven Lemoine went back to his table. Kerry Cuccia nodded his approval. Appearing a little more nervous than usual, Sean Gillis smiled. He knew that if his attorneys convinced the jury he was mentally ill, he could not be put to death under Lousiana law. For all of the times he had broken the Sixth Commandment—"Thou shalt not kill"—this killer did not want to die.

Connecting the Victims

This portion of the trial should have been easier on the prosecution. The defense had already admitted that Sean Gillis was a serial killer, that he had killed three women in an "incomprehensible" manner. But for this prosecutor, it was more difficult, simply because this was the part where the pain of the families had to be faced, heard, acknowledged by everyone who watched as they told stories about the women they had loved. This part was never easy for Prem Burns. As firm and detached as she appeared when grilling witnesses, she was an emotional woman and felt the pain of the families. It's what kept her motivated. It's what justified handling death penalty cases. She decided to save the families' testimony for last, when it would have the greatest impact.

Throughout the next few days, the jury was once again subjected to witnesses who revealed the most horrifying aspects of humanity. Burns carefully guided the jury through the details. As she had with Donna Bennett Johnston, she established early on that the two new victims were prostitutes and drug addicts.

Barbara Mason, a criminal record analyst with the state police, told jurors that Katherine Hall had been arrested on September 18, 1994, for possession of cocaine. She had pled guilty on April 7 of the following year. Burns also produced the arrest record of Johnnie Mae Williams, who had been arrested on June 17, 1998, for prostitution and crimes against nature; she was arrested on August 13, 2001, for prostitution; and on November 9, 2001, she was arrested for possession of drug paraphernalia.

Ledell Blakes described how he had found a jacket, a zip tie, and a food stamp card on his property. "I feed and water my cattle every day, and I knew it wasn't there the day before. The jacket was just hanging on the gate," he said.

Prem Burns showed the jury photos of the field while Sean Gillis looked on.

Kenny Kwan, with the Crime Scene Division of the East Baton Rouge Parish Sheriff's Office, had responded to the call about the items Ledell had discovered. He told the jury that he had taken pictures of the jacket on the gate, the card, the zip tie. He had also attended Katherine's autopsy. He identified photographs of injuries to the back of her neck and other evidence.

Herbert K. Jones explained that he had been out squirrel hunting the afternoon he'd found Katherine's body. "I could see she was cut up real bad," he remembered. "I put my truck in reverse and backed up to the street. I called 911." Herbert identified photos of Katherine's body, the dead-end sign where she had been posed, and other pictures of the body. As usual, Sean Gillis couldn't keep his eyes off the photographs.

Detective Richard Mohr, with the East Baton Rouge Parish Sheriff's Office, described how he had been dispatched to Cujo Street and had observed a nude black female lying on the ground next to a backhoe. "I photographed and fingerprinted her, then placed her in a body bag," he said. "I also drew a diagram of the crimes scene."

Jim Churchman told the jury that he and Natasha Poe had observed the autopsy. "We were there to see if we could lift fingerprints from her skin," he said. "We did not recover anything of value. There was too much damage to her skin from cutting. We collected a hair from her mouth and brought it to the state police crime lab."

"Did you test the hair at all?" Steven Lemoine asked.

"No," Churchman replied.

Sean poured himself a cup of water from the pitcher on the defense table.

Natasha Poe told the jury that the state police crime lab did not begin testing DNA until 2001. "We ran a dampened sterile swab along the zip tie to try to get STR (short tandem repeats). We found Katherine Hall's DNA on the zip tie. We also tested the hair and found a male profile. It lay dormant until 2004. I was later asked to compare profiles between DNA contributed in Donna Bennett Johnston's case to Katherine Hall. They matched. I then compared the DNA with Sean Gillis. It was consistent. The probability of finding another person with that DNA is one in 3.8 trillion."

Dr. Edgar Shannon Cooper then testified that he had reviewed the autopsy that had been performed by Dr. Lim on June 6, 1999. He vividly described Katherine's wounds. "She bled to death from a stab wound to the jugular vein," he said. "There is a jugular vein on each side of the neck, with internal and external branches. Two veins run together and drain blood from the brain. A person would bleed out in eight to twenty minutes. She suffered sixteen wounds before death—two in the left breast, eight in the abdomen, one above the pubis bone, three in the left

eye. She had a small laceration over her eye from a fist
and inside of her mouth. All of the wounds were similar,
like they had been made by a knife blade that was narrow,
then wide, then narrow. She had two parallel lines on each
side of her neck from ligature."

As the doctor explained the wounds, Sean Gillis
became increasingly upset. He began jerking, resting his
chin on one hand and then the other, as he watched the
doctor. He started talking loudly to Kerry Cuccia, obviously disturbed by the testimony. Cuccia could not shut
Sean up.

"We need a recess, Your Honor."

Judge Jackson had been watching the tantrum as it developed. "The jury is excused," she said. "We'll reconvene
in an hour."

An hour later, obviously medicated, Sean Gillis looked
at pictures of Katherine's wounds calmly as Prem Burns
displayed them for the jury, one by one. He listened quietly as Dr. Cooper identified them. "The width of the zip
tie is similar to the one used on Donna Bennett Johnston,"
he explained. "This victim had hemorrhages to her eyes
and a subdural hemorrhage to the left side of her brain.
A blow to the head is how these injuries usually occur.
She also had hemorrhaging in her abdominal cavity."
The doctor went on to describe the postmortem wounds.
He mentioned that cocaine was found in her system.

Satisfied, Prem Burns directed the testimony to Johnnie Mae Williams.

Robert Reames told jurors how his son, Ethan, had
found her body in the woods near their home. "The new
pastor of our church was over. We went directly to the
spot. We saw the body but tried not to disturb it. I could

not tell if she was male or female upon initial observation. I thought she was very young, because she was so small," he said.

Nicole Compton described how she had gone there to preserve the crime scene and stayed all night. "I started at the roadway and worked my way down to the gully where the body was. I used flags to mark evidence and prepared a crime scene diagram. The body was found three hundred eighty-three feet from the road. A car could have driven the trails to the body. I found tire tracks."

Compton went on to describe Johnnie Mae's condition. "The body was facedown. She was African-American. Her skin was slipping. There were cuttings, and the body was decomposing. She had no clothing. There was insect infestation—a maggot collar. She had no identification and no valuables. The first thing I found and noticed was that she didn't have any hands. I looked for them but couldn't find them. She was not identifiable."

Dr. Cooper was recalled to the stand. He had performed the autopsy on Johnnie Mae. He described multiple blunt-force trauma wounds from punches and being hit against a tree. He placed the date of her death as October 9. "Her hands were missing at the time of the autopsy. There was head trauma to the left side of her head, contusions to the right thorax, buttocks, and lower extremities. She also had postmortem injuries, including multiple sharp-force injuries to her left buttocks, upper right leg, and lower left leg. There was no bleeding in the tissues. Because of the decomposition, you couldn't tell what kind of weapon performed the amputation of her hands," he said.

The jury was not unhappy to watch Dr. Cooper leave the stand. His testimony turned their stomachs.

Mary Manheim, a forensic anthropologist from the FACES Laboratory at LSU, who was also known as "the

Bone Lady" and had written a book with the same title, testified that she had attended the autopsy of the then–Jane Doe. She told the jury that she had been asked to identify a bone found at the crime scene and determine from where it had been severed. She identified photographs of the bottom half of the left humerus and the distal part of the left humerus near where the elbow bends. She observed seven cut marks on the humerus, ulna, and radius. She said that they had occurred around the time of the death or postmortem. "I would have to defer to a medical doctor," she said.

Ginesse Listi, who worked with Mary Manheim at the lab, explained to jurors that she had discovered a limb hair and fiber in the distal left radius. She said that she removed it with tweezers while looking through a microscope. She obtained a reference limb hair from Johnnie Mae by scraping hair off her forearm tissue.

Mark Kurowski, with the Acadiana Crime Lab, tested the hair for DNA. "I laid out a sheet of white paper. I thought the sample was empty because the hair was so light in color. I knew immediately it wasn't a head hair or a pubic hair. It had to be a limb hair or auxiliary hair," he said. "I compared it to a head hair from Johnnie Mae Williams. They did not match. I released the hair to Bryan White."

Judge Bonnie Jackson stopped the proceedings. "Let's reconvene at ten-thirty tomorrow morning."

Terri Lemoine stood up, staring straight ahead at Sean Gillis. She seemed upset by the day's testimony.

"Are you okay, Terri?" a reporter, noticing that she was shaking, said.

"I do not know that man up there," Terri whispered, still staring at Sean. "I do not know that man."

Why, Sean, Why?

The following morning, Bryan White testified that he had traveled to the Acadiana Crime Lab and had brought the hair sample to Nicole Compton. Compton explained that she released it to Jeff Methvin. "I requested that the FBI Crime Lab look at mitochondrial DNA and compare it to the DNA for Katherine Hall and Johnnie Mae Williams," Methvin told the jury.

Deborah Polanskey, a forensic mitochondrial analyst at Quantico, explained to jurors that there are two types of DNA—mitochondrial and nuclear. "Nuclear DNA is found in the center of the nucleus like the yolk of an egg. It is unique to you. One comes from mom, and one comes from dad. Mitochondrial DNA is found outside of the nucleus or could be considered the white of the egg. It comes from the mother and is not unique to one individual. There are many more copies of mitochondrial DNA," she said. "The structure of DNA is like a twisted ladder with two strands. We look for common base between samples on each position. The mitochondrial DNA from Johnnie Mae Williams and Katherine Hall had a common base at each position. Sean Gillis could not be excluded from both samples."

Sean Gillis, quieter and calmer on this day, was chatting with Steven Lemoine.

Clayton Reeves, who had been with the attorney general's office, explained to the jury that he had retrieved three pictures of Johnnie Mae Williams after Geoff Black had dropped them out of a Norton SystemWorks book found on Sean's desk.

Prem Burns showed the pictures to the jury. Sean watched quietly.

Joshua "Josh" Benjamin Noel was called to the stand. Sean Gillis had confessed to Josh when he had been a reporter for *The Advocate*. Because Burns had been forced to compel his testimony, her scope was limited, and she knew Judge Bonnie Jackson would be more careful than usual about allowing her to step across the lines.

Josh Noel explained that he had interviewed Sean Gillis in July of 2004, with Terri Lemoine standing next to him. "I was not allowed to tape the interview," he said. "My understanding was that I was not allowed to take notes, so I did not take a notebook. I was required to rely on memory."

Josh said that Sean agreed to speak with him because "'I did it.' He said he killed at night when he became restless. We discussed Johnnie Mae Williams, and he said they had been friends for about ten years. He told me he picked her up on the street. I asked him why he killed her, and he said that she had become a steady user of crack cocaine and he couldn't restrain himself. He felt a certain contempt for his victims. He said, 'It's like they were already dead to me.' He told me he had taken digital photos of one of the victims after he posed her. He said he felt horrible about the crimes and would give his own life to take them back. He also said that if untreated medically, he would be at risk to kill again, but if treated medically, he would not kill again. He was calm, pleasant, clearly interested, respectful, forthright, and honest."

At times when testifying, Josh had to refer to the story he had written. Steven Lemoine asked him what he thought Sean had meant by "They were already dead to me."

Josh shrugged and sidestepped the question. "You are always evaluating the information that is given to you," he said.

Josh was excused to go back to Chicago.

Prem Burns called Lauren Williams to the stand. Earlier, Judge Jackson had ruled that Lauren could not give a victim impact statement because Johnnie Mae had not been a part of the guilt phase of the trial. Lauren could only identify pictures of her mother and tell the jury that she had reported her mother missing to police.

"How old are you, Lauren?" Burns began.

"Twenty-eight," said the pretty young woman.

"I'd like to show you some photos. Could you identify the person in the picture for me?"

Lauren looked at the photograph.

"That's my mama."

"And this person in this one?"

"That's my mama at her best friend's wedding. She was matron of honor. I didn't see her that often because she didn't want to bring that lifestyle around us. She called all the time," Lauren said.

"Objection," Steven Lemoine interrupted.

"Remove the jury," the judge told the bailiff.

"This is not admissible," Lemoine told the judge. "We are not having victim impact for the other two victims."

Lauren was looking at Sean Gillis. Sean was mouthing the words "I'm sorry. I'm sorry."

"Why? Why? Why did you do this to my mama?" Lauren asked him from her seat on the stand. Steven Lemoine had asked to approach the bench and was not paying attention to his client.

"I don't know. I don't know. I'm sorry. I loved your mama. I love you, Lauren," Sean answered, a little louder this time.

"Judge, the witness cannot talk to the defendant," Kerry Cuccia said loudly, trying to draw attention to what was going on.

Judge Jackson admonished Lauren and excused her from the stand. The young woman, who had struggled so much with her mother's death, would never get the opportunity to tell the world how much she loved her mama.

Prem Burns decided it was time to let the jury know that the families of these women had loved them. She called Donna's mother, Johnnie May Bennett, to the stand.

Burns smiled at the elderly woman. "How old are you, Mrs. Bennett?"

"Seventy-nine," Johnnie said.

"How many children do you have?"

"Six."

"Are you married?"

"My husband, Joseph, is dead. He was a welder. Donna was my fourth child and the second child I've lost," Johnnie explained.

"Where was she born?" Burns asked, compassion for the woman filling her voice.

"Donna was born in Monroe. We moved to Baton Rouge shortly after she was born. She liked to do gymnastics. She went to church and played sports."

"So she was a normal little girl?"

"Yes." Johnnie smiled sadly at her recollections. She told the jury about Donna's teenage years, how she had become pregnant and then married twice.

"She was always close to me," she said, then described how Donna's second marriage had been full of ups and downs. She admitted that Donna had developed a drug and alcohol problem while she was married to Jimmy.

"Before the crack, she was such a good mom. She cleaned. She cooked. She believed in God. She was Catholic. When the drug use started, she started staying away from them. They've always lived with me. She just started not coming home."

Johnnie explained that Donna had gotten worse in 2004. "She was [a] prostitute, I guess. That's what I was told."

"When was the last time you saw her?" Burns asked.

"She needed a new ID, so I took her to the DMV. I drove her on February 20. She needed it to get a new food stamp card. She gave me the ID card. She wanted me to take her to North Baton Rouge, but I wouldn't. I knew what she was going to do. That's the last time I saw her," Johnnie said, her voice quavering while tears streamed down her face.

"I'm sorry," Burns said. "I know this is difficult, but can you tell me how you found out she had died?"

"I found out when two detectives came to the house and told me," Johnnie said, trying to regain her composure, but not quite succeeding. "They left her casket open, but I didn't want to. All they could show was her head."

"And where are her youngest children now?"

"Jesse, we call him 'Woody,' he's eleven and Savannah's fifteen. I take care of them. It takes a lot of energy. Woody don't say too much, but he thinks a lot. He tells me he'd like to have her back. He mows the grass at her grave, keeps it up."

"And Savannah?"

"Savannah is quiet, don't have a lot to say. Sometimes she don't pick her boyfriends too good, but she's a good girl."

"What about Donna? How do you feel about her?"

"Donna was a very loving, caring individual. She loved those kids dearly. Even the drugs couldn't keep her away all the time. All she ever wanted was a loving husband and a home for her kids. Every day I look forward to her coming to my front door, but she doesn't come to it no more, not even for a little while." Johnnie bowed her head to wipe at her tears.

Some of the jurors were also wiping their eyes. Burns showed them pictures of Donna during happier times. Sean Gillis stared at the pictures of Donna with her children.

"Mrs. Bennett, I'm Sean's lawyer. I just want to tell you I'm sorry," Steven Lemoine said. "No questions for this witness."

"The state calls Justin Bennett."

Donna's son took his place in front of the jury.

"How old are you, Justin?"

"Twenty-four."

"Are you married?"

"Yes. My wife's name is Casie, and we have two children, Chelsea and Kayla. We have another one on the way."

"How did you find out your mother had been killed?" Burns asked.

"Me and my younger brother, Tony, were playing

basketball. I heard my dad's ringtone. I lived in Lafayette then, and he said I needed to come home. He said, 'They found your mom.'"

"How old were you then?"

"I was nineteen, Tony (James Anthony) was seventeen, Michael was twenty-seven, Vanna was ten or eleven, and Woody (Jesse) was seven or eight."

"What did you do after you learned of your mother's death?"

"I went home. I couldn't drive. My wife drove us. It was the worst feeling in the world to bury my mom. I've always been a mama's boy. Tony was closer to my dad. She'd come home and stay months at a time. She was everything to me," Justin said, tearing up. "She would call me mostly every night to tell me where she was and how she was. We'd expect those calls. I've been with my wife nine years, and my mom loved Chelsea, even though she was my stepchild. She taught me a lot about life, about how rough it is out there. Mom would always help anyone to the best of her ability."

"What was it like when she came home?" Burns asked.

"She'd sleep for a whole week, then it was like she was never gone. She'd cook, clean, get us ready for school, go to the park. We did a lot when she was home. I love my mama more than words can explain.

"For the last four years, it's been a big change. . . . For the first year, I'd call my brother and grandmother in the middle of the night just to say, 'I love you,' just in case. I don't get that call anymore."

Three members of the jury were openly crying as they listened to Justin's testimony. Family members in the audience were struggling to keep from crying as well.

"On Mother's Day, we cut the grass at her memorial

site, the area where her body was found. We put flowers there. Pretty soon, we hope to get a headstone."

"What's the best memory you have of your mom, Justin?"

"The best memory I have is when I was sixteen and had just got into basketball. My dad was a coach, and we got a team together, played for three summers. We'd go to Kansas, Texas, and she was at nearly every game. Our whole family was together."

"If you could have one more moment with your mom, what would you do?"

"If I had one moment, I would just hug her and kiss her and let her meet my babies."

"The state rests," Prem Bruns announced.

A Loving Son,
a Good Friend

"The defense calls Yvonne Gillis to the stand."

Yvonne would spend the next hour explaining to the jury what a good son Sean had been. Slender and fragile, with a thin face and graying hair, Yvonne was sincere in her beliefs about her son. The jury perceived her as everyone in the courtroom did—as a woman who had tried hard to be a good mother, to raise a good Catholic son. As Yvonne discussed her life with Sean Gillis, even the victims' family members understood what she must be going through and felt sorry for her. No one in that courtroom would have ever believed that Yvonne had done anything to create the evil that was her son.

Steven Lemoine questioned Yvonne about her background. She told him that she had worked in Baton Rouge at a department store and television station before moving to Atlanta in 1992. She described her relationship with Norman, how they had met and married. She explained that Norman had threatened to kill them and that she had divorced him. She told the jury about the time Sean had gone to New Orleans to pick up his father's things. "When he got back, there were some pictures of gay men there at his dad's. He was very peeved at his dad." Yvonne described the relationship Sean had with his father after that. "When Sean was a senior, Norman wanted to give him money to buy a car. Sean told him to give the money to me to pay for school, that he could drive my car. Norman started giving me money after that."

Yvonne said that Sean had graduated from Redemptorist High School in 1980 and had continued to live with her afterward. She told the jury that Sean had friendships that had lasted a lifetime, mentioning John Green and John Rosas. She explained that she had been raised in a very Catholic environment, that her brother was a priest and her sister a nun.

"A one-parent family always has drawbacks," she said, "but Sean was well fed and clothed and attended good Catholic schools. The other kids sometimes kidded him about not having a dad."

Yvonne shared memories of Sean's childhood, expressed how she had always thought he was a genius, talked about his favorite toys. As she talked about her memories, she would sometimes look at Sean, and the two would share a smile. It was evident that if they were not close now, they had been when Sean was younger.

"Sean was a sweet, loving little boy," Yvonne said. "A very respectful kid, but he could be tacky. We did a lot of things together. He was always so much in awe of things. Sean loves to read," she said proudly. "When he was a baby, I encouraged him to read. He gave me books as gifts."

"Did he like girls?"

"Oh yes." She laughed; Sean laughed with her.

Yvonne identified pictures from Sean's childhood for the jury. "He did have a special teacher he liked, Mr. Bumm," she recalled. "Sean mentioned that Mr. Bumm helped him."

"How?" Steven Lemoine asked.

Yvonne grinned. "Well, he needed an athletic supporter, and Mr. Bumm helped him."

Sean laughed out loud at the memory.

"How did you find out Sean had been arrested?"

"Terri called me at work. I didn't answer because I was in a meeting. I called her back and she told me. I felt like I had been run over by a Mack truck."

It was Prem Burns's turn to question the witness. While Yvonne Gillis seemed nervous at first, she soon settled down and seemed to enjoy talking about her remembrances of her son.

"It was groundbreaking for a woman to work like you did back then, wasn't it?" Burns asked. "That much responsibility was quite exceptional for a female."

"I was just a hardworking person. I'm not sure how much groundbreaking I did," Yvonne replied.

"Did you have any trouble with your pregnancy?" Burns questioned.

"No. My pregnancy was normal. I never felt healthier in my life."

"Do you remember Sean ever being unconscious?"

"No. He may have gotten the wind knocked out of him."

"Do you remember a wreck where he lost a tooth?"

"He spent a couple of weeks with Mr. Gillis and my parents. So if it happened, it would have happened there."

"Was Sean upset when you moved?"

"My son did not express that he was upset that I moved.

He did not want to go with me, because he had interest in a girl," Yvonne said. "Later, when I asked him to come to Atlanta, he said, 'You left, Mom. You have to come visit me.' We saw each other once or twice a year. I was lonesome. I saw him in June on his birthday and at Christmas."

"Do you remember any injuries he sustained as a child?"

"He had two injuries. I remember he was climbing stairs and fell and hit his forehead and started bleeding. The doctor said they bleed a lot right there. He said, 'Don't worry. It's not serious.' Then he had an accident playing basketball and popped his knee out."

"Do you remember an incident when he was ten when he fell into a drainpipe and was knocked unconscious?"

"No."

"Were you ever told [that] at fourteen he had an accident at school and was knocked unconscious?"

"No. At seventeen, he got in an accident when he drove my car. He had learned how to drive, but would turn his head when a cute girl walked by," Yvonne said.

Sean smiled.

"Did you ever spank him?"

"I did spank him one time, but the whole thing hurt me more than it did him. When he was older, I disciplined him by taking away television privileges."

"What did you use to spank him?" Burns persisted.

"I used a thin belt. It left marks on his leg but didn't bleed."

"Did your husband ever molest Sean while you watched?"

Yvonne was appalled by the suggestion. "No," she said angrily.

"Did Sean ever sleepwalk?"

"I think he did once. One night, he just walked up and

said something, then walked back to his bed. When I went in there, he was asleep."

"Did he drive his car sleeping?"

"No."

"Did he mention being watched by ghosts?"

"No."

"Vampires?"

"No."

"Did he mention having implants in his brain?"

"No."

"Ants in his brain?"

"No."

"Did he mention ants coming out of his nose?"

"No."

"Did you ever catch Sean looking at Web sites of dead bodies?"

"No. None of this seemed to manifest itself until after I was gone. I saw him as a happy, sweet, loving person. He enjoyed life. He enjoyed his friends. I did not see this coming, period. My first thought was 'Gosh, I must have been an awful mother.'"

"How has this affected you?"

"This is the person I loved most in the world," Yvonne said. "It's too hard to believe. It's hard to sleep at night. I miss my baby. I stay tense all the time. It's a mother's worst nightmare. The victims' mothers are also going through a nightmare. I feel so sorry for them. I know it occurred, but it's hard to believe."

Yvonne was excused. She walked quickly back to her seat, glancing at Sean as she passed him. He smiled, quietly reassuring her that she had done well.

* * *

Sean Gillis's cousin Pam Bordelon took her place on the stand and explained to the jury that she and Sean spent a lot of summers together when they were young. "Sean always worried about me," she said. "He was great to me, kind. He was the same way with my sisters. I thought he was a great young man, thought he was doing fine."

She described her family dynamic for jurors, saying that the family was "not very affectionate, not huggy kissy. I saw Sean with his mother a lot. Yvonne loved him."

Although they did not see each other much as they got older, Pam said, Sean would drive to Lafayette to see her now and then, and they always kept in touch.

"What did you think when you heard he got arrested?" Steven Lemoine asked.

"I couldn't believe it. That's not the boy I grew up with, not the person I know. I don't understand it."

Prem Burns asked Pam if she'd known Sean to have girlfriends. "I'd always joke and ask him if he had a girl-friend. He had a few. Nothing abnormal. Sean's never been violent," Pam said.

Sean's teacher Robert Bumm had a different opinion of Sean Gillis as a child. "I've known him since he was a real young boy," he told the court. "He was a lonely-looking child, stood off from the other kids. I wondered if he had problems. I felt he needed attention. He was reaching out to me as a male mentor. I didn't do a very good job of helping him. Sometimes he would come by and talk to me about *Star Trek*."

Robert remembered that Sean had once been kicked out of an English class for calling his teacher a "damn bitch."

"He asked me what to do, but I told him I never come

between a student and another teacher. That was the only case I ever knew of a conduct problem. He was more quiet than other students, sat in the back of class. He had his own world he lived in. I liked him."

John Green, Sean's childhood friend, testified next. He began to describe the trip he and Sean Gillis took to New Orleans to collect Sean's father's things. Norman Gillis stood up and walked out of the courtroom. He did not want to sit through this testimony. John described getting lost near the Superdome, and Sean started laughing. He was enjoying seeing his old friend and taking a trip down memory lane.

John described how Sean had been forced to take care of himself while Yvonne worked. "He was more like an adult than other kids. It made him a survivor. He is a strong individual and handles himself well. Around my parents, he was respectful and helpful. He had a fantastic sense of humor, very funny, funny and smart. I never saw Sean do anything mean. I love Sean sincerely. I know what he did, and I still love him."

Norman walked back into the courtroom.

"Sean didn't cringe in the face of adversity. He was like his mom in that respect. He faced things head-on. He was a good person to have by your side in a difficult time," John Green continued. "I'm actually probably the one that introduced him to the idea that there might be Devil worshippers in Baton Rouge." John related the incident when they were teenagers and had gone to look for the Devil worshippers. "But I've never known Sean to be interested in Satanic things."

* * *

After John Green was excused, John Rosas walked to the stand. He testified that he had met Sean in the seventh grade, and the two boys had become like brothers. "After high school, we got even closer," he said. "We went to the movies, to the mall, to each other's house. He's friendly, a good listener. He made me laugh. I could count on him. I love Sean. Still do."

John remembered that he and Sean had been good drinkers and sometimes smoked marijuana together. He said that he had heard that Sean had smoked marijuana with Christine, John's daughter. "I forgive him," John said. He described how Sean had gone with him on weekends to visit his daughter. "They were like brother and sister. Sean gave her presents for holidays, sometimes stuff he made from things around his house."

"How did you find out Sean had been arrested?"

"I was at work. My ex-girlfriend called me to tell me about Sean. I was totally shocked. Couldn't believe it. Would never have predicted he could do something of that nature. Growing up, I didn't go to church. Now I go every Sunday. I'm a better person now. It's like something hit me. Sean was like a brother. I'm closer to him than my own blood brother," John Rosas said.

Christine Rosas, John's daughter, told the court that she had fun, happy memories of Sean. "Sean is my godfather. We had a very close relationship all my life. He was always there to talk to me, to inspire me." Christine said that she had been molested at the age of seven and had to help raise her little sister. "I swept the floors like Cinderella. The good times I had were when Sean and Dad picked me up. I love him." Christine started crying.

Sean looked upset.

"I still love him. It's not up to me to judge. In my eyes, he's the Sean I always knew. Him and Terri were like my own family."

"How did you discover what Sean had done?" Steven Lemoine asked.

"Me and my husband lived in Milton. A sketch came on the TV. My husband said, 'Baby, it's Sean.' I said it couldn't be. Sean wouldn't do that. That day, Sean came over, and the sketch came on again. My husband said, 'That's you. You did it.' Sean said, 'Yeah.' I never saw that evil side of him."

Then Christine made a startling announcement. "He told me his father had molested him, and his mother watched. I was kinda down, and he told me that to comfort me. I always talked to him about me being molested."

The court recessed. Yvonne Gillis was crying. She hurried toward Christine. "I can't believe you said that," Yvonne cried furiously. "That is not true."

Yvonne marched up to Kerry Cuccia. "You know that's not true. You know that's not true," she said angrily, wagging her finger in his face. "Why did you make her say that?"

Cuccia tried to appease the distraught woman, but to no avail. Yvonne had spent her life trying her best to live right, and she could not handle being maligned this way. She hurried out of the courtroom, still crying.

"How often do you have seizures?" Steven Lemoine asked Terri Lemoine, who had taken the stand.

"A couple of times a week. I had one this morning, and one at noon yesterday. I got out of the car, came up the elevator, sat down in here and couldn't remember how I got here. I lose memory and time. It usually lasts three to ten minutes."

Steven Lemoine asked Terri to describe Sean's relationship with her children. "Katie is twenty-eight. I didn't raise her. She came to live with me when she was seventeen. Sean started visiting after Katie came back. Me and Katie had differences. I hadn't seen her since she was two, and she wasn't ready for another mother. She already had one. Sean got along better with her because he wasn't trying to be her mother or her daddy. He was patient. They would get on the computer for hours like two kids while I was in another room. He was the one who made me realize she already had a mother."

"Tell me about your sexual relationship," Steven Lemoine said.

"It wasn't really intimate. We had sex twice or three or four times in ten years . . . when we first met," Terri said. "That didn't matter to me. We had the same likes and dislikes. His computer got in the way of our relationship. He spent twelve to forty-eight hours on it at a time. That was the other woman. I felt like he paid more attention to it than to me."

"No further questions."

"Did you ever get a call saying he had passed out or had a seizure?" Prem Burns asked.

"No," Terri said.

"You never took him to the hospital?"

"No."

"Did you know what he looked at on the computer?"

"No."

"Did he ever beat you?"

"No."

Did he ever tell you about ants, worms, or implants in his brain?"

"No."

"Did you ever see him sleepwalking?"

"No."

"Urinating in a cat box?"

"No, ma'am."

"If he had been doing the things we've discussed, would you have gotten him help?"

"Yes," Terri Lemoine replied.

"Thank you. No further questions."

Conflicting Testimony

Steven Lemoine and Kerry Cuccia had carefully chosen the experts who were to convince the jury that Sean Gillis was mentally ill. They knew that if the jury had any doubt at all about Sean's sanity, they could not put him to death. Steven Lemoine would spend an unusually long time establishing each of their credentials as they took their turns testifying.

Dr. Thomas Reidy, a forensic psychologist with a Ph.D. in psychiatry, specialized in neuropsychiatry. He explained that he regularly did evaluations for courts to determine sanity and competency. He also performed research on violence risk assessments in capital cases.

"Violence risk assessment is a way to look at factors about whether an individual engages in violent practices. I can only talk from a statistical viewpoint. I did not interview Sean," he informed the court.

"I would like to voir dire this witness," Prem Burns piped in. She wanted to question Reidy and his qualifications to act as an expert witness for Sean.

Judge Bonnie Jackson nodded.

"You've never examined Sean?" she asked.

"No. Information was provided to me," Reidy said.

"What information?"

·"His age, lack of prior record, lack of violence in four years of custody."

"You are aware there are three victims in his case, aren't you?" Prem Burns asked, her tone disbelieving.

"I have not reviewed police reports," Dr. Reidy replied.

"Have you seen pictures of Donna Bennett Johnston?"

"No."

Members of the jury laughed.

"Are you aware that Sean used a nontraditional weapon?"

"I was not told that. I have not reviewed Mr. Gillis's makeup. The best predictor of future behavior is past behavior to a point," the psychiatrist said.

"I object to this psychiatrist's testimony," Burns said.

"Overruled."

"How someone commits a homicide is not related. How many is not related," Steven Lemoine explained. "Age is related. Frequency of acts of violence in prison is related."

Dr. Reidy explained that when a person goes to prison, he or she is classified. "What we have found in our research is that issues like diagnosis are not terribly related to risk of violence. The actual rates of violence in prison are quite low, which may surprise some people. All felons by definition are dangerous, but we don't know if they will be dangerous in a particular context."

The doctor said that he uses a statistical probability method that models patterns of behavior. "Seventy-five percent of prisoners have diagnoses of antisocial personality disorder. You can't say for sure whether an individual will commit a violent act. You look at degrees of improbability. We also look at impulsivity. Everyone in prison is impulsive. For Sean, the context is prison, looking at how murderers do in prison."

Reidy was referring to articles that he had written in the past as reference points throughout his testimony. He presented a slide show for the jury to emphasize his points. Sean was interested in the slides.

"Age is the most powerful predictor of behavior in prison," Reidy continued. "Those who enter prison while they are young are much more likely to act out. As people age, they mellow. The age group of nineteen- to twenty-four-year-olds has the highest number of infractions. If you are young and enter prison with a short-term sentence, you'll commit more infractions than a long-term sentence. If older, the infractions are smaller for long-term and short-term. If you go into prison at an older age, you commit less infractions."

Prem Burns looked frustrated and impatient with the testimony. The look on her face said, *What does all of this have to do with Sean's mental state?*

Reidy droned on, determined to explain his slide show that was intended to impress jurors. They did not look impressed.

"In an Indiana study, we looked at prison infractions. We looked at nine thousand five hundred ninety-five offenders. The frequency rates for first-degree murderers was thirty-five percent commit acts of violence. That is lower than the rate of other offenders. Regular prisoners had forty-five percent frequency rates. Less than one percent of prisoners commit assault with injury."

It finally became obvious what the doctor was trying to accomplish. He was trying to convince the jury that if given a life sentence, Sean would not be violent in prison.

"Sean Gillis is forty-six. He is at the bottom of the graph for probability to commit a violent act."

The jurors looked bored. Some asked the bailiff for water.

Prem Burns objected again to the witness. "It's your testimony," she said, "that you mellow with age? Sean Gillis killed Katherine Hall when he was thirty-seven and Donna Bennett Johnston and Johnnie Mae Williams when he was forty-two. You cannot say he will not kill again. Anything's possible."

Dr. Reidy stepped down. The judge recessed for lunch. She could tell the jury needed a break.

After lunch, Dr. Ruben Gur, an expert in neuropsychology from Jerusalem, walked to the stand. Steven Lemoine quizzed him extensively about his expertise, articles he had written, his background. Finally he allowed the doctor to articulate his knowledge of positron emission tomography (PET) scans. "They are no longer used predominately to link activity in brain to activity," he said. "The Functional MRI is used now. With PET, you can measure glucose metabolism to the brain and blood flow. PET also measures neurotransmitters. Magnetic resonance imaging (MRI) dots reflect a real number that indicates the intensity of a signal in that image—three-dimensional pixels called voxels. In quantitative analysis of MRI, multiple sclerosis shows in white matter. You can have significant damage that is not visually apparent."

Gur explained that in the brain there is gray matter, white matter, and fluid. "Traumatic brain injuries can be diffused and dispensed and sometimes cannot be seen. The MRI detects what radiologists cannot see," he said.

Prem Burns interrupted. She had heard enough. "It took an hour to establish him as a witness, to link brain function to behavior, neuropsychologist, neuroradiologist, doctor who reads MRIs and PETs. Sir, isn't it true that your methodology has previously not been accepted?"

"Yes."

"Have your findings and methodologies been opposed?"

"There's obviously experts on the other side," the doctor agreed.

She reluctantly tendered him as a witness.

Gur spent the next hour giving the jury an anatomy lesson in the science of the brain using quantitative analysis. He finally got around to Sean Gillis.

"He is within normal range in his frontal lobes," the doctor said. "Sean was born with a large brain, but some regions are smaller. The gray matter in his brain has a one to one-and-a-half standard deviation. The amygdala is abnormal. The occipital lobe is also outside of the standard deviation. The corpus callosum is two standard deviations below normal, showing that he has little ability to communicate between the sides of the brain. On the right ventral, Sean is two standard deviations above normal, indicating a loss of tissue, similar to an individual born with schizophrenia, although a bit more severe."

Although he had not examined Sean Gillis outside of reading his MRI, Dr. Gur determined that Sean had schizoaffective disorder, which is a flat affect—not happy, not depressed. "You are more depressed when you are more intelligent," Gur said.

The doctor went on to give his diagnosis of Sean's

PET scan. "Mr. Gillis values in most regions right above normal," he said.

Sean was listening intently. This was fascinating to him.

"However, in the amygdala, he is five or six standard deviations lower than normal. The corpus callosum is also abnormally low. There is too much action on the left side. Most of the damages are more right hemispheric. There is abnormality in the right portal, which can lead to dissociative experiences. In the temporal limbic area, every little thing activates the region. He is overwhelmed with urges. Looks like a seizure disorder on a PET scan. We're dealing with more than schizophrenia. There are additional abnormalities," Gur declared. "If we put the two together, I'm convinced we're dealing with a brain that had abnormalities to begin with, but also sustained a brain injury later on. There is moderate brain damage definitely. The amygdala, it's about as bad as I've seen. The main role of the amygdala is the detection of threats, but it is at the heart of gray matter and emotion. This can produce a propensity for violence."

It almost seemed like the defense's experts were testifying against each other. One said that Sean had no propensity for violence, while the other testified that he had an accelerated propensity for violence.

Likely feeling pretty violent now herself, Prem Burns pounced on her prey. "Quantitative analysis has not been allowed by the FDA, not for clinical use. The FDA does not approve this kind of thing. This is not something in clinical use. It's far from an exact science."

"This is as exact as you can be," Dr. Gur retorted.

"How do we know what a normal brain is?" Burns asked.

"We take measurements from a large sample of normal

brains, twelve to fifteen," Gur replied. "We have to use the smallest number of people, approximately fifteen people. It's best to use all males for males and all females for females. We have values from all over the world, not much variation geographically. There are variations due to age and ethnicity."

"We are taking your numbers on faith," Burns replied. "The date on your report is February 4, 2008, written '4-2-08.' If you transposed numbers on your chart in the date, how can we rely on your numbers?"

"My European background, where you put the day before the month, might account for that," Gur said.

Burns continued with her attack. "Have you studied Asperger's? There is no model that fits those with that disease. Can you diagnose if a person will kill if they are bipolar?"

"We can't predict if they will kill or not. The diagnosis is only as good as the information you receive."

"You did not see crime scene photos, police reports, the amount of thought that went into the planning, the three victims the same size, prostitutes, drugs, late at night, unique choice of murder weapon? You did not know that he photographed victims and brought a camera?"

"I did not see those pictures," Dr. Gur admitted.

"Pictures showing his body parts touching the victims, you did not see this?"

"No."

"Videotapes?"

"No. I was just asked to do imaging. That is not relevant to what I was asked to do."

Steven Lemoine addressed the jury. "You have to remember, he still has a lot of brain activity. Parts of the frontal lobe are damaged, not all of it. Nothing is in conflict with the other testimony. Mr. Gillis has a brain that can go from point A to point B."

After a few more questions, Lemoine finished with his witness. Family members in the courtroom let out a sigh of relief. The testimony had upset most of them. Everyone knew the psychiatrists were paid to be there. They felt like they would come to whatever conclusion was expected of them. They hoped the jury would see through the charade. The next day would prove even more trying.

Illness versus Evil

Kerry Cuccia and Steven Lemoine had saved their most persuasive expert for last. When the courtroom door opened on July 28, family members of the victims were unprepared for what they would hear. Even Sean Gillis's family— Yvonne, Norman—and Terri Lemoine would listen in disbelief as the defense witness explained Sean's particular psychoses to which they had never been exposed.

Dr. Dorothy Lewis flitted up to the stand. Slim, with short black hair framing a pixieish face, she smiled a big, happy smile at the jury. Steven Lemoine asked her about her background in psychiatry. It was impressive.

Lewis had been a psychiatrist since 1979. She had studied at Radcliffe College, Harvard, and Yale School of Medicine. She currently worked as a professor at the Yale Child Study Center. "I've always been interested in issues of justice, behavior, and aggression," she said, looking at the jury and smiling while she tried to win their confidence. Lewis was an expert at this. She traveled the country testifying in capital cases of killers, including the case of Arthur J. Shawcross, who was later convicted of eleven murders. Lewis had testified that Shawcross suffered from child abuse, post-traumatic stress disorder, and multiple personality disorder. He was given a life sentence. She had also examined Ted Bundy in 1987 while he was in prison awaiting his death sentence to be carried out. She had diagnosed Bundy as a manic depressive. Serial killers were her specialty. She had even penned a book, *Guilty by Reason of Insanity*, on the subject.

The defense had hired her to examine Sean Gillis, and over the course of twenty-six cumulative hours of interviews, Dr. Lewis was confident she knew exactly what was wrong with the killer. She told the jury that she had brought together a team: a neurologist, a psychologist, and a radiologist, who studied his school history, medical history, and psychiatric history.

"There are two reasons to do the history," she explained. "There are dispositions to having a disorder, and if an individual is raised in a household with a disturbed parent, the child can also be affected." It was obvious that Lewis believed that nature and nurture were contributing factors.

She told the jury that Sean's father had experienced numerous hospitalizations between 1957 and 1981, and had been given seven different diagnoses. "He moved out of the house when Sean was very young," she said. "One hospital dismissed him as sociopathic. Eight days later, he tried to kill himself."

Dr. Lewis said that on different occasions Norman Gillis had tried to cut his wrists, overdosed, and put guns to his head. "He was confused about his sexual identity and threatened to emasculate himself," she added. "There were several violent episodes before he had a religious epiphany." After Norman "saw the light," Lewis said, he began speaking in tongues, saying that the church had healed him, but that disorders have different manifestations at different times.

Lewis smiled again at the jury. No one smiled back as she continued to describe the mental illness in Sean's family history. She said that Norman Gillis suffered from migraines and noted that Sean did, too. She explained that migraines can cause a neurological disorder, which can result in multiple episodes of déjà vu and epiphanies.

She related that Sean's paternal grandmother had also been in and out of mental hospitals during her lifetime and had received electroconvulsive, or shock, therapy. She described a history of schizophrenia through Sean's paternal great-grandmother, who thought she could put spells on people. Dr. Lewis explained that everyone thought the woman had poisoned her husband because poison was found in his system after he died, but she had not been arrested. "His paternal grandmother's brother was a drag queen," Dr. Lewis continued.

She said that Yvonne Gillis denied any history of mental illness in her family. "Sean described some mood swings to me, but said she was a nurturing mother," Lewis said. "Others have said her father was a womanizer and an alcoholic, but she denies it. Sean's maternal grandmother could drink Sean under the table." Dr. Lewis said the tendency here was toward bipolar disorder.

She went on to discuss a head injury Sean experienced as a toddler. "He went headfirst into a table," Lewis explained, still smiling and bubbly. "He bled a lot and went to the hospital. Damage to the frontal lobe of a young child is not good. It affects control, logic, and executive function. Sean also said he had an injury at ten or fourteen when he fell into a storm pipe, and another injury sustained while playing basketball. He told me he was unconscious for twenty minutes. I documented scars on his head."

Lewis told the jury that in another incident, Sean was rear-ended and hit his head on the steering wheel, breaking his front tooth.

"From MRIs and PET scans, we can tell he has deficiencies in the frontal lobe. He came by them naturally," she joked. "Any of these could have affected the amygdala. He also has a long-standing history of migraines," she said, mentioning complex partial seizures and dissociative disorders as by-products of the headaches. "He said he had multiple episodes of falling to the floor."

By this time, the state experts sitting in the front row were having difficulty containing their laughter as Dr. Lewis cheerfully rolled out her laundry list of disorders. Kerry Cuccia noticed.

"Judge, the people in the front row are making disparaging remarks and making faces during the testimony. Dr. Hoppe is being dismissive, smiling, and shaking his head," Cuccia said.

"I would expect professionals to act professional," Judge Jackson admonished. "You do not have the right to do anything that might influence the jury."

The "professionals" were hard-pressed to keep from busting out laughing at Lewis's next statement.

"Sean believes his brain is like a library operating system. He believes a worm has infiltrated his brain or a virus has infiltrated the operating system. He thinks he has ants in his brain. He says the government has devised a way to teleport people to other geographic locations," Lewis said, ignoring the psychiatrists in the front row whose shoulders were shaking as they tried to contain their laughter.

She continued to describe a variety of symptoms Sean

Gillis was experiencing from hyperactivity to bipolar disease to grandiosity and periods of episodic rapid indescribable speech.

"Sean told me—"

"Objection," Prem Burns said.

"Overruled."

"I went to Dr. Robert Blanche (Blanche had treated Sean in prison), and he said yes, he had discussed bipolar disorder with Sean. He talked about how Sean is so happy and exuberant one moment and stable later on. Dr. Zimmerman reported the same thing. His grandiosity, his belief that he is a high-ranking officer on a mission only he knows about. He has stationery with a picture of himself in a high-ranking *Star Trek* uniform."

Obviously, Dr. Lewis had not bothered to ask Sean where he had gotten the stationery. He could have told her that Louis Gaar had created the image and made the stationery for him as a present.

Dorothy Lewis mentioned Sean's complex partial seizures and dissociative behavior. "People can have very complex behaviors but do not fall to the ground and do not froth at the mouth," she said. Then the bubbling psychiatrist laid it on even thicker.

She told the jury that Sean had a female self that lived inside him. "He felt that this 'Goldilocks' was a very strong part of him and still believes she inhabits him. An imaginary friend usually disappears at five or six years of age, but with extensive disturbance in children, the imaginary companion lives on. Sean hates this part of himself. On more than one occasion, he has said, 'I'll rape her. I'll kill her.'"

("Bullshit," Terri Lemoine would say later, laughing.

"That's hilarious. I've never heard Sean mention Goldilocks. If he told that psychiatrist that, he was screwing with her.")

Dorothy Lewis wasn't finished. "Sean often refers to himself in the third person. He calls himself 'Bobby.' He says things like, 'I don't want Bobby in my head,' or with Goldilocks—'I wanted to kill the bitch. Get her out of my head.' He says things like, 'This is Admiral Sean Gillis.'"

Sitting in the courtroom, listening, Terri smiled. That had been their special way of communicating with each other. Sean called her "Admiral Lemoine." She wondered if that meant she was crazy, too.

"Sean said he saw pictures on his computer of Terri's daughter Katie, dead and decomposing on the computer screen. When the two girls were home, he would go out and drive because he was terrified that he would hurt them," Dr. Lewis said.

Terri rolled her eyes. Sean had never laid a hand on any of her children, had not even raised his voice to them.

"In the case of Johnnie Mae, he cut off her hands and painted her fingernails. He said, 'I thought she should look nice when she goes to meet her Maker.' He forgot her body in the trunk of his car."

This testimony was becoming more and more unbelievable. Sean had disposed of Johnnie Mae's body the same night he killed her.

"I asked Sean's father why he had taken off, and he said, 'I thought something was wrong with me. I thought maybe I was gay.' Sean always thinks there's something wrong with him. Like a female, Sean could have feminization in his brain."

Finally Dr. Dorothy Lewis got to her true diagnosis. "He has all the signs of schizo-affective disorder. I can't argue with anyone who says that. He comes by it naturally. There is additional damage, abnormality of his brain."

"At the time of the offense, was Sean Gillis affected by mental disease when he committed these acts?" Steven Lemoine asked.

"Objection. That's for the jury to decide," Prem Burns said.

"Overruled."

"Did he appreciate the criminality of his offense?" Steven Lemoine persisted.

"Yes, as I understand it. When Mr. Gillis set out that evening, he had been driving around. Whatever was going on in his head passed. He was going home when he saw in the distance a female. He looked at her and thought, 'Yes, she is meant to die,' and killed her. Damage to the temporal lobe does cause animalistic behavior. Suddenly he hacked off the arm, then bites it."

Dr. Lewis mentioned that Sean Gillis was taking Elavil, an antidepressant that sedated him. "I believe I have examined him when he was not taking Elavil, because he was far more animated. He was high as a kite, chattering, going on and on. We talked about *The Joy of Sex* and the *Kama Sutra*."

Steven Lemoine tendered the witness.

Prem Burns stood up and asked Dr. Dorothy Lewis how many serial killers she had evaluated.

"No, Prem, no," Tony Clayton mouthed quietly from his seat in the courtroom. He had dropped by to watch Burns work her magic. He admired the assistant district attorney's calm and methodical approach to trying cases, although it was so different from his own. "Stop," he muttered. "Say, 'No questions for this witness.'"

Clayton worried that the longer Dr. Lewis was on the

stand, the more time she would have to convince the jury of her various inane diagnoses. The doctor had already been testifying for way too long, for hours. "Show the jury that she's insignificant, not worthy of questioning. Get her off the stand."

Prem Burns didn't hear Tony Clayton's mutterings, and if she had, she wouldn't have paid attention. She knew what she was doing. She was determined to discredit this witness.

"I have evaluated twenty-two serial killers. I've testified for the defense seven or eight times," Dr. Lewis answered. "I don't believe in killing children, but I don't believe severely mentally ill people should be executed."

"In your book *Guilty by Reason of Insanity*, you said, 'evil is not a scientific or medical term, it's a religious term.' Did you say that you believe people kill because they are evil?"

"No. Evil is a judgment. Doctors are no more qualified to say someone is evil than dentists. It is not a medical or scientific term."

"Do you believe someone will hurt another person for the sheer pleasure of it?" Burns asked.

"Yes."

"On April 2, 2008, an MRI was taken at LSU Shreveport. A board-certified radiologist read it to be normal. The same thing for the PET scan and sleep studies. You evaluated the sleep studies and cannot give us your findings?"

"Parts were missing," Dr. Lewis said. "I could not evaluate it because there was not adequate data. I think I saw the report. Other aspects were not made available."

Burns asked for the definition of "sociopath."

"'Sociopath,' I would have to look at the *DSM-IV* (*Di-*

agnostic and Statistical Manual of Mental Disorders).
I don't think it's a term anymore," Lewis hedged.

"Do you know what page?" Burns asked. "Doctor, I'll
let you look because you're a psychiatrist, and I'm just
an assistant district attorney. I'll defer to your expertise."

"There are no references to sociopath," Dr. Lewis said.

"Did you look under antisocial personality disorder?"
Burns said matter-of-factly.

The doctor flipped through the pages of the bible of
psychiatry. "Here it is," she said. "'It is a pervasive pattern
of disregard for, and violation of, the rights of others that
begins in childhood or early adolescence and continues
into adulthood.'"

"So anyone's diagnosis is only as good as the information you have?"

"Yes," Lewis agreed.

Burns moved on to Sean's parents.

"What did Sean tell you about his mother?"

"Sean said she could fly into angry states. She beat him
with a thin black plastic belt until it broke. I looked at his
buttocks, and he had scars. His mother also stated that she
did beat him once. He could not have inflicted this on
himself."

"If everybody else says he had a nurturing mother, and
he says severe beatings, would you agree there is a difference?"

"Yes. But his grandmother's brother was a drag queen,
his grandfather was a gambler and a drinker, his grandmother also drank. All one can say is there may have been
a history."

Prem Burns addressed the injuries Sean had sustained
in childhood. "Is there a record of when he cut his head on
the table?"

"No," Dr. Lewis said.

"Of the storm pipe incident?"

"No."

"When he fell at school at fourteen?"

"No."

"When he was in the wreck at seventeen?"

"No."

"In the first report that you cited, it says Sean recalled an incident where he fell at ten years old. The report says, 'According to his sister that was there.' He has no sister."

"That was a misstatement," Dr. Lewis said.

"Or it could be bullshit. You know what I'm talking about," Burns said.

"Objection," Steven Lemoine said.

"Overruled."

Prem Burns and Dorothy Lewis then discussed Sean's sleep patterns and his statement that he had walked in his sleep and urinated in a cat litter box.

"I have not made a diagnosis of parasomnia," Dr. Lewis said.

Burns asked her about Sean's female persona.

"He alternated between a male voice and a high-pitched female voice. He would say, 'Between us girls.' He said, 'I try and I try to lower my voice to sound like a man.' It happened frequently. I said, 'Yeah, you kinda sound like a girl.'"

"Would he lose a job over it?"

"I don't think he would."

"Did he lose a job because of falling down or Goldilocks?"

"He does have the job history of a man who could be violent. His left hemisphere is very active, and he's smart. He should have been able to keep a job."

"Or he's a man whose mother pays the rent and utilities

and a girlfriend who carries the load. It could be laziness," Burns stated.

It was time to talk about Terri Lemoine. "There were inconsistencies with Sean's stories and the answers given by his girlfriend. His perception is that they had sex a lot, and hers only twice in a long time," Dr. Lewis said. "He said he would go into states at night where he would beat up on her and not remember it. Terri suffers from seizures. Her memories could be distorted."

"Are you saying she doesn't remember him beating her because she was having seizures?" Burns questioned.

"People do have periods of sleep where they don't remember."

Prem Burns showed the jury a report based on interviews with Sean Gillis that were conducted by Dr. Dorothy Lewis on January 10, 20, and 21, 2008, at East Baton Rouge Parish Prison. She handed out additional reports from June 28 and 29, as well as interviews with Sean's friends, family, and neighbors. She also introduced four hours of taped video of Sean from April and May of 2004.

"Objection," Steven Lemoine said. "She agreed not to use those interviews, which she agreed were obtained illegally. She is making reference to materials she said she was not going to use, or we would have made a motion to suppress. I move for a mistrial."

"Whenever we gave notice of this, I said I would not use it in my case-in-chief, but retained the right to use it in the penalty phase. Dr. Lewis used interviews to make findings. It was the defense's choice to send her the tape," Burns argued.

"The tape is admissible. Motion denied."

"Did you view these tapes?" Burns asked.

"I skimmed the tapes but did not review them. I was sent a bunch of transcripts. I reviewed some of them. I don't recall. This was such a long time ago." Dr. Lewis's upbeat demeanor was rapidly changing to nervousness.

"Look at page fifty-four," Burns said. "Mr. Lemoine, why don't you go up to the stand and look at it with her? You told Sean he was a good actor. You said, 'A good liar and a good actor.' He talks about following the case through the media. On page fifty-nine, he's talking about living women. He says, 'I treated them like ladies. I couldn't wait to get them into my car.'"

"Objection."

The jury was again removed from the courtroom—one of a multitude of times during these proceedings.

"Judge, I move for a mistrial," Steven Lemoine said again. "Since she does not recall the interview, she could not have used it for the basis of her findings. I ask that the tapes be suppressed."

"The tapes are out," Judge Jackson said.

"This is a violation of my client's constitutional rights," Steven Lemoine said.

"There is no basis for that. I don't believe there was anything said that would cause the jury to go on a wild speculation. Motion denied."

The spectators in the courtroom had been hanging on every word of this testimony. It was like something out of *The Twilight Zone*. They rose as the jury was brought back in. "You don't have to stand," Judge Jackson said, laughing.

Prem Burns continued: "In a report by Dr. Blanche dated March 17, 2005, Dr. Blanche stated that Sean has no psychotic symptoms evident. He experiences flashes of light but is doing things he always wanted to do. The report says Sean is coherent and organized but does complain of severe headaches."

"Dr. Blanche recognized the disorder but bent over backward to do what the prison wanted," Dr. Lewis said.

"Isn't this sad? He knows what's wrong with this man and is not putting it down. This guy refused to make the diagnosis. When I read this, I thought, 'How dare you? Sean reports headaches, numbness of his side, mood swings.'"

"Isn't that normal for someone in jail waiting for the death penalty?"

"Objection," Steven Lemoine said.

"It was a simple slip of the tongue."

"I move for a mistrial on the grounds of prosecutorial misconduct."

"Denied."

"Were you furnished crime scene photos?" Burns asked the doctor, who had by now been testifying all day.

"I reviewed the current case."

"Were you able to look at forty-five pictures taken after the homicide?"

"Yes, some of them."

"Were you aware of similarities?"

"One was white, one was black. It mentioned ages."

"Are you aware of their occupation?"

"Was it the oldest occupation in the world?" Dr. Lewis quipped.

"Did you see the pickup site, murder site, disposal site?"

"I didn't focus on physical evidence."

"Are you aware that initially there was a denial?"

"Yes."

"Did you know he deleted the pictures before police arrived, that he committed the first-degree murders of three women?"

"He made the statement to me, 'They were already dead.' He would have the feeling that this person was meant to die. He would look at a person, and he would feel, 'Well, she's already dead,' if she didn't pay attention to him. He felt he was saving them. To him, they already looked dead."

Judge Jackson yawned.

"Each time we talked, he said they were already dead," Lewis continued.

"If he said that to a newspaper reporter in 2004, what does that mean?"

"He does perceive that they were already dead because he had seen delusions of their deaths. He looked at his mother once, and he had a knife. He thought, 'No, this is not her time to die. She still looks alive.'"

Dr. Lewis went on. "He tries very hard to seem normal, to not appear crazy. I wasn't hacking away at him, I just sat back and listened. After a little time, some of this bizarre behavior came out. He was going and going, talking and talking, going hither and yon, then a day later, he's back to normal."

"Why do his friends still love him?"

"It's like a baby with Down syndrome. You might ask how she can love him, but even that baby can be loveable."

Prem Burns was done. "No further questions."

"Thank God that fruitcake is off the stand," a reporter whispered to another sitting nearby. "At least, the jury won't buy a word of that."

Prem Burns called Dr. Donald Hoppe's name. She needed him to rebut the doctor's testimony. One of the experts who had laughed at the preceding witness took his place on the stand.

Hoppe had been a clinical psychologist for twenty-seven years and had done an internship at Johns Hopkins. His current position was chief psychologist at Baton Rouge

General's Chemical Dependency Unit. He also had a part-time practice in Baton Rouge. He explained that psychology was the science of behavior, and clinical psychology was the study of behavior as it applied to mental issues.

"I am here to testify about Dr. Lewis's opinion," he said. "The *DSM-IV* allows us to have a shared language for diagnosis. Her data was astounding, but I'm not sure that her opinion is correct."

"I object to this witness," Steven Lemoine said.

"Overruled."

"Did you hear Dr. Lewis's testimony?" Burns asked.

"Yes."

"Did you hear testimony about ants, sleepwalking, alleged abuse, alleged molestation witnessed by Sean's mother, the testimony of his live-in girlfriend who denied all of this?"

"Yes."

"Would a red flag be raised if there are disparities in the information given, if his girlfriend says differently?"

"Yes, but my greatest concern was the large number of diagnoses given. If we receive facts A, B, and C, and then get to D, we should go back and revisit diagnosis, not add another diagnosis."

"Objection."

Judge Jackson rolled her eyes.

"Overruled."

"For all the talk of science we've heard, we're forgetting that the biggest principle of science is parsimony, which requires that given competing explanations, the simplest is always the best," Dr. Hoppe said.

"If someone has the large number of disorders, and he's had those disorders for many years, how is it that he lived for thirty-seven years undetected?"

"It's not likely that someone with that many disorders could have functioned," Hoppe said.

"If you look at the list of diagnoses, it's a wonder he can even get up and put two feet on the floor," Burns said.

"Objection."

"Overruled."

"Sean has symptoms of Asperger's syndrome," Hoppe said. "Emotional neglect, considered odd by his peers, can relate better to adults, well versed on narrow topics, very narrow esoteric areas of interests. With Sean, it was *Star Trek.* If you want to see what someone with Asperger's looks like, go to a *Star Trek* convention. People with Asperger's are often described by adults as little professors. There is compartmentalization. They learn not to talk about things. Very often they have a façade and become very good at playacting. They don't know why they do it, but they play the role. There is usually moodiness, low stress tolerance, substance abuse. They avoid sexual behavior because it's too complicated emotionally."

"Is there a correlation between Asperger's and violence?"

"No. I'm not making a diagnosis, just asking why this wasn't considered. She made six diagnoses. Asperger's would account for all of Sean's symptoms and behaviors and explain why he could still function in society."

"What is Asperger's?"

"It's a developmental disorder, high-functioning autism. They are labeled as odd, nerds, bully. They have a severe deficiency in social skills, in forming relationships, in understanding emotions. They have highly developed verbal skills but don't use language as others do. They talk about the same thing over and over. I had a man I treated who was only interested in hands. The fascination with body parts is very telling. Sean was very interested in body parts. There's definitely enough here to ask, 'Does this man have Asperger's?'"

Prem Burns knew it was imperative that she show the jury that Sean was not mentally ill. She had to convince them he was simply evil.

The ADA called Dr. David Lilien to the stand. Lilien, a nuclear medical physician who had been with LSU since 1965 and had moved to Shreveport to become the medical director of the PET Center there, described how PET uses radioactive tracers to produce images. "We inject radioactive forms of sugar into the patient and wait an hour, then put it in the scanner like a CAT or MRI," he said. "The data is three-dimensional. We are looking for gray matter. This is quantitative analysis not yet approved by the FDA. We don't use it on a daily basis."

"And you performed this PET scan on Sean Gillis?" Burns asked.

"Yes. I look at all orientations of the brain. We found neither subjective abnormality nor anything more than two standard deviations from the mean," he asserted.

Dr. Mardjohan Hardjasudarma testified next. A neurologist employed at the LSU Health Science Center in Shreveport, the doctor told the court that he had received a copy of an MRI under the name "John Doe." He told the court that he had studied the MRI carefully. "An MRI is a device that collects pictures of parts of the body by using magnetic fields and frequency pauses. A brain MRI looks at the whole brain. It determines shadows, dark and bright. You know what normal looks like both in shape and shading intensities. I did not find anything abnormal in his brain."

"No more questions." Prem Burns kept the testimony of

her expert physicians short and sweet. She did not want
the jury to get any more confused with another onslaught
of medical terminology, technology, and procedures.

Steven Lemoine had saved Norman Gillis for last. He
felt certain that if his experts had not convinced the jury
that Sean was insane, Norman would.

Sean's father carefully sat his Bible on the bench and
walked to the stand. As he took the court through the most
humiliating moments of his life, Norman sat tall in the
seat and spoke steadily and clearly. He had prayed that
God would help him through this. He knew he had to try
his best to help his son. His history of mental illness could
help to save Sean's life.

Norman described how he had spent years trying to kill
himself and being committed to hospital after hospital. He
listed all of the times that he had been committed or committed himself and explained why. He told the jury that he
had received shock therapy, as well as other treatments not
commonly practiced today.

"I got more and more lost in myself. I started on tranquilizers, and my mind started bringing me to different
ideations. I became a Buddhist, because I thought as a
Buddhist, I wouldn't hurt anyone. Then I became Catholic.
The Knights of Columbus taught me about Catholicism. At
twenty-seven, I was the oldest altar boy. I was twenty-five
when I married Yvonne."

Norman wiped away tears and bowed his balding head
as he began talking about his son. "I really believe that
part of his problem is heredity. I really don't see how me
abandoning Sean had an effect. That's why I want to save
my son. Angola has a faith-based program. I would hope
that Sean would be given the opportunity to search for his

faith. He could not do that if he was sent to death. I think he's responsible for what he's done. But I knew my name and address but didn't know who I was."

Norman recalled the incident when Sean had found "things of a homosexual pornographic nature" in his hotel room. "I assumed he had written me off after that," he said.

Now at age seventy-two, Norman had finally come to grips with who he was. He told the court that he had married twice after Yvonne and finally found the Body of Christ Church, which turned his life around. He had become an ordained minister.

"How did you find out Sean was arrested?" Lemoine asked.

"I heard from a newspaper reporter. I was stunned. I couldn't register it. I went to my wife and prayed. I told people in my church the next day and asked them to pray for us."

Lemoine tendered the witness.

Prem Burns stood up and walked toward Norman Gillis. "Do you know what your son was doing on January 4, 1999? He was murdering Katherine Hall," Burns said.

"Do you know what your son was doing on October 11, 2000? He was murdering Johnnie Mae Williams," Burns emphasized.

Norman looked down.

"Do you know what your son was doing on February 27, 2004? He was murdering Donna Bennett Johnston. No further questions."

"The defense rests," Lemoine announced.

Norman Gillis hurried out of the courtroom. He had to catch a plane back to California, leaving his son behind once again—this time to face certain death.

Death for a Killer?

Gray clouds loomed over the courtroom on the morning of July 31, 2008, as the prosecution and defense waited for court to commence. Each had worked diligently to prepare their closing arguments, the summation that would hopefully persuade the jury to vote their way. Each knew that Sean Gillis was a sociopath, a killer who had taken the lives of eight women. The jury would never hear *that* in a courtroom. They were to determine Sean's fate based on the three murders that had been presented.

Typically, in Louisiana, an "eye for an eye" mentality exists. Along the back roads and in alligator-infested bayous, justice is often swift and brutal. If the death penalty was chosen as his punishment, Sean would be injected with drugs that would put him into a peaceful sleep before he died. Sean didn't want to die. But if he did, he would never know the terror of running through a field with a zip tie around his neck.

He would never know the fear of lying on the ground with a knife slicing at him, fists beating on him until he was dead.

He would never suffer the humiliations he forced on his victims after they were dead.

No one would ever place his body parts in their mouth just to experience the taste of human flesh.

His death would be quiet, serene. He would not feel anything more than the prick of a needle.

The victims' family members wanted him to feel the prick of that needle and were not overly concerned about the verdict. They had heard the testimony. They had watched the jury. They felt confident that Sean would be sent to Angola's death row.

As they took their seats in the courtroom, they greeted each other with hugs, bonded now over the deaths of their loved ones. They watched as Sean Gillis took his seat at the defense table, his nervousness apparent. They stood as the jury walked in. They prayed. They held hands with the person closest to them.

At 10:03 A.M., Prem Burns stood up, her heels clicking across the floor as she took her place facing the jury in front of a podium. Once again, she said, "Ladies and gentlemen, whoever commits the crime of first-degree murder shall be sent to death or life imprisonment without parole."

In her beige suit, coordinated with beige glasses, Burns looked as confident as ever as she read the statutes associated with the case. "In making the determination of sentence, the state of Louisiana is asking you to use your common sense. Weigh carefully the impact of these killings on family members."

Again, Prem Burns reminded jurors the dates of when Katherine, Johnnie Mae, and Donna were murdered. She asked the jury to consider the testimony of the best historian in this case—Terri Lemoine. "Look at the facts. Weigh that against what was told to you by Dr. Dorothy Lewis, who was retained by the defense. Weigh that against Terri Lemoine, his mother, his friends, evidence that was made up and told to Lewis. Prior to Donna Bennett Johnston's killing, there were two others who had been killed by Mr. Gillis. This was not his first killing, rather his third. You now know that he is a serial killer."

Burns reminded the men and women who sat listening intently that Sean Gillis had stolen Donna Bennett Johnston's belt, that he had committed armed robbery. "In Louisiana, we have specific intent. You can use premeditation as an element of what you consider. This jury should consider that there was great thought and planning in this case. He used a very nontraditional weapon. We know this was not the first time he used this tie. We know he tried to use it on Katherine Hall. She was a little bit bigger. She was able to give him a better fight. By the time he got to Ms. Johnston, he knew how to use it. Practice makes perfect. These are not the actions of someone in a dream state or a dissociative state. He knew it would have to be someone who would get into his car—a female street person, someone he could control, someone disposable.

"This was a stranger," Burns continued. "It could have been anybody's mother, anybody's sister. We learned from Dr. Cooper that he had to bring at least two cutting instruments. Donna's arm has seven cutting marks to it, whereas the tattoo was a smooth-cutting instrument. In October 2003, he had removed the hands of Johnnie Mae. It was planned.

"He brought a digital camera—not the actions of someone in a dream state. His killing kit is in the car. His documenting kit is in the car. He sure managed to take forty-five pictures. If he was crazy and demented, how come not one of those pictures showed his full license plate? His hands were touching the tattoo area of the leg. He didn't show his face. He did nothing that would connect him absolutely to the case.

"The DNA on Katherine Hall was in her teeth. Only one in 3.8 trillion people could have contributed that DNA. You know how that hair got there. In Johnnie Mae, a limb hair in her cut. This is not someone in a dream state with worms in his head, ants in his head, delusional. This is someone who is calculating. If the murder of Donna was the only crime in this case, you would be justified in choosing death.

"You heard that Yvonne Gillis was a lady, a good mother. She always put her son first. Then you heard that she beat him, that she watched while her husband molested him. Filthy lies. Not true.

"In 1999, state [exhibit] 15 was placed around the body of Katherine Hall," Burns said, holding up a zip tie. "She was a drug addict. A prostitute. She managed to fight for her life and get this off her. She had a chance to live. What was she thinking? 'I may get out of this. I have a chance.' That knife went into the oral cavity of her eye. At what point did she know it was over? 'I will never see my family again.' And where did he leave her? Next to a dead-end sign. That's like saying, 'Screw you,' flipping the bird, 'Catch me if you can.'

"He was thirty-seven years old. You heard Dr. Hoppe when he said if someone had the problems Dr. Lewis said, he wouldn't be able to put on his shoes. Not one documented report that he ever had anything bizarre going on for thirty-seven years. When I asked his mother about the ants coming out of his brain, she laughed. It was so outrageous.

"Somebody's mother, daughter, sister," Prem Burns's

voice chimed like a bell throughout the room, where all of the mothers, daughters, and sisters sat with tears streaming down their faces. "Were it not for the limb hair, there would have been nothing to connect him to Johnnie Mae. Very well done. Good work.

"Donna wanted to be a good mom, to have a home, someone to love her. She didn't get those things. She dealt with unfaithfulness, and that's hard. At some point, she began drinking and doing drugs. Her mother raised her kids. But there were good times." Burns showed the jury pictures of Donna with her kids at their birthdays. "She always came back. She'd cook. She'd clean. Now there will never be the possibility of a knock or a call. 'Hey, Mom, I'm here.' Forty-three is too young to die. Sean wouldn't hurt his friends. 'I'll take my frustrations out on these women. They are trash, second-class citizens.'

"What would you have said to Dr. Lewis if you were Sean? Four years later, he says he has ants, pictures standing over his mother with a knife. Think of the things you would say."

Sean Gillis was writing on a yellow notepad as Prem Burns spoke.

"There were no instances of delusions in childhood, not even a doctor's visit. It's baloney. You heard Mrs. Gillis testify to the one time she took him to the emergency room and got a little Band-Aid. Then when he fell in the storm drain, the report said his sister . . ."

Sean was getting agitated. He began patting the arm of his chair. He handed Kerry Cuccia a note labeled, *Read before you speak.* Sean began crying, sobbing uncontrollably, yelling at Cuccia, who asked for a recess. Sean was escorted from the room, his steps unsteady as he tried to regain his composure. Even he knew he was going to die.

"That is Sean Vincent Gillis," Prem Burns said, pointing to Sean, as she resumed arguments following the recess. "He has logic, reason. He is not delusional, this man who killed three women. That is the man who had a normal MRI, PET scan, who does not have disorders, who was not beaten by his mother, molested by his father. This was all made up for this trial. Look to who Sean Vincent Gillis is, at his denials, at his speech. Terri lived with him for ten years. Look to her testimony and the woman who raised him. Look at his character and propensities, at the impact on the families. The state of Louisiana submits to you that the maximum penalty of death is warranted in this case."

Burns sat down and prepared her notepad. She would be writing notes on Steven Lemoine's argument to rebut later.

Steven Lemoine stood up. Cuccia stayed in his seat, tasked with keeping Sean under control. The last thing he needed was another outburst in the middle of Lemoine's speech.

Lemoine smiled at the jury. Several members smiled back. They liked his soft-spoken manner, his friendly face.

"There has been so much pain for the families of the victims. These are horrible crimes. Horrible. I'm not gonna thrust pictures at you to make you feel how horrible. They are acts that could not have been committed by anyone other than someone who was seriously mentally ill. We think about murder as someone who has something to gain—rape, anger. We understand those things. We hate them. 'Okay, I can see how that happens.' But what is there to understand about the killing of women and the dismemberment after death?

"How? How?

"It isn't hard to understand that these acts are evil. Why in the world would someone kill for pleasure? The act of depriving someone else of their life causes pleasure. Katherine Hall—no attempt made to conceal her identification. Johnnie Mae—both hands cut off. What in the world? I don't know what his purpose was, but it was not the purpose of a sane man. Donna Bennett—one of her arms cut off. I can't get inside of Sean Gillis's mind and tell you his motive."

Lemoine went on to describe the history of mental illness in Sean's family, the fact that his father had abandoned him, the fact that his father had been gender confused. He reminded the jurors that Sean had seen those pictures in his father's room, that his mother had left him when she moved to Atlanta. All of these things contributed, he told them.

"That's not to say that Sean Gillis was raving, blithering, foaming at the mouth. He knew it was wrong. He concealed things. He hid things. Sean lived his life like a number of people. You could call him a screwup. He couldn't keep a job. His mom paid the mortgage. He had relationships with people who loved him. He had a relationship with Terri for ten years. He was kind to her. She wanted to make sure she wouldn't get involved with another man who hit her. She slapped him. He got confused and cried.

"Sean goes with his friend to visit his daughter every other weekend, drives two hundred seventy-five miles. That's of infinite value to Sean because he becomes her de facto godfather by being her friend. Sean helps her, talks to her, reassures her. That evil man. I don't think so.

"Sean comes from a place we cannot precisely understand, a diseased place," Lemoine said. He went on to reiterate the things that Dr. Gur had said about Sean's brain. Then he moved to Dr. Lewis. "She doesn't believe everything he says, but it's important how he says it. It may come from left field, but she's been to left field before. She would not come to court and say something she doesn't believe. When I heard about the ants in the brain, I thought, 'What a load of poop.' He was in a manic phase when she saw him.

"So what happens? He's got the bad amygdala. How do you explain getting in your car driving around searching for a woman? Not the actions of a sane person. Then to do it again and again. It's not all his fault, not freely committed crimes. He's impaired, really impaired. I've seen signs of it.

"It's so horrible. Imagine the phone call—your wife, your sister. It's horrible. We have revulsion. We have to stop this. We have to condemn this in the worst way. It's not that simple. Not that simple. I bet a lot of time he was just holding himself together. He knew he was weird, and you get weird friends. What triggers it? I don't know. Web sites? In some sick way, it makes sense. When you see pictures of dead women, something inside you says, 'I like this.'

"Does that happen to people who are not mentally ill? No. Sean came by his mental illness naturally. Sean tried to win, but then he and three women lost. Sean should die in jail. He should never get out. He's too damaged. I ask you to send him to the biggest prison in Louisiana and let him die in jail. It's enough. We don't need more heartbreak. It's enough.

"Ms. Burns gets to talk again. She's brilliant. This is a personal moral choice for each one of you—your personal, individual moral decision. If you know it, believe it. It's your choice. In the future, we all have to live with our choices," Steven Lemoine concluded, hoping that if nothing else worked, the guilt trip he had just put on the jury would.

Sean Gillis had no reaction. He had been quiet since he came back into the courtroom. The medication he had been given to calm him down had worked.

Prem Burns was furious. She couldn't believe the things Steven Lemoine had said in his argument. "If any child who had grown up without a parent could use this as an excuse. People grow up without a father and do not kill. To use this as an excuse is offensive. To use gender problems, which millions of people have, is ridiculous. He said, 'I was pure evil.' He did it three times in the ultimate way. Because his father left? Because he saw photos? Because he didn't have sex? That is not sufficient. It's offensive.

"Yvonne did everything at a difficult time for women. She worked hard. He did get a degree. He worked at Shamrock for four years doing highly technical work. There is nothing wrong with his brain."

The medication was wearing off. Sean was getting worked up again. Kerry Cuccia watched him nervously.

Burns once again attacked Dr. Lewis's diagnosis of Sean Gillis. She noted for the jury that the good doctor had not even bothered to look at the police interview of Sean when he sat laughing and smoking while lying to them about being on Ben Hur Road. "Wouldn't you want to see the very best evidence? That would be the first thing a credible doctor, an impartial doctor, would do. She would look at not what he's saying to her, but what he says in an impartial setting. Dr. Lewis tried to create a history of medical head injuries.

"Do you believe Sean or his mother? There is no issue.

His mother said she took him to Our Lady of the Lake and they put a bandage between his eyes. Dr. Lewis said his head was split wide open. She is theatrical and goes on about things that are tangential to this case. Garbage in. Garbage out. Goldilocks, baby ants, sleepwalking, sleep driving, migraines. I submit to you that when people have migraines, they lie down in a dark room. They don't go out and take pictures of women they killed. It's ridiculous, and done by a doctor who is on the fringes."

Again, Prem Burns discussed each of the murders. Sean Gillis was becoming more and more agitated.

"On January 4, 1999, this defendant attempted to strangle Katherine Hall. She defended herself, got out of the zip tie, right before being viciously, viciously beaten to death."

Sean began talking loudly to Kerry Cuccia again, upset by what he was hearing. Cuccia tried to calm him, but Sean started sobbing. It seemed that something about Katherine Hall's murder disturbed him. This was the second time that he'd suffered a meltdown during discussions of her murder.

Judge Jackson called another recess. This time, it took forty minutes to get him calm enough to bring him back into the courtroom.

Burns picked up where she had left off, as if nothing had happened, discussing with the jury what Sean had done to Johnnie Mae Williams and Donna Bennett Johnston. "This is what we know," she said. "Nothing outweighs what this murder has done to the five children and mother of Donna Bennett Johnston. They will never see her again. As Justin said, words cannot express the love he had for her. As for Sean, well, it was like they were already dead to him.

"Were this only Donna Bennett Johnston, we submit

the merit would be death. But there are two other murders. There are reasons we have the law. Sean Vincent Gillis is that reason. The state of Louisiana asks that you return a verdict of death."

Judge Bonnie Jackson gave her instructions. "You must consider the circumstances of the evidence, circumstances and propensities of the defendant, and the impact on the family."

Sean Gillis was quiet once again.

Jackson told the jurors that they must consider aggravating and mitigating circumstances, that they must believe the evidence beyond a reasonable doubt. She said the vote for death must be unanimous. "You may consider a verdict of death, but that does not mean you must find death. Life is another option. You must also consider any mitigating circumstances. Each of you must individually determine the weight of the mitigating circumstances."

The judge explained that armed robbery and kidnapping were other circumstances, but that the prosecution was only required to prove one. She said that mitigating circumstances could be no sign of prior history, influence of mental disturbance, influence of another person, that the offender believed the acts were morally justified, if the offender could not appreciate or conform to the law, etc.

"Even if you find no mitigating circumstances, you can still impose a life sentence. In addition to the evidence presented at this hearing, you may consider the evidence presented in the guilt phase and the impact statements," she said.

At 3:03 P.M., the jury retired to consider the verdict.

The Final Verdict

Kerry Cuccia was nervous. After the jury left, he sat at the defense table and tore a tissue into strands. He balled up the shredded paper, then put it in his mouth and began chewing. Since he had begun handling capital cases, he had not lost. No client of his had ever been sent to death row. But this was different. He was defending a serial killer in southern Louisiana. He knew the jurors would feel like Sean should die for his crimes. He had watched their faces, their reactions, throughout the trial.

Prem Burns was not as nervous. She had faith in the jury. She knew they had seen right through that doctor, as had everyone else in the courtroom. She smiled at family members, reassured them, held their hands and waited like everyone else. It was out of her control now.

In the waiting room, sisters Virginia Valentine and Patricia Dawson sat next to each other. The two women were deeply religious; yet they hoped Sean would get the maximum penalty. He had taken their Lillian away. He had done unspeakable things to her. They knew. They had read the police reports. Forgiveness was not even possible at this time.

Justin paced back and forth, praying for justice for his mama. The trial had been beyond unbearable for the young man. He hoped he wouldn't have to wait long. His wife stood beside him, patting him every now and then. She knew better than anyone how his mama's murder had affected him.

Lauren Williams talked with Yvonne Gillis for a few minutes. She had come to like the woman and understood how difficult it would be for a mother to face the death of her son at the hands of the state of Louisiana. But that didn't take away the fact that this woman's son had killed her mama. She hoped Sean would be sentenced to death. Her brother, Larry Williams, trying hard to hide his angst, waited like the others. The emotion written on the faces of everyone in the hallway was tangible.

Terri Lemoine was nervous. She smiled when someone looked at her but stood mostly by herself in a corner. The trial had revealed so much to her, had destroyed her illusions about the man she loved. No longer could she believe her Sean wouldn't do these things. She had heard the details. There was no doubt in her mind now. She had lived with evil for ten years and had seen only good.

The reporters sat in a row on a bench and took notes, documenting how the families were reacting in this untenable situation. They made bets with each other about how fast the jury would come back. Many thought it wouldn't be an hour. They tried to bet on the verdict—life or death. No one took the bet. Everyone knew Sean Gillis would be sentenced to death. Occasionally they would look at their watches and write down the time.

4:03 P.M. The jury has been out one hour.

5:03 P.M. The jury has been out two hours.

At 5:45 P.M., the courtroom door opened. "The jury is coming back," the court officer announced. Everyone rushed for the door.

As they waited for the jury to be seated, family members held each other's hands fiercely. Yvonne clasped her hands in her lap. Terri sat on her hands, rocking slightly. Burns feigned confidence. Attorneys Cuccia and Lemoine talked quietly with Sean. Judge Jackson watched the assembled crowd dispassionately as she had throughout the trial, her keen eyes missing nothing.

"In the case of the *State of Louisiana* versus *Sean Vincent Gillis,* how do you find?"

The foreman of the jury, a big teddy bear–looking man with a military haircut, stood up.

"We cannot reach a verdict," he said.

"Please rise," the judge said to Sean. "Sean Gillis, you are hereby sentenced to life imprisonment at hard labor without the benefit of parole."

A collective gasp went through the courtroom. No one could believe it. The jury had hung. Any other judge would have sent the jury back into deliberations with an Allen charge to come back with a verdict. This jury had only been out for two hours and forty-two minutes. But Judge Bonnie Jackson had a reputation for being firmly against the death penalty, and she wasn't about to send them back.

"What just happened?" the families wondered aloud. "How could this have happened?"

Prem Burns, disbelieving of the outcome as well, hurried to comfort them as they cried on her shoulder.

Sean Gillis was crying, too—tears of joy as he hugged Kerry Cuccia again and again.

Lillian Robinson's family watched with disgust. It

wasn't fair. Lillian was dead. Sean had not spared her. Why was he spared?

Terri Lemoine hugged Yvonne Gillis. The two women who had bonded over their love for a killer were experiencing one of the happiest moments of their lives. "I've got to go call Norman," Yvonne said, hurrying away. Terri sat back in her seat, the weight of the world lifted from her shoulders. Sean would not die.

The courtroom cleared quickly. Justin hurried past the reporters who had set up their cameras on the steps of the building, ready to capture all emotions as the families exited. Justin, so upset by the verdict, could not even speak to them. He and his family, tears streaming down their faces, simply walked away.

Lauren comforted Larry, whose shoulders were shaking as sobs wracked his body. "I just can't believe it. I just can't believe it," he cried.

"I know, I know," Lauren said, hugging him tighter to her.

Virginia and Pat were furious. "I'm very upset, very angry," Virginia told reporters. "I see an evil, wicked man there. I saw him laughing in there, but this isn't funny. He who lives by the sword should die by the sword."

"It's very disappointing," Pat added, shaking her head. "This has been like reliving her death all over again."

Yvonne, on the other hand, shared her elation with reporters. "I'm just thrilled," she said, before hurrying off to visit with her son. In a back room of the courthouse, the mother and son hugged each other and cried tears of happiness.

Burns made her way outside, fully expecting the barrage of reporters, who shoved microphones in her face. She saw Lauren standing nearby and reached for her hand.

"There's something spiritually wrong with that man," Lauren said. Burns wholeheartedly agreed.

"Prem, what happened? Prem, give us your thoughts. Prem, how do you feel about the verdict? Prem, are you going to try him again?" they cried in unison.

"Obviously, all of the families were hoping for a verdict of death. I hurt for them," she said.

"Are you going to try him on another case?" a reporter yelled.

"This was our strongest case, the best case we had. We presented the best evidence we had," Prem Burns said, effectively telling them no before she walked away.

This trial would take a toll on her. She was a prosecutor known for winning cases. She had worked hard, fought discrimination against women and won, fought the Colombian drug cartel and won. She had put numerous murderers behind bars. The families of the victims had counted on her. She knew she had let them down. A serial killer had escaped the death penalty on her watch in a state known for vindictive justice. She had underestimated the jury. She had counted on the fact that they would see through Dr. Lewis's testimony. She had been wrong. She had not taken fully into account the fact that the jury would look at those pictures and believe that only an insane person, a mentally disturbed person, could commit such evil acts for the pleasure of it.

Kerry Cuccia, with Steven Lemoine by his side, walked proudly up to take his place in front of reporters. This was his moment, and he would glory in it. "The jury was introduced to Sean Gillis, not just his victims," he said. "I can't say what the defining moment was in the trial. We're just very pleased with the outcome." Families who had stayed behind looked at him with disgust written on their faces. Cuccia was oblivious as he smiled for the cameras.

Steven Lemoine stood there, smiling bigger than ever.

"We don't know how many jurors were holding out," he said. "I'm just very gratified with the result."

It would come to light later that the vote had been eight jurors for death, four against.

As the steps of the courthouse cleared, Terri stood off by herself waiting for her ride.

And on February 17, 2009, in a Lafayette courtroom on the day his trial was scheduled to begin, Sean pled guilty to the first-degree murder of Marilyn Nevils.

He received another life sentence. He would not be tried again. The families of Ann Bryan, Hardee Moseley Schmidt, Lillian Robinson, Katherine Hall, and Johnnie Mae Williams would never experience the sweet taste of justice. They simply had to live with the fact that their tax dollars were being used to feed and house the man who had taken so much from them.

Terri Lemoine had to live with it, too. Since the trial, she no longer corresponded with Sean. She and Louis were very happy together, still living in the house on Burgin Avenue, where so much evil had taken place. So many years after Sean Gillis's arrest, his books still line the bookshelves, his toys still fill closets, bloodstains still lurk under rugs and floors and in closets. Terri has tried not to think about it, to live her life safe in Louis's love.

However, every now and then as she washes dishes at night, standing in the very spot where Sean mutilated several women and forced himself into their dead body parts, a chill runs up her spine as she remembers.

Redemption

On June 9, 2004, about six weeks after he was arrested and charged with the vicious slayings of Katherine Hall, Johnnie Mae Williams, and Donna Bennett Johnston, Sean Vincent Gillis was saved.

A little over a year later, Sean explained his redemption through answering questions in a prison ministry pamphlet:

My name is Sean Vincent Gillis. I was born at 11:45 PM, CST, June 24, 1962. I was raised in a very Catholic family with one of my mother's brother's a Catholic priest and her little sister a nun. I spent a lot of time learning church doctrine, but never read the Bible for myself until last year after my arrest and incarceration awaiting trial. I read it three times and was shocked to say the least. I became involved with United Prison Ministries International, The Living Church of God, Kenneth Copeland Ministries and you fine people at the Voice of Prophesy. I asked for a booklet and got a great lesson instead. Cool to say

*the least. I really see the U.S.A. as in the process of
making an image to the beast in the Middle East right
now. I can tell you from personal experience that
Satan is more "a foot" than people think. As the
Rolling Stones said, "he'll lay your soul to waste." He
tried, did a lot of damage, but he's on the ropes now.*

When asked in his *Discover* pamphlet, *How can the
Sabbath make a difference in your life today?* Sean answered, *It has caused a few raised eyebrows, snickers and
out and out disbelief. It gives me a clear picture of God
and His intentions for me in the days to come. It feels
right, if you know what I mean.*

In response to the question *Is there anything in your life
that is keeping you from making a complete commitment
to God?* Sean wrote, *Lust & coveteousness are my real
weaknesses and sexually immoral fantasies. I've asked
God to send his Holy Spirit to help me. Every day, it gets
better. It's slow going but I know with the Holy Spirit we
can beat this thing. I've come too far to quit now.*

When asked, *If we accept Jesus, do you believe He
really forgives us completely? Have you accepted Jesus
as your savior? If not, would you like to?* Sean answered,
*Yes, completely, no exceptions! Yes, on the ninth of June,
in the year of OUR LORD, two thousand and four. Life's
changed from a "bitch" to a "dream" that's true. Thanks
and praise be to God, my Father, and yours.*

In a prayer request, Sean wrote, *Pray for peace, that we
may stop the killing of our brothers and sisters, here and
around the world.*

Apparently, in his euphoric state of redemption, Sean
had forgotten that he was responsible for the killing of
eight of his "sisters." He answered much of the correspond-
ence he received from prison ministries and talked some-

times with a nun from New Orleans, Sister Kathy, who worked in Kerry Cuccia's office and came to visit Sean.

Sean loved to discuss the intricacies of the teachings of the Bible. As he familiarized himself with the Old Testament, he often had questions, and Louis Gaar became his go-to guy for that. He often wrote long diatribes to Terri's boyfriend asking questions about this or that, or explaining what he thought about certain chapters or verses of the Bible.

On June 10, 2005, Sean asked Louis for an explanation in a letter:

> I could use your point of view here on the status of the prophet Elijah. In one of my study courses it is the opinion that he was alive and on earth some seven years after being caught up in the whirlwind because of a letter from him to King Jehoram of Judah. They say this proves he was still on earth. I can not say it proves anything except he was a prophet doing what prophets do, prophesying. Nothing I can find says specifically that Elijah wrote this letter at the time it was read.
>
> This sort of thing bugs me and I don't know why. The more I search the scriptures for the truth, the more I don't like what I find. But "ours is not to question why." Still, I question.
>
> I'm not even going to ponder the reunion of Jesus, Moses and Elijah on the mountain in the "transfiguration." I feel confident that Elijah was not roaming aimlessly on the earth those many years untill then. Please send me your thoughts on the matter of Elijah. Love and thank you,
>
> Sean V. Gillis

Sean also wrote Louis Gaar other letters, asking for things he felt would make his life in prison easier. He sent Louis a picture of a naked, pregnant Britney Spears bent over as if she were giving birth. *I'm sending a picture I would like you to find and make a 7 X 5 or 6 X 4 or whatever you can send me,* Sean wrote. *Britney's perfume is from Elizabeth Arden Inc. EA Fragrances. If it's there, good but if not, I'm sure there is a good one somewhere else. Maybe even the Dillard's web site.* In a P.P.S.S., he wrote, *Don't use any from Britney Spears.com, her official site. They have the smallest pics and don't blow up worth a crap.* Sean often asked Louis and Terri to send him pictures—of Britney, Buffy the Vampire Slayer, and other celebrities he had a hankering for.

But at other times, Sean seemed serious about looking for ways to change his life, to rid himself of the demons that possessed him, and God was one way. Reading was another. As he sat in prison waiting to be found guilty of his sins, he read extensively, copying on notebook paper, supplied by friends and family, quotes that stood out for him from the books he read. Quoting from the book *The Greatest Salesman in the World* by Og Mandino, Sean wrote:

> *Today I will begin my new life.*
> *   I. I will form good habits and become their slave.*
> * II. I will greet the day with love in my heart.*
> * III. I will persist until I succeed.*
> * IV. I am nature's greatest miracle.*
> *   V. I will live this day as if it's my last.*
> * VI. Today I will be the master of my emotions.*
> * VII. I will laugh at the world.*
> *VIII. Today I will multiply my value a hundred fold.*
> * IX . My dreams are worthless, my plans are dust,*

my goals are impossible. All are of no value unless
they are followed by action. I will act now!
    X. I will pray for guidance, and I will pray as a
salesman in this matter.

As the years went by and Sean Gillis became more and
more caught up in the teachings of the Bible, he became
convinced that he had indeed been redeemed—that God
had forgiven him for his sins and that he, like all of the
other good people in the world, would go to Heaven to
meet his Maker.

The families of the victims he mutilated, the investigators who took his confession, the people who still lock
their doors in Baton Rouge ever fearful of the evils that
lurk silently in the night, might disagree.

And for all his newfound religious beliefs, it's very difficult to forget that Sean told detectives and *The Advocate*
reporter Josh Noel, "Without being medicated, if I get out
of here, I *will* kill again."

Author's Note
From Susan D. Mustafa

I moved to Baton Rouge because my sister, Bridget, told me it was a safe place to live. That was the year before Derrick Todd Lee went on his rampage and began killing women in their homes. Like everyone at the time who felt that Baton Rouge was safe, I was unaware that Sean Gillis lived in one of those "safe" neighborhoods, next door and down the street from families who trusted that they could sleep peacefully at night. But it was Derrick Todd Lee, not Sean, who shattered that illusion for me and so many others.

As Sue Israel and I researched this book, shock and disbelief rose up each time we learned a new sickening detail. We had heard none of this in the media. We had to dig through police reports, watch confession footage, and interview police and those who knew Sean to discover the horror that he inflicted upon his victims. The murders of most of the women Sean killed—with the exception of Hardee Moseley Schmidt and Ann Bryan—were relegated to small stories. Between 1992 and 2002, more than sixty women in the Baton Rouge area were reported missing or found murdered. Until 2003, most of these cases remained unsolved. Police in Baton Rouge knew that a serial killer was targeting prostitutes, but they did not make the connection for the public. None of the killings received much publicity, at least not until Derrick Todd Lee began killing women who were more acceptable to polite society.

When police formed a task force to track the Prostitute Killer, everyone in Baton Rouge went about their daily lives—for the most part—oblivious. Some police officers believe the Prostitute Killer has killed as few as six, as many as nineteen, women in the North Baton Rouge area. The posing of their bodies, naked, with legs spread open in an effort to humiliate them, was their greatest indicator that the crimes were related. In early 2010, DNA finally made a connection between three women—Florida Edwards, Sylvia Cobb, and Renee Newman—and a man, Jeffery Lee Guillory, who had been incarcerated since 2008. Few in Baton Rouge even remembered hearing anything about his victims.

On February 2, 2010, in a Lafayette courtroom, Guillory was found guilty of the attempted robbery and attempted murder of Johnnie Martinez, a woman he attacked while she was standing at a bus stop. According to Johnnie, Guillory grabbed her and dragged her to a line of nearby trees as she fought him. He took her purse and strangled her. Thinking she was dead, he left her there. Martinez is the only known survivor of this serial killer. He was sentenced to fifty years in that case and faces trials in Baton Rouge for three murders.

As in the Sean Gillis case, no one—not even police—had any idea how many women he had killed. It's a scary thought that three serial killers could be operating at the same time in a city the size of Baton Rouge.

But it doesn't stop there. In the past decade, Louisiana has become a popular hunting ground for serial killers.

Across the Mississippi River in the town of Port Allen, in 2006, a pack of killers would brutally attack and rape a transient woman in front of her boyfriend while they took turns holding him down before viciously stabbing him to death. Michael Garcia and his brother, Daniel, and their friend, James Edward Nelson II, were arrested for these crimes. The three men are also suspected of murders in Michigan, where the Garcias once lived, and in Florida, where Nelson lived.

"Michael Garcia is one of the meanest killers I've ever seen," Judge Robin Free told me. "It was about control with him. He had an 'I can kill you because I can' mentality. He was a coward who used the ability to take lives as a way to be better than those he killed."

And in the rural town of Houma, Louisiana, on September 24, 2008, Ronald Joseph Dominique pled guilty to the rapes and murders of eight young men. In 2006, he had been formally charged with the killing of eleven men, but police believe he is responsible for twenty-three murders that spanned throughout Louisiana—from New Orleans to St. Charles, Lafouche, Terrebonne, Assumption, and Iberville Parishes.

This serial killer lured his victims much the same way Sean did—sex for money. He brought them to his house, tied them up, and raped and strangled them. Sometimes he produced a picture of a pretty girl, said she was his wife, and asked if they would have sex with her. The ones who agreed died—a single bad decision that was life-changing for families who waited sometimes for years for them to come home, not knowing what had happened to them. Many of their bodies were found in sugarcane fields or along the banks of bayous. Most were found partially clothed with their shoes missing, a clue that eventually led to his capture. The task force that had been formed to catch this killer arrested him in a homeless shelter called the Bunkhouse, which was operated by a Houma police officer.

Believe it or not, there is yet another serial killer operating in Louisiana, one who has not yet been caught. In the small town of Jennings, a town that averages one murder per year, eight young women have been killed by the same person since 2005. On May 20, 2005, Loretta Chaisson Lewis's body was found floating in a bayou. Between 2005 and 2008, Ernestine Patterson, Kristen Lopez, Whitnei Dubois, Laconia Brown, Brittney Gary, and Crystal Benoit Zeno were found on roadsides either strangled or with their throats slit. At the time of this writing, Necole Guillory is this killer's latest victim. Her body was found off Interstate 10 in Acadia Parish in August 2009.

These women were between the ages of seventeen and thirty and, like Sean's victims, lived high-risk lifestyles, according to police. It was not until the discovery of Necole that police in Jennings finally admitted the murders were connected, something residents of the rural community had believed all along.

In a press release, Jefferson Parish sheriff Ricky Edwards Jr. stated, *"This investigation pertains to the murders of Loretta Chaisson Lewis, Ernestine Daniels Patterson, Kristen Gary Lopez, Whitnei Dubois, Laconia 'Muggy' Brown, Crystal Benoit Zeno, Brittney Gary, and Necole Guillory. I use the term 'murder' because we are treating them all as murders unless we can prove otherwise. As we have stated in previous releases, it is the collective opinion of all agencies involved in this investigation that these murders may have been committed by a common offender. For that reason, the label 'serial murder' is applicable; however, we have not used that label when referring to this investigation because it does not benefit us in our goals to identify and apprehend the offender, nor does it prevent further loss of life. Labels are sometimes confusing and are subject to misinterpretation."*

The label "serial murder" confusing and subject to misinterpretation?

Really?

What is so confusing about the fact that a serial killer is killing innocent women? How can that be subject to misinterpretation? How can women protect themselves if they are not told about the dangers that surround them? None of Sean's victims were informed that a serial killer was targeting women. None were informed that another killer was targeting prostitutes as well. Would that knowledge have saved them? We will never know, but it might have given them a sliver of a chance.

The writing of this book was difficult on so many levels, and certainly the reading is not easy, either. We don't like to think such evil exists in our communities. But it does, and if this is happening here in friendly south Louisiana, evil can be anywhere.

This book took on more of a personal note for me after I met my husband, Scott, whose sister, Sherri, was raped and murdered in Baton Rouge years ago when she was only eighteen years old. Sherri was walking to a nearby store when she went missing. Her body was found on Thanksgiving Day. She had been shot twice in the back of her head, her young life brutally stolen from her much too soon. It took years for police to narrow the suspect list down to one, but by then it was too late. Her rape kit had been misplaced. Sherri's killer is still a free man, and her case remains forever unsolved. But what her killer couldn't take was the love that her family still feels for her. Even murderers can't take that away.

I urge women and men everywhere to be vigilant, to take self-defense classes, and to be careful when someone approaches. Even seemingly nice, normal-looking people can be killers. Do not live your lives in fear, but be aware and be certain that the Sean Gillises of the world live quietly among us.

It took more than two years to compile the information necessary to write this book. So many people along the way helped us by providing information, support, and all the little details that can make a difference. We would like to take a moment here to thank these folks.

To the families of the victims who shared with us their memories and their sorrows. We will always keep you in our prayers:

To Richie Johnson—Thank you so much for all you did to make this book become a reality. Your help was invaluable!

To Terri Lemoine and Louis Gaar—Thank you for your honesty during our many interviews and for the insight you gave us into the mind of a serial killer.

To Todd Morris—Thank you for your service to the Baton Rouge community. Residents can sleep better at night knowing you are protecting them.

And to Tony Clayton—We sure missed you on this journey.

To my husband, Scott—Thank you for being the incredible man that you are. Your love has brought such light into my life during those times when I am writing and so surrounded by darkness. To Angel, Gasper, Brandon, and Jonathon—You all make being a parent such a joy. I'm so glad God gave you to me. To Sue—Thank you for always taking my words and making them so much better.

You're simply the best. To Michaela Hamilton—Thank you for your belief in us and for making our writing dreams come true! To Mike Kinnamon, of Music Central in Nashville—I couldn't ask for a better manager or friend. I love you. To B. G. Dilworth—Thank you for all you do and for being such a great advisor. To my mom and my brothers and sisters—Thank you for all of your feedback and support.

—Susan Mustafa

To Suz—You're truly amazing and an inspiration. To my husband, Bob, and my family—As always, thank you for your love and tremendous support.

—Sue Israel

GREAT BOOKS,
GREAT SAVINGS!

When You Visit Our Website:
www.kensingtonbooks.com
You Can Save Money Off The Retail Price
Of Any Book You Purchase!

- **All Your Favorite Kensington Authors**
- **New Releases & Timeless Classics**
- **Overnight Shipping Available**
- **eBooks Available For Many Titles**
- **All Major Credit Cards Accepted**

Visit Us Today To Start Saving!
www.kensingtonbooks.com

All Orders Are Subject To Availability.
Shipping and Handling Charges Apply.
Offers and Prices Subject To Change Without Notice.